W9-BBA-920

One Foot in the Cradle

BY THE SAME AUTHOR

Spiritual

THE YOKE OF DIVINE LOVE
THE INNER SEARCH
THE CHOICE OF GOD
THE GOSPEL PRIESTHOOD
APPROACH TO PRAYER
APPROACH TO PENANCE
APPROACH TO CALVARY
SANCTITY IN OTHER WORDS
PRAYER IN OTHER WORDS
DEATH IN OTHER WORDS
SUFFERING IN OTHER WORDS
OUR LADY IN OTHER WORDS
THE PSALMS IN OTHER WORDS
THE MASS IN OTHER WORDS
THE GOSPELS IN OTHER WORDS
CHURCH HISTORY IN OTHER WORDS
THE OLD TESTAMENT IN OTHER WORDS
WE DIE STANDING UP
WE LIVE WITH OUR EYES OPEN
WE WORK WHILE THE LIGHT LASTS

Monastic

THE HOLY RULE
THE BENEDICTINE IDEA
THE BENEDICTINE NUN
APPROACH TO MONASTICISM

Devotional

THE WAY OF THE CROSS
A BOOK OF PRIVATE PRAYER
PRAYING WHILE YOU WORK
IDEAS FOR PRAYER

Miscellaneous

FAMILY CASE-BOOK
WILLINGLY TO SCHOOL
DOWNSIDE BY AND LARGE
APPROACH TO CHRISTIAN SCULPTURE
ORIGINALS DON'T FADE
KALEIDOSCOPE

One Foot in the Cradle

AN AUTOBIOGRAPHY

Hubert van Zeller

HOLT
RINEHART AND WINSTON

NEW YORK CHICAGO
SAN FRANCISCO

Library of Congress Catalog Card Number: 66-22064

88973-0116

Printed in the United States of America

Gratefully to
Frannie and Johnny

Contents

	Preface	xi
1	The Cradle	1
2	The Nursery	9
3	The First Uncertainty	25
4	The Preparation	35
5	The Junior School	54
6	The Upper School	83
7	The Wait	111
8	The Early Years in the Monastery	127
9	The Middle Years	163
10	The Change	189
11	The Second Dawn	199
12	The Second Noon	223
13	The Second Evening	246
14	The Cycle Repeated	268
	Index	279

Illustrations

FACING PAGE

The author, 1937. *Photo: Anthony Rochford* 20

The Camberley House 21

The London House, 109 Lancaster Gate. *Photo: M. Haighton* 21

The author's mother and Yolande 52

The author, age two, 1907 52

The author and his brother, 1912. *Photo: Aziz and Dorés* 52

The author's father with "crew" sailing *Water-Witch* in 1912 53

Mother and son at the fort, 1913 53

Deposition. Now at Downside. *Photo: K. B. Eachus* 188

Stoneshed 189

Christ Dead. Now at Downside. *Photo: K. B. Eachus* 189

Ronald Knox. *Drawn by the author* 220

Siegfried Sassoon. *Drawn by the author* 220

Head of a soldier 221

St. Christopher. Now in the possession of Mr. Willard Bunn of Springfield, Illinois 221

Preface

Religion is ordinary or extraordinary according to the way you look at it. So is sculpture. The same may be said of travel, friendship, books, education, enjoyment of life and the distaste for it, growing old and adjustment to change. There is nothing particularly original to be said of any of them. Solomon admitted that there was nothing left that was new. Anyway these subjects will form the matter of this book. Material of autobiography may properly, but should not be exclusively, the author. If the author can remain the ring-master so much the better for the circus. Ring-masters may have to be present all the time in the ring, but their aim is not to focus attention upon themselves. The spotlight plays elsewhere. Who, having spent an afternoon at the circus, remembers what the ring-master looked like? Where the following pages are concerned I like to think of myself as assembling material, re-arranging it, flicking it into movement with a little crack of the whip, and then letting the performance speak for itself. If this simile suggests nothing but clowns, paper hoops, spangles and the snapping of silver pistols, it should be remembered that sweat sometimes mingles with the sawdust and and big top has been known to go up in smoke.

In conclusion I must thank the Hon. Mrs Patrick Chorley for reading the text and making suggestions which in every case have been followed up, and my brother for deciding about the illustrations and providing psychological support.

CHAPTER ONE

The Cradle

Believing that writers who delve deep for early memories tend to attach too much relevance to experiences held more or less in common with everyone else, I rather disqualify myself from producing a string of nursery anecdotes. Nor, when I reflect upon them, could I point to more than a very few remembered emotions, sensations, occurrences, insights into life, or even personal exchanges which deserve to stand in a category of their own. And yet there remains a certain separateness about oneself, the general awareness of which goes fairly far back and becomes increasingly clear as one grows older, which has to be borne out by illustration. Out of the relation between the early inward and the early outward, and indeed out of the sense of personal separateness, adult life takes shape. The fact that everyone else has an inward and outward too, has a sense of separateness, does not contradict this. It merely makes it inadvisable to go on at length about it.

'Everyone's childhood', says Heimito von Doderer in *Every Man a Murderer*, 'is plumped down over his head like a bucket. The contents of this bucket are at first unknown. But throughout life the stuff drips down on him slowly, and there's no sense in changing clothes, for the dripping will continue.' In my case the stuff has dripped more in the form of feelings than in the form of events. Events have either occasioned the feelings or come in afterwards to corroborate them. But it has always been the feelings that have had the last say. I am not saying that this has been either good or bad; I am merely stating a fact.

If the mood looms larger in my memory than the incident which gave rise to it, I do not repine. I would prefer to have it so than the other way round. Often on returning to a place which I have not seen for years I have been able to remember exactly what

I was feeling when I was there last. Why I was there, what I did while I was there, how old I was when I was there, may have faded completely: whether I was in a good or bad mood, whether other people reacted to me favourably or unfavourably, I can recall with embarrassing clarity. Not long ago I attended a meeting at a London hotel which I had not visited since I was a boy at school. I remembered nothing about the former occasion except that I was wondering at the time whether it might not be thought too bold a venture to appear wearing suède shoes.

The reverse process, whereby one remembers the features and forgets the feelings, may be more useful if one has to give an account of oneself before a magistrate. Here it is a question of the immediate. In the long run, however, the way in which memory works with me is more satisfactory. Certainly it provides me with better copy in my job. Not in the job of writing only, but in the job of preaching and trying to help with advice. If ever I come to the stage where it is easier to recall facts, still more if ever I shall prefer to re-live occurrences rather than impressions, I shall know that I am ready for the knacker's yard.

So it is that though many may lay claim to recollections which go back to the age of two or even younger, I mean to boast of nothing earlier than about my fifth year. A friend tells me he remembers being given sips of tepid beer at the furthermost point of a seaside pier when he cannot have been more than eight months old, and that he preferred it to milk. Moreover, he tells me that there was something furtive in the nursemaid's action when she gave him his beer, and that his suspicions were aroused. But I think this man lies.

Reluctantly, and only because it has its bearing upon an aspect of the thesis outlined above, the earliest recollection to be recorded is that of the resentment I used to feel when my toes were imperfectly dried after I had been bathed. As I have always disliked telling people that they were doing things badly, I had to spread my toes apart, keeping them in this position for a while until dry enough to be brought together. It was a nuisance, but it seemed preferable to telling a grown woman her job. Another bath memory is that of introducing a rhythm into having my hair rubbed. Instead of allowing it to be done all anyhow, with one hand while the other hand was squeezing out a sponge or turning off a tap, I not only insisted on two hands plying the towel at once but contrived so to yield my neck to the movement as to secure a regular even beat. By bending my head backwards and forwards metronomically I found I could impose my will upon the immediate authority. Some would say I have been trying to do this ever since.

It is a lifelong weakness of mine that having gained an objective I am not content to rest there but must either come back the way I went or else try to improve the position with circus-tricks. Dominion in the matter of having my head dried no sooner established than I turned to experimenting with the alphabet, racing it against the escaping bath water. I doubt if symbolism has much part in this.

So much for practices and attitudes. The first actual incident which I want to pull out of the toy-cupboard is one which is slight enough in content but rich in implication. If by the simple act of plucking a chord the little Beethoven sent vibrations ringing which nothing but the end of civilisation will silence, then by the simple act of visiting a kitchen I can say that my childhood mind first began to tick. One day early in the summer of 1910 (the year is fixed for me because it was before my brother was born) I left the breakfast-table in my grandmother's London house and went downstairs into the kitchen to ask the cook if she would be so good as to make a *brioche* for my aunt Yolande, who did not care for the ordinary English scone. The cook did not know what I was talking about, and almost at once I was whisked upstairs again.

I was then five years old, and though I remember the scene very clearly I remember still more clearly the sense of confusion which resulted in my mind. First, I was puzzled that it should be thought odd by my uncles and aunts for anyone to leave the breakfast table before my grandmother had given the sign which sent the whole family into the morning-room. Secondly, I wondered why I should be so swiftly pursued from upstairs and swept off as though the kitchen belonged to a world not to be frequented by the family. In the third place I was bewildered by the discovery that one whose business it was to cook food had no knowledge of how to make a *brioche*. To my cosmopolitan mind, which had been developing all too slowly in surroundings less stately than those in which I then found myself, the *mores* of English urban life appeared unreasonably complex.

What was this ritual about breakfast in a big house? Why this gulf between life on the ground floor and life *under* the ground floor? How could a competent cook, working in the then fashionable neighbourhood of Bayswater, and with a whole team of underlings in their uniform of pale pink gaberdine to help her, be unable to bake the roll which appeared so abundantly in the meanest French street? I should explain that I had spent more of my five years in Egypt, where I was born, than in England, to which my mother and father and I came each year. In Egypt I had been accustomed to walk in and out of the kitchen at will, making friends with anyone who happened to be there. If pressed I would probably have pointed to the kitchen as being the most important room in the ugly little house which we occupied at that time in Alexandria. Though my father and mother would not have been found there, I could count upon meeting the gardener and some of his children, one or two of the orderlies, an Italian groom, a smattering of beggars, more than one goat. As a social centre the English kitchen, approached from the outside down a flight of area steps, was uninviting.

So on that summer morning in 1910, restored to the breakfast-table under my grandmother's frown, I awoke to the idea of social inequality. A new dimension, that of class, lay open before me. Though the knowledge grew gradually, fed for the most part unconsciously by my elders, it provided me with assumptions and evaluations from which I have never wholly been able to free myself.

Although until the age of nine I continued to live more of my life in Egypt than in England I look back at the time spent at my grandmother's house, 109 Lancaster Gate, as having had a more formative effect than the time spent in Alexandria. It is in this sense that I think of Lancaster Gate as the cradle in which one foot (at least) still rests. I have described this house in a collection of biographical essays called *Family Case-book*, so must not repeat myself here. Nor would an account of the rooms, lit by gas and oil-lamps and heavy with Victorian and Edwardian furniture, serve much purpose. It was the attitude of mind which was engendered by my grandmother's two houses (the other was at Camberley in Surrey) that matters.

Since religion has been the main force in my life, and sculpture my main interest, it is a pity that I can say so little about either of them as influencing my early years. Awareness of religion was, I am gratified to find, the first of the two to reveal itself. Nevertheless, and I have to rely upon hearsay for even this evidence, it was not an awareness which made much difference to my life. On our annual journeys to and from Europe we used to spend one night in a large hotel in Paris. It seems that during one such visit I stared, until corrected, at three men who happened to be reading or writing in one of the public rooms, each of whom wore a long white beard. In the lift on the way up to our floor was yet another man in a long white beard. This fourth man took off his top hat and looked gravely down at his cloth-topped buttoned boots throughout the ascent. When we reached our rooms I put to my mother the first of my theological problems. Was there one God the Father, I asked, or did he distribute himself according to the needs of his faithful? And if multiplied in this way, I further wanted to know, how was it that no less than four of him were lodging at the same hotel as ourselves? Having spent most of my five years in Egypt where gods were plentiful, and preferring the legends of Greece to any other for bedtime listening, I must have felt that the monotheistic claim warranted a stronger apologetic than my European experience provided.

My mother, never much of a hand with the catechism but viewing the possible direction of my thought with misgiving, so far succeeded in weaning me from paganism as to remove for good whatever difficulties I entertained regarding the Fatherhood of God.

While at my grandmother's, such religious formation as I received came from Miss Georgina Barrington, the resident seamstress, and who, being saintly beyond the aspiration of anyone else I knew, was the right person for the job. While in Egypt, until the birth of my brother introduced an Austrian nurse called Josephine Tonitz into the household and I picked up something of the subject from her, my religion went by default.

I have mentioned sculpture. The earliest remembered piece of carving I can point to is that of a standing bear. Unfortunately I cannot remember where it was or what particularly attracted me about it. I know it was carved and not modelled, because it was white, and therefore presumably of marble. I know it was standing and not on all fours, because at first I identified it in some way with my grandfather. My paternal grandfather, like the four gentlemen in the Paris hotel, wore a long white beard, so the association is, if not immediate, at least understandable. The fact that I had never seen my grandfather on all fours may have helped the illusion.

In any case the feeling for sculpture comes later. There would seem to be a cycle in a child's visual appreciation. From the first stage which recognises things in the round, going out to golliwogs and teddy bears, the mind graduates to pictures. Then the interest in pictures gives place to things in the round again. Tin soldiers and forts for boys; china (now plastic) dolls and prams for girls. In my case I have only the haziest memories of stage one, of attaching myself to anything stuffed. At the period of which I write I was vastly enjoying pictures. A few years were to elapse before I would get back to three-dimensional objects. That is why the marble bear stands out in my mind as a notable exception. Indeed, I can remember the bear more clearly than I can remember the grandfather.

Psychoanalysts have probably by this time found out exactly how the memory works. In case they have not, I would like to say something more about how mine does. Where the minds of an increasing number of people can be brought to perform conjuring tricks which enable them to juggle with statistics and pull unlikely but significant things out of a hat, the mind which I am now talking about cannot be relied upon for special service. It may serve well enough in ways other than those demanded, bringing to light much that pleases its owner, but it seems incapable of answering to the demand on the label. It is like the rocket in the box of fireworks which instead of sending a dazzling display into the sky falls flat on the lawn and splutters out in a shower of sparks among the flower beds. There are some, for instance, who can dismiss the irrelevant from their minds even as it is being presented to them, and never think about it again. Others can switch their memories on and off at will, eliciting and discarding scenes as though editing a reel of film. But is such facility to be coveted? Not by me. Admittedly it would be convenient to be able to drop into the waste-paper basket of oblivion the tedious or regrettable days, but there would always be the danger that among the rubbish something was being dropped which would come in useful later on. One reason why I do not envy the work-to-rule memory is that experience seems to show how selective even the most haphazard memory can be. It gets rid of a lot of the rubbish on its own, without being told to do so. Memory has an eye for the significant. Some years ago I attended a fire, and, while the ashes were still warm, wrote a detailed account of it. A year later, and without reference to the earlier report, I wrote a second version of the same incident. The second version was shorter, clearer, no less accurate. The moral of this story is not that some writers must wait a year before embarking upon composition, but that if they have had to wait fifty years they can believe that with any luck memory has jettisoned the waste material.

If a good memory is one which enables a man to carry in his head the numbers of cars and telephones, to recite a column of newsprint after a single rapid glance, to give you the dates of every important battle in history, then I am quite content to jog along with my bad one. If my kind goes about with a caricaturist's pencil and sometimes exaggerates, at least it carries away something against a rainy day. An impression, though it may have to be corrected later on, is worth a dozen figures. Telephone numbers, on a rainy day, are regrettably cold potatoes.

Accordingly I remember the impact which natural beauty made upon my mind for the first time. (I do not count the bear.) It was when, from a P & O liner, I saw the glow of a smouldering volcano against the night sky. Which particular mountain it was does not matter, and in any case I forget names. My mother was up on deck; my father was holding me, wrapped in a blanket and wearing pyjamas, for it was after my bed-time, against the round brass rim of the porthole. Besides the glow in the sky I remember the reflection on the water. The beauty of it, which in later years I might have judged to be too theatrical, left me with a feeling of sadness which I was unable to account for. I am unable still.

I remember the first time I was transported by the flow of oratory. It was while listening to a sermon preached by Father Robert Hugh Benson at Spanish Place in London. The effect was all the more electrifying because the delivery, anyway at the beginning, was poor. Once under way, and with the words, 'if you are honest you will ask yourself this' coming again and again, the waves broke with devastating effect. I remember nothing of what the sermon was about.

The impact of ugliness, seen in the figure of a drunken man who lurched about on bumbling feet, remains as a vivid memory. The scene of this was the winter-garden of the Ramleh Casino, Alexandria, at the improbable hour of four in the afternoon. I was too young to understand what I saw; I knew only that I did not like it. This also marked, since I do not remember being afraid of the dark, my first conscious experience of fear.

Homesickness, which I have always regarded as the worst of all human ills, came much later. Never away from one or other home for so long as a single night until the age of nine when I went to school, I had no occasion to be homesick. Though I had occasion to be lonely and bored, for I knew hardly any children of my own age either in Alexandria or in London, I have no recollection of loneliness or boredom at any time in my childhood. Only when I began to mix with people did I come to feel these things.

Initiation into the emotion of love, of whatever kind, defies the pinpointing of date or place. Hate? I am surprised to find that I cannot remember the first stirring of hate. I am a poor hater at the worst of times, more inclined to hate places and occupations than people. It is no virtue to have got through life without properly hating anybody. On the rare occasions when I have come anywhere near to it I have felt so uncomfortable that it seemed not worth while to proceed.

There must always be a margin of self-deception in accounting for one's infant sentiments and recording one's cradle reminiscences. But, allowances made, I know now beyond doubt that the first five years of my life were, in a placid and perhaps negative way, the happiest. If the remaining fifty-five have never quite risen to the opening, the fault is my own. I do not propose in the rest of this book to tell a tale of gloom.

CHAPTER TWO

The Nursery

In the days when Egypt was virtually a British possession, a sort of extra hand granted to the Empire for purposes of operating dams, there was often an interchange of personnel between the British and Egyptian armies. English officers would be seconded for special service: Egyptian officers did some of their training with English regiments. For my part I was never very clear as to when my father was drawing a salary from the Egyptian government and when from our own. Nor was I very clear as to the nature of the work he did in either service. As Major van Zeller he served under the Union Jack during the First World War. As van Zeller Bey he held office, both before and after the war, in what was called—in England—the Coast Guards. My mother was constantly having to explain to friends at home that her husband's job did not involve walking round the sea shore with a telescope. Later my father was appointed Governor of the Red Sea Province. What this final appointment involved none of us was quite able to determine. We hoped that with inauguration would come a palace and perhaps a private army. My father's governorship left us more disappointed than proud.

When my brother was born, in October 1910, in our house on the outskirts of Alexandria, I knew we were in for changes. At first, and I am sure he will not mind my saying this, he was a disappointment to me. I hoped that we would be able to explore together the mysteries of the grown-up mind, to find an explanation of such incidents (the *brioche* episode being one of them) as were constantly baffling me, to form a coalition of two which would present a jointly framed policy. By the time he was old enough to be of any use in this way, I was some years ahead in my discoveries. He probably had problems of his own by then. People have to find things out by themselves.

With my brother's birth came a re-arrangement of rooms. Hitherto I had slept in my father's dressing-room, which opened out of my parents' bedroom, and had the day-nursery to myself. Now, when the new member of the family was ready for it, a night-nursery was established on the west side of the house and we shared this as well as the day-nursery. We had a nightlight in the room and a nurse who slept within hailing distance. I felt I was too old for both. The day-nursery was a cheerful place which had a balcony connecting it with a spare room also facing south and overlooking the garden. Since guests rarely used the balcony, and since it would have meant a tight fit if they had, we of the nursery enjoyed virtually exclusive possession. Indeed barricades were not unknown.

The night-nursery had access to a balcony too, a longer and more spacious one, but was a cheerless room smelling of paraffin and ironing. I think of it as a place I used to visit during the daytime only when I was sulking. No recommendation to a room. It should have been gay enough, with its open-air approach to two other rooms on that side of the house and with a fine view of the sea, but if associations are against a place nothing redeems it. From its windows could be seen two forts, any storm which happened to be going on inside or beyond the bay, and the most spectacular sunsets which anyone could wish for.

Immediately below, the house being two storeys high, stretched a strip of grass which my father required to keep watered and mown the whole year round. Nobody ever sat or walked there. It might have come from Eastbourne. Though not in fact tenanted by painted plaster gnomes holding fishing rods, the lawn, as my father grandly called it, was liable at any moment, had the house not been occupied by us, to sprout a birdbath or a sundial.

It may be gathered from what has been said that with the perversity of Egyptian planning the house had turned its back on the only thing worth looking at, the sea. It faced, at the end of less than an acre of front garden, a municipality wall which was as blank as it was high. In the garden, from beds which at my father's command were forever altering their outline, grew some reluctant, uncompeting, apologetic roses, some leathery but recognisable violets, and a fig tree so reticent as to produce only a few stiff, dry, unyielding green knobs every three or four years.

My mother, driven by a stern sense of duty, would occasionally put on leather gloves and wrestle with the undergrowth. Nature invariably winning, she would return to the house in a vile temper. Though gardeners seemed to be always in attendance, and though the hiss of the sprinkler and hose are part of the well remembered orchestration, the only thing I can vouch for as ever coming up at all regularly was crop after crop of tomatoes which Josephine, our Austrian nanny, produced from a window-box.

The night-nursery, so well suited to bad moods, became to me more of a haven as my brother learned to walk, climb, and destroy. I would spend what must have been considerable periods of time looking out of the window at the sea, at the men who leaned against walls and spat at the veiled women who gossiped and gesticulated and whose arms glittered and rang with bracelets, at the buggies which moved up and down the coast road as if in their sleep, at the squads of Egyptian soldiers in khaki shorts who used to drill on a piece of waste ground between our house and the encroaching town, and at the two forts. It is one of the unconscious luxuries of childhood, impossible to recapture, that time can be wasted without the least sense of guilt.

Fenestrating in this way I was able on one occasion to witness a house falling down, a sight I have not seen since. The house was being built on the far side of the compound where the soldiers paraded, and was nearing completion. It was a tall house, probably a block of flats, and I had watched it grow from its foundations. Though the work of building commanded my admiration I had come to view the enterprise with distaste, because to my father, and so to me, it spelled the end to our privacy. Soon we would be enveloped. Suburbia, my father said, was breathing on the glass of the dining-room window. There was nothing for it, according to my father, but we must pull up our tent-pegs and press farther up the Nile into the desert. Such a change was evidently something to be warded off until the last minute, so, when in my already bad mood I stood gazing out with a jaundiced eye at this house, now virtually a writ of eviction, and then saw the walls wobble, crack, and fall to the ground in a great cloud of dust, I believed myself responsible. I was overwhelmed by my guilt. Whom should I tell? If I explained to Josephine, who at this period knew only German, would she grasp what I was driving at? My mother would understand about it being all my fault, but what if she died of shame and grief, falling down like the house itself? My father was the only one left to go to.

It was in the early evening that the house had fallen down, the workmen having fortunately gone home and left me to perform my act of destruction without danger to life, so I knew I would find my father downstairs in the study reading the paper before going up to dress for dinner. With tears splashing from my cheeks I opened the door and stood in front of him. As manfully as I could I confessed I had just pulled down a house.

'Which house?' my father asked without looking up from his paper.

'The one we don't like . . . the one that's nearly finished . . . you know; the house you said a lot of other ones are coming after.'

'Oh, *that* house,' said my father a shade less absently, 'so you have pulled it down. Well done.'

Then I suppose my crying must have made itself heard, because he put the paper away and asked me to tell him more about the supposed calamity. When I told him where I had been standing, and how I had wrought the havoc from the night-nursery, he hoisted his large body from the chair, took my hand and came upstairs with me. He was humouring a lunatic son.

'Good Lord, the feller's right,' he exclaimed, removing his eyeglass, which was what he always did when he wanted to look at anything, 'the damn thing *has* fallen down.'

Together we surveyed from the nursery window the distant wreckage now reddened by a dazzling Alexandrian sunset. Once roused, my father's interest never slackened until it had, to use an expression of his, brought back the fox in the bowler.

'What time do you go to bed? Let's go and have a look at this house of yours.'

In no time he had led me away to the stables, which were by far the best part of our modest property ('Who in this family wouldn't gladly be a horse?' my mother said), and was shouting for a groom. Seated astride in front of him on the pony which he rode for exercise and not for transport I went on suffering from my conscience. We did not dismount at the site, my father being a punctual man and wanting to be in good time for a bath before dinner, but trotted round the great heap of rubble from which dust was still rising. From the crowd of bystanders which had collected we learned that there had been no casualties apart from the insurance companies. Everyone was explaining how it had happened but nobody knew. There had been no earthquake. The other houses round about looked firm enough, heartlessly indifferent. To me they looked accusing.

'Could it have been a cannon-ball?' I asked my father, hoping that I could shift the blame. We reviewed the peaceful scene. Not even out at sea, where battleships sometimes broke the line of the horizon, was there anything more warlike than a fishing boat. My father shook his head.

'The bally thing just collapsed. And for goodness sake don't you think you had anything to do with it. Some fool of a builder mixed the wrong plaster or something, and then a puff of wind came or a rat nibbled through a piece of scaffolding, and the whole show toppled over. You were jolly lucky to see it happen, if you ask me, so shut up about being the one to have done it.'

It was kind of him to reassure me like this, and it was pleasant to be staying up later than usual, but of course I did not doubt for a moment that I had been responsible.

My habit of nursery fenestration brought me to a circumstance more psychologically representative than that just recounted. Less dramatic but deeper in implication, it is connected with one of the forts alluded to above. Over the years I conceived a growing curiosity about the more distant of the two forts, each of which lay on the opposite horn of the bay. The nearer fort I judged to be of no consequence. I had not then acquired the affection which I have now for the dilapidated. Against the crumbling walls of this near-by fort poor families had built themselves homes of mud and tin. Some of the dwellings were so ramshackle as to make it difficult to see from the road which belonged to human beings and which to animals. But even those which looked too rickety for human habitation must have been built to withstand rough handling because apart from the storms which would beat upon that line of coast with great violence I remember a week of Moslem wedding celebrations which called for much banging about.

Though my mother had put it out of bounds for the afternoon walks which I took in the company of Josephine and the baby, my uncle Marcel, ever scornful of bounds, took me on a tour of this nearer fort whenever he came to stay with us. Uncle Marcel frankly enjoyed humanity in every form, and here he knew he would find it. Humanity at Fort Silsileh was abundant, noisy, intimately adjacent, smelly. Mixed with it were goats, dogs, donkeys, hens, lizards. Clouds of flies hung and swung over offal. Rubbish gave off the sweet-sickly vapours of rotting matter.

Pondering my superficial inspections, I felt fairly sure that this untidy squalid fort bore little relation to its counterpart at the other end of the bay. The far one, stretching out on its promontory so that it seemed to have its rocky boots in the sea, might also be a ruin, might also hum with insects and stink to high heaven. But I came to see it as having an aura. To me, who had never been within a mile of the place (easily seen across the water, it would be four or five miles from the house by road), the low rambling pile of masonry spelled romance, mystery, power, grace, manliness. It was Achilles' spear, King Arthur's sword, Ronsard's horn.

This may sound fanciful but I can say that looking out upon the sweep of the bay more than half a century ago, and idealising one place from my knowledge of another, I developed a dream fort in my imagination comparable to the fictitious character whom many children invent for themselves. Perhaps because I had less attraction than most children for toys, and still less affection for fairies, I fastened on a fort, a demonstrably real piece of architecture. It stood for a supposedly inaccessible, unattainable, unknowable, and clearly three-dimensional structure to which I felt in a particular way committed. If I ever got there it might turn out to be another labyrinth like the one on the island of Crete, or just another slum like its counterpart close by, but at least it would not be paste-board flat like the pictures which I drew of it, a mere back-drop to decorate the bay.

Considering the importance I attached to the fort it surprises me in retrospect that I never asked to go there and have a look at it. Surely I cannot have felt at that age that contact would break the spell. Whatever the reason, it was not until my seventh birthday, after at least two years of wistful wishing, that I set foot on the empty barrack square. Here comes the disappointing part of the story: I can remember hardly anything about it. That the occasion of the visit was my birthday I know because the choice of how to spend the afternoon was left to me. At breakfast, the first to be enjoyed downstairs and not in the nursery, I was given my presents and told I might invite as many friends as I liked to a party. If I chose to ask a lot of friends the party would have to be on another day; if a few it could be arranged for today. Until bedtime the hours were mine. The only friend whom I would have wanted to invite, indeed I had few others, was a flute-playing son of the gardener whose name would not have been approved of on a list of guests. Ali, the flautist, was about two years my senior. The idea of a party interesting me not at all, and the idea of the fort uppermost in my desire, I came out promptly in favour of a drive to the other end of the bay and a picnic tea in the shadow of the battlements.

Every child must be familiar with the way in which adults, the moment a plan is projected, seek to divert the intention into alternative channels. So now. 'That seems such a dull sort of birthday outing . . . are you sure you wouldn't rather the Yacht Club? . . . there are those nice people who have taken a house near the Cathedral.' It was my day and I remained firm. Evidently I had kept to myself the interest I felt in the fort, because I remember how puzzled my parents were to find me so emphatic. It was arranged that my father should take me in the pony-trap immediately after luncheon, and that my mother, brother, Josephine, and the tea-basket should follow in the carriage later on. The morning dragged on heels of glue.

We must have got there all right and had tea. A blurred picture hovers in my mind of a more orderly group of buildings than ours next door, of having to get a key from a soldier in order to get in, of some empty sentry-boxes and a flagpole without a flag, and the whole place looking smaller than I had expected. All I can remember actually doing is clambering barefoot over the rocks down by the water's edge, sitting with my legs dangling over the edge of a concrete mole or breakwater, and hiding my sense of anticlimax.

If the others noticed my disappointment they tactfully made

no mention of it. Nor did I for a moment regret not having chosen the Yacht Club or the people who had taken a house near the Cathedral. I was glad to have spent my birthday finding out. It was coming back that was the difficulty. During the next two years, until I went to school in England, I was to do a lot more looking out of the night-nursery window, trying hard to make the fort what I wanted it to be. It was not a mirage, but neither was it the place I had chosen to visit. This fort which I had come back to and which looked exactly as it had always looked, was, though I did not admit this, pretty much like the one just down the road.

The reason for devoting a good deal of space to the fort episode is that I have spent most of my life too eagerly wanting this or that, getting it, and then trailing back to actuality.

My seventh birthday behind me, it was time for riding lessons. I had ridden before, both in Alexandria and in the grounds of my grandmother's Surrey house, but strictly as an amateur. 'Jump up and have a go . . . see how long you can stick on.' But this was to be something different, the real thing. It was my father's intention that each year as I grew up I must add one more item to the list of my athletic accomplishments. At the age of five, and much against my inclination, I had been taught an elementary, but stylistically correct, form of boxing. At the age of six I had learned to swim. I was now seven, so the task for 1912 was riding. My mother opposed, annually, each venture as it came along, pointing out that by the time I came of age I would be jumping on to the backs of whales from an open boat.

A factor which inclined my father towards horsemanship for this year, rather than towards shooting bison, for instance, was my cousin Tommy's gift to me of a high-spirited young mare. I call him my cousin but Tommy van Zeller was in fact my father's cousin, and today must be getting on for eighty. When I asked him about this, the only horse I have ever possessed, he told me that the reason why he chose it for me was not because he thought I would tame it but because he thought it would tame me.

Until quite recently Tommy van Zeller still rode to hounds, and even now would rather ride to the village to post a letter than walk. He has a length of metal in one leg and a patch over one eye (he was wounded in the First World War) and has fired my imagination since I was a boy as possessing all the characteristics which I would most like to possess myself. In another age he would have been a pirate; in our own he maintains a reputation for engaging eccentricity. A buccaneer, a nomad who wanders over Africa and lingers only in Scotland, a swashbuckler of the old school. We never write to one another, but to me his always unheralded visits are invariably stimulating. He has a large family and no money. 'I'm so poor that I've got more children now than horses, and you can guess what a grief this must be to me,' he says cheerfully.

Though not able to share Tommy's devotion to horses, still less to justify my father's hopes for me as sportsman and athlete, I preferred riding to boxing and swimming. The riding lessons were not altogether successful, partly because of a lack of sympathy between instructor and pupil, and partly because techniques can seldom elicit my full co-operation. Whether in the arts, manual skills, study or religion, I tend to be impatient of what might be called the carpentry of the subject and want to sit down on the furniture. This is a flaw in my character which I inherit from my mother, the least curious of women when it came to knowing how a thing was done. For my mother it was always the short cut, and in her case, more often than in mine, it worked.

Where my father delighted in taking trouble to reach proficiency, my mother disliked trouble of any sort. Having no ambitions, my mother confidently expected to reach, on the minimum of effort, levels which suited her. So she scorned method, trusting not so much to luck as to flair. 'You make such a religion if it,' she used to tell my father when she saw him charging into a new hobby. Conscientious in his job as in his play, my father took lessons in Arabic and made himself master of the grammar. When language difficulties arose in the household the servants would get my mother to interpret. For a time my father took up photography: it meant a dark-room, chemicals, apparatus, textbooks, and a camera from Germany. The photographs which survive today are those taken by my mother with a box Brownie.

My father's enthusiasms were not only pursued with such thoroughness as to make them a nuisance, they were also entirely unpredictable. If he were alive today his family would certainly bet on his wanting to become an expert in surfing. But he would be just as liable to put the surfer with the cubist, the vegetarian, the spiritualist, and say, 'absolute bosh, the whole thing'. Again we would guess that on balance he would vote today against pop music. But there would be no knowing. He can well be imagined buying every record and subscribing to every pop magazine. I can see him studying every modern trend. Perhaps my mother was wiser after all. Book study produces a race of mechanics, engineers, even craftsmen. The book does not produce men of culture. An increasing number of articles can be read today—and I say this knowing how pompous I sound—which tell how the film has been made, how the stars have found their appropriate firmament, how the set has been assembled, how the novel has come to be written, how the melody has come to be composed. The concern is not with ends but with means. Give me my mother every time.

So it was that my coolness towards riding lessons caused my father disappointment. Two factors however tended to lessen his dismay. The first was the zest which I exhibited that same year in England for the rides which were accompanied by my grandmother's elderly coachman, Ellwood. It was not the smart kind of riding which my father would have wished—the hunting bowler on a string, dark cutaway coat, top boots, crop, string gloves, which made up the uniform even for children when they appeared on horseback—but a more informal business of jersey, socks, shorts, and sandals. Though he did not presume to the role of riding master, Ellwood taught me more than I had learned from my Egyptian mentor. Such was Ellwood's tact that he never in so many words corrected my bad seat and my fumbling with the stirrups, but always 'advised'.

'My advice to you would be, General,' he would say by way of introduction to corrections so veiled as hardly to appear as corrections at all; and I would dust myself and remount in a spirit of hardy optimism. 'Let me tell you what *I* do, General, when the saddle slips away from under me.' I am sure that the saddle had never slipped away from under Ellwood. 'You know what Red Indians do when the reins get shot out of their hands? Well, they just grip with their knees, lean forward, and pick 'em up again. They never dismount, Red Indians don't, unless they bloomin' well have to. When the bullets are flying they press hard with their bare legs, same as yours are now, and their ponies know what's wanted.'

I can remember more of our conversations than of our rides. Ellwood had been in my grandmother's service for a dozen years or more, and there were few outside the family whose friendship I valued as much as his. At one time I thought of being a coachman when I grew up, and when I told my mother of this I was surprised to discover that she thought it would be a funny life to choose. When asked why, I said it was because of the noise which the heels of Ellwood's boots made in the coach-house. Thus is youth moulded.

The second reason why my father was reassured about the chances of my one day becoming a rider was that I began to take an interest in camels. Camels, with my father's military background, were two a penny so far as I was concerned, and very soon I was enjoying a lofty hump. The camel's easy swinging lope gave me the sense of being carried on the waves of the sea, and by comparison the horse's trot seemed to me very small beer. At the age of seven and wearing the enormous pith helmet which appears in the photographs of me at this period, I must have looked, up there on the back of the stately animal, like a mushroom, and I wonder that I was allowed to ride camels at all. Certainly my father would have been all for my riding any animal which was prepared to carry me on its back, from an elephant to a crocodile, and it was only because I was bitten a year later when trying to feed a camel that I was encouraged by my mother to have another try with horses. When my father was told that I had narrowly escaped having my hand bitten off, he hid his concern by the comment that I had probably been asking the poor brute some of the damn fool questions I was for ever asking him.

Though we went back to England only once a year the journeys assume in retrospect a disproportionate place in our lives. Breaking into routine existence, travel, like periods spent in hospital, can awaken a whole range of sensibilities normally asleep. As I write, with nothing to help me in tracing the sequence of these voyages, impressions crowd close. Whiffs of train smoke float across the page, and a liner's dinner gong sends an echo which booms through the tapping of the typewriter in front of me.

In every journey there comes a particular moment when the traveller feels he is under way. It might be thought that the moment comes at the point of departure, or immediately after it, but this is not what happens. Neither the drive to the station nor the boat train, whether on the Egyptian or the English side, marked for me the real start. These were no more than preliminary movements, manœuvrings for position. Even the Customs, which in Egypt meant pandemonium and in England aloof unconcern, did not spell for me the magic of take-off. The significant moment came when I heard the anchor being drawn up into the ship's great nostril and I saw the lozenge-shaped pads, wasps' nests to a landsman like myself, being pulled over the side of the deck. Early in the course of my travels I learned not to be misled by hoots, bells, sirens, whistles: these might mean any number of things. But there was no mistaking the anchor and the pads. Even then it was only when the gangways had been stowed away that I allowed myself the luxury of smelling the hot oiliness of the engine-room, the tang of hemp and tar, the mixed ozone of salt water and clear soup. The adventure had begun.

It is forty years since I have sailed on anything larger than a channel steamer, so for all I know the sights, sounds, smells may have been replaced by new ones. I hope the gritty white nail-heads, bolts, and nuts still look down from the ceiling of the cabin upon the occupant of the upper bunk, and that brass and mahogany still make the dominant combination. I trust that as you turn the pages of your Children's Annual in the saloon, hoping that someone will come along and volunteer to read to you, you can still hear the slap of deck-quoits, the burr of propellers, the thud of bare feet, the ticking of the news-tape, the flapping of tarpaulin, the squeak of a deckchair. If these things are no more, why not go by air?

On one of these sea voyages from Port Said to Marseilles I was discovered to be ignorant on two points about which I should by then have acquired a knowledge. I did not know how to tie my shoe-laces and I did not know how to tell the time. It places the incident early in my career. Both defects might have

The author, 1937

The Camberley House

The London House, 109 Lancaster Gate

escaped notice indefinitely had I not on the same day, and by want of presence of mind, gone almost out of my way to betray myself. The mistake with the laces was to stick out my feet when a steward came along in the middle of the morning with a tray: he did not know that I expected him to tie my shoes. The other mistake was, when my father sent me below to find out the time from the clock in the card-room, to guess. It was now afternoon so when I came back and reported that it was half-past nine I knew from the effect I produced that I should have taken the trouble to ask somebody.

'Can't the boy even read the time?' My father was in full tornado. My mother, who knew how easily the waters could be troubled, was never without oil to pour. She said that perhaps the clock in the card-room had stopped at nine-thirty. 'Of course it hasn't. Clocks on this line never stop. And if they did, there would be some chap up on a ladder to put them right. The fact is the boy doesn't know how to tell the time. Or how to do up his shoes. O my God.'

In spite of what I have said about my attitude towards technique I am pretty sure that as I lay in my bunk that night, under the white goose-pimples of the metal beams and while listening to the band which played in the saloon, I decided to mug up the technique of tying laces and telling the time.

On one of these voyages, and shortly after we left Port Said, a Lascar sailor jumped overboard. An alarm bell, shrill as breaking glass and as imperative as a baby's cry, rang. The ship swished round in a graceful curve like a duchess sweeping up her train, and came to a chugging uneasy halt. Boats were lowered. Passengers went to the deck's rail, and said, but with solicitude rather than with morbid interest, that they thought they could see something bobbing up and down. My father held his field-glasses, set with his usual efficiency at 'marine', to my nose. Could I see anything? No. 'You just twiddle that little wheel in the middle until you find the outline has settled down. How is it going?' After a lot of twiddling and a steady look, I said I was afraid I could see a red smudge on the surface of the water.

'Then the bally old propeller must have got him,' he said, adding in a voice which was new to me, 'so the best thing you can do is to go below and pray for the feller.'

Today whenever I am served with a slice of melon, my mind goes back to yet another sea voyage. Encouraged to fend for myself, a phrase used often by my father, I was sent to the dining saloon to have breakfast on my own. This, in the light of my shortcomings over doing up my shoes and telling the time, was designed as part of a policy. Still a very backward child, I could not read what was on the card, so, noticing what a fellow passenger was eating at the next table, I told the waiter I would like melon. When I had finished the melon I asked for porridge. Feeling manly and grown-up over my porridge, I noticed the man at the next table getting up and leaving. His melon had not been followed by porridge or bacon and eggs, so I argued that melon was supposed to come at the end and not at the beginning of breakfast. Once again my ignorance was shown up. What must the other passengers think of a small boy who knew no better than to take melon before and not after the main course? Was the waiter with whom I had placed my order telling other waiters about it in the hot pantry behind the screen, and laughing about it? I finished the porridge as quickly as I could, and, feeling that every eye was mocking, left the saloon. In their cabin my parents were having breakfast; they had not ordered melon. In his cabin with Josephine my brother was having breakfast; he was not old enough for melon. I could get no help from my family. Years later I discovered two truths: first that I had been right all along about eating melon at the beginning, and second that nobody minds in the least what you do about breakfast so long as you do not take it all.

If crossing France by train was less of an adventure than crossing the Mediterranean by boat, there was still much to excite and amuse. We used to start from Marseilles in the afternoon, travel overnight, and break the journey for one or two days in Paris. An early instance of this arrangement remains in my memory because heading north in the early evening from Marseilles, the train, unlike the trains in Egypt which moved irregularly, maintained a speed so even and fast as to make me wonder aloud about it to my father. The observation which he made puzzled me at the time, and I have speculated about it since. He said that by counting the telegraph poles which were spaced at exactly measured intervals along the line you could tell to within a few seconds the speed at which the train was travelling. He took out his watch, frowned, muttered a calculation, looked at a few telegraph poles, drummed his fingers on the padded arm-rest in the compartment, an activity which I took to be a further aid to his arithmetic, and told me the number of miles we were doing per hour. Never had he so commanded my admiration. Here was something which I too could do if I tried hard enough. Even though I could not multiply and divide, and was still none too sure about interpreting the hands of the clock, I could at least count up to a hundred. Perhaps this primary facility would bring it off. Accordingly I counted telegraph poles until it was dark, and I had to climb into my sleeper. Nor was this the end of it because during the night I went back to the corridor of the train, and stood in my pyjamas and slippers counting telegraph poles. If I counted enough of them, and there were certainly plenty between Marseilles and Paris, would not the knowledge come? I must have stood in the corridor a long time, and grown muddled with sleep, because my mother told me next morning that I had come, sooty and barely coherent, into their compartment and had asked my father for a further explanation of the system. It was an admission that the short cut cannot always be relied upon.

I can remember another all-night train journey across France when there was a storm, and again I spent a long time at the window in the corridor. I see lightning bouncing along the rails and looking like silver stair-rods, and the rain on the glass tracing complicated road maps which shivered and altered their pattern every time the thunder broke or we went over the points.

When I discussed with Ellwood the whole matter of travelling by train I was recommended a practice which, it seemed, had served him throughout a long life. It was to say repeatedly, working the refrain into the noise of the wheels, 'to Manchester, to Manchester, to fetch a pocket handkercher'. I tried this at our next journey and it worked so well that I handed on the information to my father. It was an exchange for the information which he had given me about the telegraph poles. My father was reading at the time, cushioned in the velvet of his First Class corner seat facing the engine, and did not hear the advice I offered. My mother, after listening to the refrain carefully articulated by me, said she wondered why I bothered and that in any case she was not likely to adopt the couplet on the way to Paris.

Whether on the same journey or another, but certainly in Paris (which I remember from that visit only as a city of pigeons, bicycles, baskets of fruit, smells of hot coffee and drains, angry blasts of whistles and motor horns) I was sick on a station platform. My mother had gone on ahead to sit in the carriage which my father had hired in advance, through an agent, and with her were Josephine and the baby and I think also my aunt Yolande. When we travelled we did so in quantity, my father liking to plan things in the greatest detail as though projecting a military campaign. My being sick had not been allowed for. The luggage, and here again it was a question of quantity acting as a stimulus to my father's powers of organisation, was piling up on the platform and being counted and re-counted. My father was striding about, with me trotting along at his side, and issuing in a loud voice instructions to the French porters. The fact that he spoke in German added to the liveliness of the scene. I had never been train-sick before so my act was completely unexpected. Perhaps I had got dizzy counting telegraph poles. For once my father was at a loss. The orders and their countermanding ceased abruptly and there was silence. Except from me. Then one of the porters took command. Dropping whatever luggage he carried, he picked me up in his arms and did not lower me until my mother was sighted and I was placed in the waiting carriage. Visiting Paris years later as a young man I found I could not even be sure which station, let alone which platform, had witnessed my (and my father's) distress. But the blue smock of the French porter, the distinctive Gallican smell of the French cigarette, the toytown toot of the French train are setting enough.

CHAPTER THREE

The First Uncertainty

I very soon discovered that living in England under one or other of my grandmother's roofs was quite different from living under our own modest roof in Egypt. What I was not aware of was that the arrangement made for a division of outlook, even of personality, and that I felt perfectly at home with each. Or so it was at first. But when I began to think, I began to question. I came to feel not quite at home either in England or in Egypt. It was not that over here we lived in princely style and over there in poverty. There was no such sharp contrast. It was simply that the change of surroundings and standards made for unsettlement.

So far as enjoyment went, I think I preferred the rather grander life in the English houses (there was a third, a very grand one indeed but rented, into which we used to move when my elders tired of London and Surrey, in Norfolk) to the simpler and healthier life in Egypt. It was not that I liked luxury so much as getting my own way. In England I was the spoiled grandchild, the pet nephew, the heir-apparent not to fortune but to favour. In England there were more servants to make friends with (Ellwood the coachman, Georgie the seamstress, Mrs McGrath the housekeeper) than in Egypt where they were mostly Arabic. Ali, the gardener's son who played the flute, was the only friend I had in Egypt at this time, and though I vastly preferred his company to that of the European children whom I met on the beach and at parties, his shyness was an obstacle to full friendship.

There was my grandmother herself, for whom I conceived an affection warmer than that usually given to grandmothers, who typified for me a state of life. A noble and agreeable state of life. She stood for authority, tradition, stability. I could not picture her in our Alexandrian setting. She might have understood about the two forts, but I did not see her climbing over their sea-washed boulders. I had been told of her two marriages, of the books and plays which she had written (the books were about court life in the capitals where she had lived, the plays were about diplomats whose embassies served romance as well as foreign policy*), about the historical figures with whom she had been on intimate terms, about the title and property which she had left behind when she had chosen to throw in her lot with the democracy of Edwardian England.

Though she rarely visited her native land, my maternal grandmother was of Swiss stock. Descended from Hans von Halwyll, the deliverer of Switzerland's armies from the Burgundians in 1476 (which won him the title of 'Sieger von Mürten'), her mother, *née* Comtesse Hydeline de Halwyll, married twice. Her first husband was a de Seigneux, her second was the Count de Launay who became Italian Ambassador in Berlin when Bismarck was in power. She had three children. My grandmother, Hydeline de Seigneux, married Arthur van de Velde, who, after being Belgian Conseillier de Légation in London, retired as Minister. Arthur's brother, my great-uncle Edward, married Baroness Louise de Zuylen de Nyvelt and was rarely seen in England; I, anyway, have no recollection of him. My great-aunt Gabrielle, Arthur's and Edward's sister, married the Marquis de la Riva Aguero, and thereafter lived in semi-retirement in Brussels. The Marquis de la Riva Aguero was a recluse and an invalid and a great admirer of Dickens. The works of Mr Dickens had not at that time been translated into either French or Portuguese, so Great-aunt Gabrielle was required to read them to him, one by one as they came out, in halting English. Since his father had been the last Viceroy and first President of Peru, his mother the Princess de Lööz-Corswarem, one wonders at Great-uncle de la Riva Aguero's fondness for an author whose sympathies were pronouncedly what today would be called left wing.

My grandmother, then, was Swiss by birth, Belgian by marriage, English by reason of the country in which she chose to live. She spoke the language perfectly, preferred to have English servants when everyone else was trying to get foreign ones, and never left

* One of my grandmother's plays was produced in London, another in Paris. Although Sarah Bernhardt and Louis Berton acted in both of them, because they were friends of hers, the plays were utter failures. It was only because she financed these ventures that they were put on at all.

England's shores if she could help it. It was probably my grandmother's preference for everything English which, as much as any other consideration, determined my grandfather's rejection of the post of Belgian Minister in Mexico. The decision was never regretted, and the van de Veldes took root, for all too short a time, in this country. As a courtesy to the British they dropped their foreign titles, and though the next generation professed satisfaction it was a decision which I have always felt was secretly resented.

If my imagination was fired by all this, it was fired even more by the tales of travel which were told to me by various uncles. Not only had Maurice and Marcel roamed widely, returning always with armfuls of photographs and trunkfuls of trophies, but Gaston and René roamed even farther and did not return at all. I do not know which two lots I admired the more. There was also an uncle by marriage, a colonel who had done much of his service in the West Indies, who for some reason symbolised a more exciting form of soldiering than did my father whose post in Egypt seemed by comparison provincial.

To most boys with English family backgrounds the thought of the Pyramids would probably be more alluring than the thought of Marble Arch, and if this was not the case with me it was because of Dickens. At Lancaster Gate and while visiting us in Alexandria my aunt Yolande used to read Dickens to me, volume after volume and some volumes twice, so for me there was more glamour attaching to a single London street lamp than to miles of Egyptian desert. It is the old story of liking to be where one mostly is not. England was the land of mystery and romance; Egypt of flies and glare. The yellow London fog was a veil more dramatic than the yashmak.

Today I count myself highly fortunate in the placing, geographical and temporal, of my early boyhood. I can look back at an interim period in the history of England and Egypt alike which those who came only a short time after me have missed. This is not to claim that 1910-1915 was more of a time of transition than any other. It is merely to state that of all times to be a boy, it is one which I would not swop with any other.

If Lancaster Gate, with the more vivid, worldly, variegated scenes it presented, made a greater appeal than the ugly house at

Silsileh, for all its freedom from social shibboleth, it must be remembered what London was like half a century ago. Admittedly it was sootier, muddier, smellier, noisier than it is now.

It may perhaps be imagined how a horse-drawn bus, painted and the upper deck open to the heavens, looked to a small boy who was used to drab bungalow trams stuffy with the smell of garlic and sweat. Instead of dusty and musty buggies he sees pair-horsed phaetons, matchbox coupés, hansom cabs, stately victorias, electric as well as horse-drawn broughams. Instead of crumpled Egyptian soldiers in tropical khaki leaning against walls and rolling cigarettes he sees scarlet-coated guardsmen walking stiffly in the Park. The Park, with its military bands and riders in the Row, is to him at once a kaleidoscope of colour and a pageant of elegance. He longs to be old enough to ride among the men with boots like shell-cases and the women with veils drawn down from their top hats. There are children riding in the Row, trotting along with a groom in a brown bowler at their side, but this would be altogether too tame. If riding in the Row was to mean anything it would have to be in the company of the cavalry moustaches and the side-saddle riding habits. No nonsense about a guiding-rein and someone whose job it was to hold the stirrups as one mounted and pick one up after a fall.

There were the old ladies sitting on canvas stools outside the Park railings in bonnets or straw hats selling balloons, paper windmills, cut flowers. There were the nannies in long dust-coats sitting on benches in Kensington Gardens, exchanging gossip and gently rocking prams while underling nursemaids in their pinks and pale blues played ball with small girls in white muslin and black stockings or else rounded up small boys in sailor suits. Feeding birds with crumbs, sailing boats on the Round Pond, tugging at the strings of a kite which never did more than zigzag ten feet above the ground and then crash.

Still in 1911 there was a wide variety of street hawker and itinerant performer which today is reduced to the seller of matches, toys which jump on the pavement, shoelaces, and, as providing entertainment, the violinist and pavement artist. Street organs could still grind out tunes which haunt to this day. German bands, composed of stout steaming men in black peaked caps like those worn by members of the Royal Yacht Squadron, could still legally blow into yards of curving brass. Italians continued to prod sad-eyed monkeys wearing a feather in Tyrolean hats into halfhearted dancing to tinkling grand opera which rolled out of a hand barrel-organ supported on a single stick. Rarest sight among the category, but distinctly remembered, was the performing bear which, with the aid of a tambourine, moved heavily in the steps of what was far removed from a caper.

But first to be driven off the streets by mechanisation is one whose name and function are now almost entirely forgotten. The 'runner' was a survival even in 1911, regarded with an affection which must have been more sentimental and antiquarian than practical as a member of diehard but vanishing species. Runners, earlier in top hats but latterly in seasoned bowlers, green at the crown and irregular in brim, used to hang about station yards and in the wings at cab ranks. They acted in a private capacity, not as porters. Some may have had customers whom they served habitually but mostly they seemed to be wisps who settled where they could: on any traveller with luggage. Families arriving at the entrance of the station and hailing a four-wheeler (or, if the family were large, a horse-brake) would find a runner hovering at the horse's head and waiting to hear what address was given to the driver. If the destination were not too distant, and it would have to be very distant indeed to discourage him, the runner would trot along behind the wheels until the final halt. All this for the privilege of helping the butler or footman to unload the trunks and carry them upstairs, an act which was rewarded with a small tip. There was no fixed tariff for runners, no union which could be appealed to in an argument, but the generally accepted rate was threepence a mile. That this was considered adequate was unquestioned, and my father's florin which covered the jogging from Victoria to Lancaster Gate was judged princely.

I remember a tired old man acting runner as my grandmother's carriage bowled along on its way every Sunday morning to the Jesuit church at Farm Street. In the more or less empty streets, with Ellwood on the box setting a spanking pace, a runner would have a job to keep up. A shilling at the end of it. Even if he was younger than I imagined him to be, and even if the value of a shilling was considerably greater in those days, there was little relation between the undertaking and the tip. Even I, at six or seven, could see that. 'But all he's done, dear, is open the door.'

I remember another old man, not a runner by profession and this time unquestionably wearing a top hat and frayed frock coat, who appeared at the door of Lancaster Gate on the fall of the first snowflake of 1911, and, bringing with him his own broom, offered to keep the steps clear of snow for the whole day in return for whatever they cared to give him in the kitchen. This is no longer the singing tapestry of style and colour and wit; it is the black-and-white of *Oliver Twist, David Copperfield, Martin Chuzzlewit.*

It would be an exaggeration to say that these glimpses of a London life other than that enjoyed by us at Lancaster Gate gave me to ponder upon social justice, new concepts of man's rights in an evolving world, the application of the Christian ethic. But what I saw did make me think. The London to which I was becoming more and more attached posed problems which my family seemed disinclined to discuss.

The same problems existed in Alexandria, indeed in a more acute form, but the lot of the *fellahin* appeared in the context of a simpler civilisation. Also I had no experience of how rich Egyptians lived. England was the background against which, for me, these problems had to be worked out. How was it, I kept asking myself, that in England, which symbolised all that was cultured and noble, so many people were poor?

At one stage I put the difficulty to my father, bringing up by way of illustration the snow-clearer and the runner. I do not know how old I was but I managed somehow to convey my sense of shame at receiving these servile attentions from the elderly poor, and to explain how it bothered me to see the dignity of some grown-ups being slighted by other grown-ups who happened to be on top. Were there any rules which governed these things?

'I know exactly what you feel,' said my father who had no idea, 'because I used to feel the same about Arabs. The thing to remember is that these chaps like being servile. They always have been, and it's second nature. Just like the natives in Alexandria. Besides, it's not a bad sort of life if you haven't known anything more comfortable. It's in the open air, and the exercise keeps them dashed fit. They are probably a lot healthier and happier than people of the same age higher up the ladder.'

If this was the official view I was not greatly reassured by it. Indeed it disturbed me still further. It made the poor a race apart, and I wondered if it could really be much compensation to know as you pounded along behind the spinning wheels of a carriage or swept snow from the steps that you were keeping in good enough condition to allow for further running and further sweeping. It seemed to me that being naturally servile was shameful and that being servile as a means of keeping alive was, though apparently inevitable, worse. Whether the poor fawned upon the gentry instinctively or because they had to did not seem to me to alter the main issues, namely that it was something which the gentry must have brought about originally, and something also which such of the gentry whom I had so far come across were in no mind to change.

It will be readily understood then that, unlike most small boys, if we are to judge by contemporary autobiographies, I shrank from the task of handing pennies to street singers, vendors of one sort or another, roadside contortionists, casual tramps and beggars. It so embarrassed me to see grown men showing obsequious deference to my more fortunate youth that I refused to go downstairs any longer with those pennies. I hope it did not cut off the supply.

For a time I think I must have become rather obsessed with the thought of fortune and misfortune. Another in the family who felt uneasy about our measured affluence was my aunt Berthe. But she at least had the advantage of being able to work off her misgivings on charitable undertakings. She not only visited prisons, hospitals, homes for the aged, families who lived in the slums, but also gave away, as I discovered later, two-thirds of her income to deserving causes. But I was too young to do anything except ask questions about poverty which seemed to annoy people. After a while I learned that it was almost as wrong to talk about the poor as it was to talk about health or death. So I stopped talking about the poor and confined myself to wondering about them. I wondered whether they were wondering as much as I was.

To correct any impression that between the ages of six and

eight (the Lancaster Gate period ended in the winter of 1913 when my grandmother died) I was the precocious introvert, frowning and guilt-ridden, censorious of my elders in their unthinking comfort, I must explain that, with all its sadness, London enchanted me as much in monochrome as in paint. With the same enthusiasm that I enjoyed the summer visits to the country where tea-trays were always tinkling and butterflies were always fussing about over the flower-beds, where there was a boat and one did not have to wear either shoes or stockings except indoors, where there were swans and a rockery, where there was never any fog and apparently no rain either, I enjoyed London in the winter.

I liked the reflection of gaslight on wet pavements, the way in which cab-horses puffed steam through their nostrils like dragons, the shop windows with their Christmas decorations, the policemen from whose shoulders hung dripping and shining black capes, the beery old ladies with their feather boas who came walloping out of pubs.

Moving backwards and forwards between Egypt and England, the camera uses different lenses and is liable to get London out of focus. This too I have noticed about my retrospective views of London, that I tend to see it in terms of a generation or two ago. The perspective of my vision is determined less by historical events than by social changes and by the literature of these social changes. When a child I saw the London of Dickens; in boyhood it was the London of Conan Doyle; as a young man I was back twenty years in the London of Saki; after that it was Michael Arlen's London, which fired my imagination. Today I am beginning to see London as described by the novelists of the Second World War. I doubt if I shall ever catch up. Nor do I particularly want to, having a list of more agreeable Londons from which to choose.

Connected with my uncertainty about the right to live in pleasant and comfortable surroundings was another uncertainty which came up when I began to learn about religion. If what the catechism said was true, why did not we Christians really live to know, love, and serve God? This was the first page of the catechism and I was already stuck. Perhaps religion appears more clearly to children anyway, but certainly to me the Christian statement could not have presented itself in sharper outline. The religious issue confused me not in its postulate but in its application. What I have called the uncertainty lay not in relation to God, but in relation to us. There, roughly, it has remained ever since.

I had, rather late in the day, learned to read. This enabled me not only to pursue my fondness for certain authors (Stevenson and Haggard as well as Dickens) without having to bother my aunt, but also to use prayer books at Mass without the help of hideous coloured pictures. It also enabled me to study anything that was going. At Lancaster Gate there was much to choose from in the way of possible subjects, my four uncles and five aunts being persons of diversified interests, but most easily accessible was the literature of religion. My grandmother, in addition to her three books of reminiscences and those two disastrous plays, had composed several works of devotion, privately printed, which were expected to form part of the personal library of every member of the household. Copies were presented to me, which dutifully, but also because I was fond of my grandmother, I read.

Despite the uncritical attitude of mind with which one who has just learned to read will approach anything in print from Chinese history to raising hens, I found my grandmother's manuals taxing. They were like pictures of guardian angels, which I have always felt to be a mistake anyway, in that they gave in one idiom something which belonged to another. Reading my grandmother's pious compositions had at least this effect, that when I came to write the same sort of thing myself many years later I decided to follow the opposite course of using the idiom of every day to urge people of every day to embark upon a spirituality of every day.

I knew that my father was not the man to solve problems of the spirit, so, having sworn my aunt Berthe to secrecy, I laid bare my new bewilderment to her. Why, I asked, did prayer books and the catechism have so little to do with the way things actually happen? Berthe did not snub me, as I feared perhaps she might, but neither did she sound very convincing. She told me that prayer books and catechism answers were in fact connected in the closest way with life as we knew it here below, but that we must take all this on faith and not expect to be able to understand the way things happened. She was right, of course, but to me there seemed something rather last-ditch about the doctrine. I was no match for her in argument so I gave it up. As after my interview with my father, when I had brought up the difficulty about another apparent inconsistency, I came away unsatisfied. Everywhere one looked there seemed to be inconsistencies.

Berthe may herself have felt that our religious discussion had not taken us far because she gave me a copy of the New Testament and suggested that I should read the four gospels when I got back to Alexandria. This I did, so in a roundabout way it was thanks to her after all that I did not sit in that last ditch trusting to luck.

I was now eight and it was my last summer, though I did not know this at the time, at Lancaster Gate and Camberley. Already, in 1913, the landmarks were crumbling. On my next visit to England in the year following, my grandmother's houses sold and a new era begun, I would find no horse buses in the streets, and though the motor buses were still roofless on the upper deck they were not the same. Four-wheelers and hansoms, the former scattering down roads which led to seaside towns where they creaked on for another four or five years, and the latter finding their way to Oxford where they were preserved in mothballs for very much longer, gave way to the taxi. Everywhere people were exchanging carriages for cars, gas for electricity, hand-delivered messages for telephone calls. Before she died, my grandmother made it perfectly clear that she would never go anywhere by taxi, instal electric light, or have a telephone. Her death came at the wrong time for everyone except herself.

CHAPTER FOUR

The Preparation

Back in Egypt, and having little more now than a year between me and a boarding school, lessons took on a new urgency. If I were to be launched upon the salty waters of serious education I would have to be subjected to some intensive cramming. Mr Carter, since 1912 my tutor, was instructed by my father to cut out the general reading and get down to business. This was just what Mr Carter had been dreading all along. So had I. After an uneasy start when my father had first engaged his services, Mr Carter had won me over and we were now great friends. The situation would have been impossible otherwise, for we were in each other's company almost all day long. So that at the time of which I speak (1913), with months of association in the schoolroom, on the tennis court, on the beach, and in excursions round about Alexandria behind us, we were on terms of almost equal exchange. He put me on to books which lay outside Yolande's range of interest, roused in me a feeling for antiquity and history generally, and taught me parlour games which he invented and which I would never have had the ingenuity to invent for myself. In return I gave to him the admiration and affection which he was too reserved to recognise, but which, in his somewhat withdrawn bachelor life, he probably needed. In this way both our minds were broadened.

I was anxious to get on with classics, which besides having a grown-up connotation would prevent my being at a disadvantage when I finally reached Downside; moreover, I had determined to resist mathematics to the last fraction. Mr. Carter minded it more, and again there were two reasons for this: first he would have to brush up his Latin, and second he would have to overcome my opposition to mathematics. That Mr. Carter was not proving himself entirely successful in either project became, early in the reform, apparent to my father. I suspect that my father took greater exception to Mr. Carter's inadequacy as a teacher and disciplinarian than he did to my intransigence in the matter of arithmetic. But he took exception to that too.

My mother was probably the one who saved Mr Carter from getting the sack. If so, she would not have asked that mercy be shown him, nor would she have advanced my liking for this austere shy man; she would have pointed out how difficult it would be to get him replaced. My mother had no great regard for Mr Carter—she thought him a booby and said so—but she knew how apt my father was to make sudden decisions and then find himself stranded. So Mr Carter stayed on. But his position became increasingly difficult because now my father as well as my mother came out openly about his being a booby.

I told myself that I knew Mr Carter better than my parents did, that they judged by the wrong standards, that nothing would deflect my loyalty, that I was learning as much as I wanted to anyway. Yet, as one whose presence in the room never toned down an opinion expressed by either of my parents, I could not remain altogether unaffected. Nor, though the civilities were always punctiliously observed, could Mr Carter. Not hearing but sensing the disapproval of his employers, he withdrew more than ever into himself.

So far as my preparation for Downside was concerned, Mr Carter's virtual retirement from the competitive march of education made no difference whatever. In English schools of that date it was assumed that new boys could read, and a start was made from there. But so far as companionship went, I found myself falling back on the flute-playing Ali who was scarcely more forthcoming than Mr Carter.

As in the case of my grandmother, who personified to me a whole category of concepts, so in the case of my tutor. My tutor stood for the Establishment, the Empire, the public school system, cricket. Neither my grandmother nor Mr Carter was any less dear to me for being a symbol. It is just that the creator of images lays himself open to loss. All through life it has been one of my weaknesses that I tend to mistake the image for the ideal, so that when for one reason or another the image fades I find myself without the support of what was represented, and a certain emptiness ensues. I see now that had I attached fewer labels to my elders, even bestowed fewer crowns, I would have benefited more from their friendship. Certainly I would have given greater value to the friendship of my own contemporaries. But at the time there were not many contemporaries about.

Not many, but there were some. A German family, the Lindemanns, had recently come with the intention of settling in Alexandria, and though there were only two children, Helmuth and Lisa, they entertained a good deal and frequently had relatives with children to stay. During the two years before the 1914 War I saw a good deal of the Lindemann family: Helmuth was my age or a little older, Lisa was three years younger. Herr Lindemann, Hugo, was a banker of about forty: dark, thickset, athletic, shrewd little eyes and a moustache cropped close. He had a face like an angry pug, which those who did not know him found alarming. The moment he laughed, and most of the time he was laughing, the pug was forgotten, and he was seen to be the kindest of men. Frau Lindemann, Helen, was big, fair, untidy, tolerant, self-indulgent, and far more intelligent than anyone would have guessed from looking at her. She was as devoted to her children as my mother was to us, but she treated them in an offhand way which suggested complete indifference. There were a German nanny and a nursemaid, but without seeming to do so Helen Lindemann left them no authority, seeing to everything herself. The indifference was assumed: part of a planned system of upbringing. Hugo Lindemann had made a great deal of money, and though he lost nearly everything during World War I, including his properties in Alexandria, he had made another and greater fortune before the outbreak of World War II. At the time when we knew them they owned a house in Bavaria, a chalet in Switzerland, and what amounted to a palace in the residential part of Alexandria. This house became a hospital when the Lindemanns moved out.

The house and too elaborate hospitality overawed me. I found the life they led on the houseboat which they kept anchored off the coast between Aboukir and Nelson Island less daunting. Fortunately I was invited more often to the houseboat than to the marble halls at Ramleh. If there were many guests and there was not enough room on the houseboat, Helmuth and I would sleep in a tent on the mainland while one of my father's orderlies slept in another tent close by in case of accidents. We took care to see that the guests were so distributed among the cabins on the houseboat as to make our tent a necessity. These evenings and early mornings on the shore within hailing distance of the houseboat are a memory I treasure: palm trees, sand dunes ribbed by the wind and stretching for miles along the coast, tufts of dry grass which was almost colourless and had a sharp edge when you touched it, cactus, inland pools now slate blue, now pale coffee, now red. As we lay under the canvas reminding one another of the porpoises we had seen hopping through the waves during the day and boasting of the sharks we thought we had seen, we could smell the seaweed and the salt, hear the reeds and pampases rustling in the breeze like paper bags, the whinnying of a startled horse, and in the dawn the call of a bugle from the camp.

On these three-day visits to Aboukir, Helmuth and I wore only swimming trunks, and when not in the water we paddled canoes. Helmuth was a better swimmer than I was, and it made me think that, for all the professional instruction insisted upon by my father, I could claim no more than possessing a superior style. Helmuth and Lisa had been sent down to the water's edge and told to get on with it. Again this had been part of Helen Lindemann's plan.

One reason why I am able to remember these Aboukir visits more clearly than much that has happened since may be because the Lindemanns were the first family of which I had experience at close quarters apart from our own. Their way of life was very different both from the formal routine of Lancaster Gate and from our Alexandrian home. It showed me that extravagance could be combined with simplicity, and that even magnificence could be taken lightly. My grandmother would never have accepted the Lindemann formula, and I am a little surprised that my parents accepted it, but I certainly swallowed it whole. It was only later, when I resumed my examinations of religion, that I began again to wonder.

Another reason why the Aboukir scene is so distinct is possibly because it is associated in my mind with the discovery of a craft, namely carving, which was to mean a lot to me throughout my life. May not such a discovery sharpen a whole range of sensibilities, each in turn leading to a new appreciation? With deeper appreciation comes a deeper lodging in the memory. Not for nothing does classical mythology assign to the woman Mnemosyne the role of mother to the nine Muses. Whatever scientific foundation there may be for my belief in the memorising effect of artistic initiation, I know that it was at Aboukir that I decided what I wanted to be good at before all else. (Thus worded, the decision does not conflict with my later decision to devote myself to the service of God.)

The occasion was a Sunday, and a picnic was to take place on Nelson Island. We, the party of boys and girls, were to be taken out in my father's racing yacht *Water-Witch* which he had sailed round the coast the day before from Alexandria harbour where he kept it moored. The grown-ups were to come on later in the Lindemann's larger and more luxurious yacht the name of which I forget. In the ordinary way the Nelson Island picnic held first place in our plans. The attraction was probably more in what it suggested to the imagination than what it afforded as a picnic site. I seem to connect it with tangled vegetation and, of all unlikely things, lilies. What lilies can have been doing on an uninhabited heap of sand, scrub, and jungle I cannot explain, yet how can I have invented them? This time the picnic had no appeal for me. All I wanted to do was to get back to the beach on the mainland where I had seen an Arab boy with a small assortment of knives in his lap cutting bits of black washed-up wood into shapes.

While Helmuth was casting off that morning in his canoe I had noticed someone about four years my senior, and obviously more interested in what he was doing than in us, sitting on a pile of nets and cork floats. The sculptor did not seem to mind when I came and stood within a few yards of him and stared. Looking at him while he whittled at driftwood was not like listening to Ali playing his home-made pipe. Instinct told me that not in a hundred years would I be able to get music out of a pierced reed, or any other instrument, whereas I might be able to cut solid materials into shapes. Sometimes the boy, sweeping the knives against his stomach in the folds of his *djellabiah*, would hold the piece of wood between his knees and push with both hands. Sometimes he would scoop as though working on a lobster. He would spit on his composition, rub it with his thumb, and then hold it up to see how it looked with a shine. Probably because he did not possess a file he used sandpaper of differing strengths.

I had been taught by my father never to interrupt an artist at work. I was content to wait. When he had finished the design which he had been carving in shallow relief he stood up and would have gone away if I had not stopped him. I knew enough kitchen Arabic to ask him to show me what else he had done. He pulled a cloth bundle from his pocket and shook out a number of objects on to the wet sand at his feet. Not all of these were of wood. Some were of a chalky substance, which he told me came in on the wash and was easy to carve. At home, he told me, he kept his big pieces.

So while Helmuth plied his paddles, swam and splashed, lay in the sun, twined seaweed round his toes and fought one foot against another, I waded out deep into new and unbelievably exciting waters. This does not imply that one morning of exploration and discovery represented any great climax in my life, still less that it gave me the advantage of Helmuth whom I now saw as an uncouth rustic, but merely to peg down in time an awareness which directed many of my energies later on. If I knew that I was in fact no match for Helmuth in the water, in the saddle, in fighting, climbing, or running, I knew also that he would not feel the least resentment should I turn out to be more skilful in a craft. My first act on finding this new interest was to tell him about it and invite his co-operation. While he showed himself ready enough to comb the beach for the blackened salted bits of wood that I wanted, many of which already suggesting sculptural shapes, I could see that the project as a project did not interest him.

'What would you like me to make you?' I asked him.

'A boat,' he said.

I told him that though I was fairly confident about being able to hollow out a boat for him, I could not promise that it would float. It would almost certainly *not* be able to float. Since I did not believe myself to be the kind of craftsman who made things which worked, might it not be better if I carved him a seated figure or a face? He chose a face. This was all very much in the future, because at that stage I possessed neither material nor tools, but so sure was I that the power lay somewhere inside me that I could afford to take risks. In the event I was able within a few days to present Helmuth with the first work of my hands: a head. The incident is still so clear to me that I can remember what trouble I had with that head. The wood, rotten with seawater, split down the middle before I had finished and had to be glued together by my father while I stood by and wept. When finally delivered at the Lindemanns, back now from Aboukir, the head was still in one piece.

Because of the morning's excitement, and the desire to collect more material before a wave came in again to wash it back into the sea, I remember particularly the mood of the picnic. The only details which remain with me are that we all drank beer, even the youngest of us, and that Frau Lindemann smoked a cigar. There was nothing unusual about either circumstance, for it was part of the Lindemann theory that the sooner the young got used to the taste of what they would be drinking for the rest of their lives the less chance there was that they would drink too much. Had Helmuth asked for a cigar he would have been given one. His mother habitually smoked cigars. She defeated, incidentally, the widely accepted view that heavy smokers are not great eaters of sweets. She ate chocolates constantly.

On Monday my father sailed the yacht back, and I was allowed to go with him. When not helping on deck I went over again and again the pieces of damp wood I had brought with me, some of it stowed among my shirts and pyjamas, fingering them and examining the grain to see what I would be able to make out of them. The first thing I did on getting home was to gather up all the old knives in the house and start cutting and chiselling. My mother's nail file proved useless, so until I could get a toothier one I used rough sandpaper. My parents believed that at this rate the craze would burn itself out in a week. But when at the end of a week I was still hard at it—though now in the stables because of the mess made in the house by the chips—they began to wonder. 'He will make us all beautifully rich,' said my mother. 'We must get him properly taught,' said my father.

I was so eager to hold my first exhibition, that the threat about being properly taught did not worry me. The exhibition took place in the dining-room because the display needed a big table. Those present were my parents, my brother (aged three), my brother's nurse Josephine, and one or two servants. I remember that for some reason Mr Carter was away, and how disappointed I felt about this. The exhibition was a good stroke: it launched me, and there was no going back. In my mother's eyes I was an infant prodigy, but knowing how readily the critical judgment can be swayed by mother-love I took no great account of it. My father did not seem impressed by the exhibition, and this dismayed me for I knew he was an artist. My brother showed a flattering desire to take all the exhibits for himself.

I never again saw the Arab boy who started all this off. Such in life is sometimes the function of one towards another. The message is delivered, and back goes the messenger into the shadows. Perhaps I should have remembered, as I worked, the old white marble bear of earlier years, and perhaps the old white grandfather too, but since I write of myself I know very well how I worked without the least recollection of either.

Towards the end of the same summer I was given a workshop. That is to say I was allowed to turn out the harness from a store cupboard in the stables, and put it to my own exclusive use. It had a skylight but no window; it was dusty and hot; it smelled of leather, rubber, linseed oil, brass-polish, horsehair upholstery. It suited me perfectly. I moved in at once with my knives, chisels, drawing materials, and a bicycle which was too big for me. The bicycle was too big for the workshop as well, so after a few days of discomfort I restored it to its place in the coach-house (which by this time was also a garage, for my father had acquired a Ford*).

The chief reason for the allocation of the harness cupboard was undoubtedly my addiction to sculpture, but there were contributory factors. It was thought that I would more effectually concentrate on the homework set by Mr Carter if I had a place to myself, stuffy after my own heart. Hitherto I had been obliged to do my homework in the day-nursery, already filled to capacity

* According to my brother, to whom in the interests of accuracy I am submitting the script chapter by chapter, there were two cars before the Ford: a De Dion-Bouton and a Talbot Darracq, one of which had a completely cylindrical bonnet like an oil-drum.

by a growing brother and his amiable talkative nurse. It was thought too that given the incentive of privacy and independence I would be drawn to cover other hobbies besides carving and painting. This I was only told about later.

My mother, in a moment of quite uncharacteristic keenness, had bought a book the title of which was *From Cot to Kindergarten*, and though I was well past the kindergarten age I had failed to reveal some of the relevant notes. When it came to the normal boy's hobbies, as described in the sequel *From Kindergarten to College*, my mother, wondering at my backwardness, consulted my father. What particularly puzzled my parents was that I had never wanted to collect sea-shells, butterflies (I never saw any in Egypt), coins, stamps, badges, or anything else. Nor have I ever since. My parents' sole reassurance was that at the age of four I had clamoured (like, as is now revealed, the infant Hitler) to have the nursery walls hung with pistols. But even this small crumb of comfort was spoiled for them when my early longing was taken to denote rather an eye for decor than a desire, as the book stated, for numerical accumulation.

To the workshop, which was my father's idea and not my mother's or mine, were accorded the immunities without which it would have been pointless: nobody was allowed in. I insisted on this from the start, and my parents understood. The only person who minded being kept out was my brother, and he was indignant. With him it was not a question of fraternal affection nor a hankering after the arts: he did not like being a little boy in the face of my status as a big one. The single exception which I allowed to the ban was in favour of Ali: he of the flute. I had wanted to keep him out too, but he looked pathetic standing by the door and I had not the heart to tell him to go away. He did not take up much room, especially now that the bicycle had gone, and I made it clear that the concession did not extend to his brothers and sisters who were as sand upon the sea shore.

Ali's father, learning from Ali what I was up to with my carving, offered to introduce me to a new medium: mud. It pays to be kind. From Ali's father I learned how the walls of mud huts were built. With the help of Ali's father I moulded enough hard lumps to last me a lifetime. 'If he took as much trouble over what he's paid to do,' said my father when I told him how Ali senior had given new directions to the industry, 'we might have some flowers occasionally. Blasted mud pies.' It must not be assumed from this observation, or from the lack of enthusiasm displayed at the exhibition, that my father meant to discourage me. He meant to prevent me from putting on 'side'. My mother told me years later how pleased he was that I had discovered a talent—at last. 'Your father was proud of you, but he thought it would be bad for you if he showed it. He believed it was better that you should go on being a flop.'

In their moist state I might have tried modelling the lumps as they were. But I was bent upon carving with the chisel and not fashioning with the hand. I lost a chance here, because the mud which Ali helped me to mix was not unlike the clay on which I had to experiment as a novice some fifty years later. In Colorado last summer (1963) I learned all over again the necessity of adding broken bits of straw to the grey paste I was preparing for the, to me, new work of modelling. If the material I used at the age of eight and nine was liable to crumble, at least it gave me practice for wood and stone. Unconsciously I was doing what the first sculptors of bronze had done namely using the material for direct carving. In parenthesis it may be noted that only much later did the idea come in which made bronze a suitable metal for casting, and even then, when the bronze had been cast from clay models, chisels and rifflers were applied to finish off the work.

Strictly speaking, if the word 'sculpture' comes from *sculpere* then only what is cut or scooped out comes under the designation. What is modelled should properly be called something else. A craftsman who shapes in clay, throwing on blobs of the stuff with his hand, may come closer to his material than the man who chips off pieces with a chisel and mallet. But since the two operations represent opposite approaches, opposite processes, it is a pity to find them classified as one. It must be rare that modelling and carving are equally well performed by the same man. I can think of three: Rodin, Maillol, Mestrovic. Of the masters who went in for both, Michelangelo was happier with stone, Epstein with bronze. In the case of most there comes a moment of choice.

So for me in my narrow workshop there was no question as to which I wanted to do. Hands covered with cuts and bruises, I thumped contentedly, and had no further ambition than to keep turning out objects which might be hideous to others but which were deeply satisfying to me. My father, as a painter, would have preferred it had I stuck to drawing and painting instead of choosing sculpture of either sort. He thought that by working in the round I would work better on the flat. I saw it the other way about: drawing seemed to me chiefly worth while as a preparation for carving. It indicates our different points of view to record that my father referred to the converted harness room as the 'studio' while to me it was the 'workshop'.

Drawing and painting were all very well as far as they went, and if playing with plasticine counts as modelling I had toyed with the next stage, but these things had been pastimes. Carving was not a game. Writing for *Liturgical Arts* a few years ago Mr Peter Watts, a noted sculptor, made the point that sculptors are for the most part men of deep seriousness. He does not give instances because a dozen names suggest themselves at once. The sculptor handles a more obstinate medium than a writer, faces a more critical public than the painter whose meaning is more easily grasped, knows that he is in for a longer run than the actor whose talent is for the effect of the moment, makes less claim upon the emotions than the musician, has to battle with limitations imposed upon him by time, space, weight, and setting. It is not that these factors turn him into a serious person, but that unless he is serious about his undertaking he will never get anything done. The writer can be frivolous, the artist can draw funny pictures, the actor can entertain with impersonations, the poet can write light verse, the musician can make gay music. But the sculptor cannot afford to be funny because he knows that his joke will be there, in durable stone, to reproach him when the laugh is over. It is true that Daumier has left some amusing caricatures in bronze, and presumably the stone gargoyles of the Middle Ages were meant to be funny, but it is not their humour which gives value to these things; it is the craftsmanship, integrity, creative inspiration—seriousness in other words—with which they were done.

Though all this was far from my thought, I knew from the start that carving was not like playing with meccano. It was not even a hobby. So the word 'studio' denoted paint, the paraphernalia of the artist. It was a fancy name, standing for something rare.

It was a good enough word for my father to use, for after all he was a painter, but it did not suit the extension of the stable. 'Workshop' was more earnest, less pretentious, less—though for all Mr Carter's literary influence this is not a word I would have used—esoteric. In the same way I would not have liked to call myself a sculptor. Nor have I since. 'Sculptor' has always seemed to me a praise name. When pressed, I call myself a carver or a stone cutter, or simply a mason. 'Studio' is a praise name, 'workshop' is not.

To this digression it is perhaps worth adding that words were already to me, since my readings with Yolande and Mr Carter, more than a vehicle of mere necessary exchange. I was reading Kipling and Barrie for fun, Walter Scott and Thomas Malory for homework.

Then my grandmother died. The death affected me profoundly, because although I may have found it heavy going at times keeping up with what was expected of me I was much attached to her. The loss of my grandmother brought about changes the repercussions of which were to be for all of us considerable. For me the first effect was, surprisingly, a religious one.

Stronger in some than in others, the tendency to ancestor worship is probably present in most of us, and lacking a more specifically devotional life I suppose I romanticised the supposedly angelic qualities of my dead grandmother. Be this as it may, I decided that she would, from her place in heaven, wish me now to read the copy of the New Testament which her daughter Berthe (with whom she had been barely on speaking terms over the past ten years) had given me as a parting gift. So, in my airless little workshop, and almost as though the pages were being turned by my grandmother's heavily ringed fingers, I read, right through, the four Gospels.

What chiefly surprised me as the result of this exercise was how much they differed from my grandmother's own compositions. On closer examination a more significant conclusion emerged: the Gospels actually related to everyday life. The miraculous element did not puzzle me in the least, and I enjoyed working out the parables and seeing how they could be made to apply. The feature which disturbed me about the Gospels, which was really the old feature about the catechism but presented now in a more graphic form, was that they pointed in a direction which was not the direction in which most of us were looking.

This private study of the Gospels, conducted more furtively than the study of sculpture and therefore without any sort of guidance, led me to make two contradictory generalisations. Over-simplifying on the one hand, I told myself that if our Lord had been reported correctly then everyone ought to become a missioner. Over-complicating on the other, I argued that our Lord's words were directed so personally to each one as to make it impossible to lay down a law and teach a doctrine which would cover everybody. Then I saw that these conclusions cancelled one another out. I was left where I was before. I look back upon this as a time when I was holding my head with both hands, wrestling with ill-assorted ideas and not knowing where to look for a formula. Mine has always been the kind of head which has room for many ideas, but just not enough room for the additional idea which will show me what to do next about them. One of the advantages of adult life is that the inability to work things out is acknowledged. In youth there is for ever the conviction that to every problem there must be allotted an appropriate solution, and that each solution is arrived at on one's own.

Though the religious conflict remains as a memory, I remember next to nothing about religious practice at this period. I know that for instructions before receiving the sacraments of penance, Holy Eucharist, and confirmation I used to go on my bicycle to the Franciscan friary where I was taught with great patience by a certain Father Dunstan. But I remember neither my first confession nor first communion, and have no recollection of disclosing the difficulties to which my piecemeal experience of religion had given rise. Confirmation, which was administered in the Cathedral with high ceremony, is clearer in my memory, but this is only because I stood out as being much younger than the other boys and girls and was also the only English candidate. In my Harrods clothes I felt out of my element among the French and Italian male *confirmandi,* who, besides showing a dark line of down on the upper lip wore striped socks and pointed yellow shoes. My father told me after the ceremony he had never seen such a band of cut-throats. 'Your chums up there on the sanctuary were dagoes to a man. I wonder you didn't bolt.'

Though we went to Mass each Sunday, in the carriage or pony trap until the cars came into our lives, I do not remember that it made much impression. Going to Mass in Alexandria was at least an improvement on the same exercise in London. The social inconsistencies which troubled me in England were here less marked. The churches were poorer, more uncomfortable, more untidy and everyday. The people who came to church were of every nationality and from every level of society. The benches were always out of line and always crowded. While very small children, brown and black as well as white, crawled on the floor with almost no clothes on, their brothers and sisters ran about the aisles giggling. I remember seeing a mother leaving her infant astride a projecting arm or leg of Guido Reni's *Saint Michael,* freely reproduced life size in plaster, while she attended to her other children. All this may have been distracting to prayer as such, but in these surroundings it was easier to think of our Lord than in Farm Street, the Oratory, Spanish Place. Among the different accents, costumes, smells, I could at a pinch imagine Christ walking in, sitting down, and feeling at home. Watching the priests moving about with great reverence on the sanctuary—whether they were bearded or merely unshaven I do not remember ('holy brigands' my father called them), but they appeared swarthier, dirtier, less well fed than their London counterparts—I could by a not too violent stretch of the imagination visualise the apostles saying Mass.

But if some aspects of Christianity were brought home to me by my reading of the Gospels, others continued to elude me. The question of poverty was still a stumbling block, and added to this was the question of disease which I began to connect with religion. Seeing flies clustering about the eyes of native children, and allowed to stay there in the name of religion, made me wonder why God did not make his wishes more clear. There was more in it, I decided, than simply a distinction between creed and creed. I suspected that the Christian and the Moslem were equally to blame, and that if the Moslem was as bad at applying the Koran as we were at applying the Sermon on the Mount it was not surprising to find unfairness everywhere. The Sermon on the Mount gave the whole story, could be read in the context of actual existence (particularly with Egypt as its setting), so why was it not taken literally? I put many such questions to myself but having experienced the futility of grown-ups I did not put them to anyone else. Instead I committed the care of Egypt's poor and blind to Allah, the care of London's unfortunates to Christ.

So the personal religious influences to date were as follows. Georgina the seamstress, or Georgie as she was known by everyone, who taught me the catechism. Berthe who listened to my confidences and gave me the New Testament. Father Dunstan the Franciscan, who prepared me for the sacraments. One more name can be added to the list: Father Bampton the Jesuit at Farm Street. Father Bampton had promised me that as soon as I was big enough to carry the missal from one side of the altar to the other he would teach me to serve Mass, and that I would wear white gloves for this. 'White gloves?' I asked. 'Yes,' he promised, 'with an Eton collar and a floppy white silk tie which fastens on with a clip.' It was the thought of white gloves, Eton collar, made-up silk tie which kept me from serving Mass until I learned to do so at Downside some years later. But by then the religious scene had changed for the better.

Whatever its emotional effect upon me, my grandmother's death affected all of us at a material level. From being rather poor we became suddenly, though not for long, rather rich. So although the particular kind of grandeur to which I felt on principle opposed, yet attracted to in practice, was now gone, a new situation arose which in terms of creature comfort amounted to much the same thing. My grandmother's houses were sold, and her nine children inherited more than they had expected. The generation of aunts and uncles who had grown up under their mother's economical eye were now free to travel more expensively, entertain more lavishly, maintain more elaborate households. Our own way of life in Alexandria did not alter greatly. But then I was perhaps too deeply absorbed in my carving and reading to notice domestic changes. When not at my lessons with Mr Carter I was in the workshop. With only the square of sky above my head, I was for the greater part of my day virtually in Noah's Ark. I withdrew so far as I could from social life, and nobody seemed to mind.

When I look back at my own occupations, which seemed at that period so pressing and time-consuming, I do not, with many of my contemporaries, commiserate with the small boys of today for having to get through their leisure hours with nothing but television. I believe that to small boys there is no such thing as a leisure hour. The people whom I commiserate with are the grown-ups. Then and now. My father was exempted by nature from boredom so does not count. Also he presumably had military and civic duties to attend to. But what can my mother have done all day? After her morning interview with the cook, conducted with dispatch, there was nothing for her to look forward to until the evening's bridge.

There was anyway one day when duty made a demand on her earlier than after tea, and I mention the occasion as eliciting from her a comment wholly in character. She had been asked by the officials of the Yacht Club to present the prizes at the most important of the year's regattas. For weeks we had prepared for the event. My mother spent hours rehearsing her speech, which all but my four-year-old brother and she herself could recite by heart. Our clothes were decided upon down to the last safety pin. For my father, who was racing *Water-Witch* in the regatta, it was straightforward yachtsman: double-breasted blue coat with silver buttons, white flannel trousers, white flannel shirt with button-down collar (because of the wind), club tie, black socks (which give the date before the 1914 War), white tennis shoes with pink rubber soles, yachting cap (which my mother said made him look like Pinkerton in a touring company of *Madame Butterfly* and which smelled of a special preparation from Paris called *Pomade Sec*). Much thought had gone into the use of the button-down collar for sailing, yet the suggestion, advanced for the same reason, that a metal tie-clip might be worn was rejected instantly: tie-clips, my father said, ranked with arm-garters for commonness. My mother wore an ankle-length white dress with a glossy white belt which matched her narrow shoes, with what would now be considered low heels, long white kid gloves, high collar kept in position by whalebone, and a wide white hat which all but hid her face and looked like an American angel-cake covered in whipped cream. Josephine wore a somewhat similar costume only in lower key. My brother and I were dressed identically: white silk shirt, poplin tie (no clip), white flannel shorts, no socks, sandals, enormous pith helmets with glazed green buckram inside the brim. My mother and Josephine carried frilly parasols; my brother and I held fly switches.

A band was playing pieces from *The Chocolate Soldier* and *The Belle of New York*. There were flags everywhere, pots of flowers, silver cups on a green baize cloth, trays of tea and ice cream. My mother read over her notes as we watched the races. *Water-Witch* came nowhere. When my father came up the steps from one level of terrace to another and exchanged his yachting cap for a panama we knew that the fun was beginning. In no time my mother was behind the green baize giving out silver trophies to bowing yachtsmen. My brother and I, only a few feet away with Josephine in the front row, peered out from under our pith helmets with their extinguishing effect, and were proud of our parents: she so gracious in her white muslins, so slender and cool, and no longer nervous about the speech which in fact she delivered word perfect; he so big and important, and now that he was not wearing his yachting cap no longer about to break into 'One Fine Day'.

Then, before the act of distribution was over and as though shot from a cannon's mouth, a little girl came forward with a bouquet and curtseyed briefly. All white frills from head to knee, and a complexity of bows, sashes, ribbons. She was Pamela Tatton-Browne, aged six, whose father was either president or secretary of the Yacht Club and who was standing at my mother's side. I knew Pamela slightly, and it surprised me that one whose excitable nature was well known should be chosen for so public an appearance. She thrust the flowers into my mother's hands and made ready to flee.

'Not yet, Pam,' said Mr Tatton-Browne very gently, 'that comes next.'

Pamela turned and took the flowers back.

'No, Pam, it's too late now. Just leave the bouquet with Mrs van Zeller.'

Pamela pressed the flowers hard against my mother's stomach.

There followed a back-and-forth sequence which looked like going on for ever and which was demonstrably bad for Pamela's nervous system. Each time the flowers reached my mother, my father's voice could be heard saying in what he mistakenly imagined to be a whisper 'Let her have the blasted thing, Nick . . . she's going to cry if she doesn't hop it soon . . . there you are, what did I tell you? The poor little chap is blubbing like a whale.'

At last Pamela herself spoke. Addressing my mother through a curtain of tears she murmured in a sad little trembling voice, 'I said I didn't want to . . . I kept *telling* them I didn't want to.'

'Oh don't cry, Pamela,' said my mother, bending down and applying a handkerchief, 'or I shall too. I didn't want to either, but they wouldn't listen. You'll find that, I'm afraid. You have your own ideas, but they never listen, do they?'

All small boys are to a varying degree fired by the desire to grow up. They would never grow up at all if they were not. With me it was an abiding concern. Partly induced by my indifference towards children of my own age, Ali and Helmuth being the only ones I cared to see, but partly also by the conviction that a moment would come when my uncertainties would be resolved. Though I had no great confidence in the power of adults to communicate certainty, I felt that they must themselves possess it. By reaching man's estate would I now possess whatever certainties were going? At each stage so far I had found myself blocked by what I assumed to be my youthfulness. Not even the acquisition of a property of my own, the workshop, nor the genuine enjoyment I derived from reading Anthony Hope, could blind me to the fact that I was still a very young person.

In an obscure way I felt that the maturing process stood a better chance in England than in Egypt. Would I not perhaps shoot into the next stage when next we sighted the cliffs of Dover? I have now so lost the ambition to span another period of years in the hope of attaining to new wisdoms that I cannot quite recapture the feel of this early desire. Another desire, about which I shall have more to say, came in to override it. Today it seems strange

The author's mother (holding baby) and Yolande

The author, age two, 1907

The author and his brother, 1912

The author's father with "crew" sailing *Water-Witch* in 1912

Mother and son at the fort, 1913

to me that after wanting so ardently in the early part of my life to grow up, I should find myself gently and automatically growing down. For only a short while, when in my forties, did I consider myself grown up. So much effort had gone into it: it seemed hardly worth the trouble.

My parents never made the mistake of talking down to me, but other people did and this exasperated me. Helmuth only shrugged his shoulders when people talked down to him. How Ali reacted I do not know; probably not at all. Wanting to be taken for older than I was must have made me tiresome. Though my father would not have tolerated any showing off, neither would he have known my correct age. Since he had shown himself to be as much as three years out he might not have noticed the disparity. But then I probably took care not to give myself airs in front of him.

When I learned that we had become richer, I thought more of what this might mean in terms of growing up than in terms of income. If it meant riding in the Row, I was all for it. So it was that money still spelled for me just those securities about which I had been so doubtful before. It spelled what it always does to everybody. The root of the matter lay in the assumption of privilege, and though I would have been disheartened had I learned this then, no amount of piling on years would make any difference to that.

CHAPTER FIVE

The Junior School

Early in July 1914 we left as usual for England. This time I knew I would be away for at least a year, because of having to go to school in England, so I was sorry to leave Alexandria. I did not in fact get back to Egypt until eight years later, and then only for a brief holiday between school terms. London seemed a different place. Not only did I miss the Lancaster Gate house but I sensed among the uncles and aunts a new mood. There was talk about money, a subject hitherto, together with disease and death, considered improper. It appeared that our new-found wealth was none too secure, and that if England ever went to war with Germany we would lose every penny. I do not know why, if this was the case, our German holdings were not transferred to bankers in England, but I suppose there must have been some reason for it.

My father, who up till now had never mentioned money, spoke of impending ruin. 'Whatever happens, Nick,' he told my mother (Nick was a corruption of her name Monique), 'we must never take the boys away from Downside.' I had not yet started my schooling at Downside, and my brother's was still five years away. Warnings followed. 'I'm afraid we shall have to get rid of the coupé.' The coupé was regarded as my mother's personal possession. Anyway my father had the car. 'And perhaps even the yacht.' My mother reminded him how, on the strength of the legacy and with the vague intention of selling one of them in the distant future, he had recently bought a second yacht. She felt that with two yachts bobbing up and down in Alexandria, with a skeleton crew idling on the slip in our absence, other economies might be planned before we decided to get rid of the coupé. 'Then when the crash comes,' said my father, facing poverty with courage, 'we'll sell the smaller one.'

When it did finally come, it was the kind of crash which many families might have envied. In the meantime we roughed it at the houses of relations and friends, and made elaborate journeys. I was measured for my school clothes, and went into practice by wearing long trousers for the first time. From the same tailor my father ordered a very complicated suit of Harris tweed which was to be for the shooting in August, so evidently the sky was not wholly clouded over by the threat of bankruptcy and war. Even when war did come, before the suits were finished, the difference was not immediately apparent. My mother jumped at the excuse for laying in a store to take back to Egypt 'for the duration', which was generally expected to last not longer than three months at most. My father, after ensuring that I miss nothing of these historic times by putting me on his shoulders in the crowd which gathered nightly outside Buckingham Palace to see King George and Queen Mary, took off for a round of visits. While he was doing the grand tour of Melville Castle in Scotland, where he had a relative, and Wardour Castle in Wiltshire, where he had another, my mother took my brother and myself to stay with her sister Rita in Ireland.

At my aunt Rita's there seemed to be no lack. Before we arrived she had bought a Daimler which in the words of the advertisement was spacious and well appointed. It was cushioned in grey velvet, panelled with polished cedar arranged with such cunning that the grain formed a pattern, equipped with extra seats, as in a taxi, which folded back into a partition which separated the occupants from the driver and anyone who happened to be ostracized. Attached to the central upright of this partition by a silver collar wrought in filigree was a slender glass vase in which sweet peas throbbed to the movement of the engine. To me the prime glory of the vehicle was the speaking-tube, a cloth-covered grey serpent through which someone sitting in a back seat could convey his, or more usually her, wishes to the driver. Among the fittings were flat and discreetly embroidered arm-rests suspended from round silver bosses. They elicited my only criticism. Why were the wrists of adults so heavy as to need support? My cousin Mildred, aged fourteen, would hear nothing against any part of her mother's Daimler, which she told me was shortly to be blessed by a bishop.

Besides possessing a machine which excelled our own modest Ford as Pegasus excelled Tommy van Zeller's pony, my aunt and uncle dispensed hospitality bountiful beyond the wildest dream. There were dances, picnics in the soft warm rain of southern Ireland, parties of every sort. If the fortunes which were either left to us by my grandmother or else amassed by individual uncles at home and abroad were in peril, we were putting on a brave front. It was with reluctance that we left Ireland to return to London where my aunt Berthe had taken a house in Lower Belgrave Street and which thereafter for some ten or twelve years became the place of assembly for all, and for all connected with, the family. On the journey from Ireland it was made clear to my brother that in stations and restaurants he must preserve, until the moment of embarking for Egypt, an absolute silence. Having had Josephine as his nurse for the whole of his four years, he spoke with a marked German accent.

The war, by the end of August, was fairly under way. My father, who had decided to attend it from a military base in Egypt rather than in England, was impatient to buckle on his armour. This meant that as soon as I was installed at Downside, my parents would cut short their European visit, leaving me to the Benedictines and the zeppelins while they confronted the U-boats on the high seas. So my last two weeks before saying goodbye, for what in my mother's case would prove to be an absence of two years and in my father's nearly four, were spent in London wondering whether I really wanted to be grown up after all. By the time the three of us set out from Paddington to Bath—I in dark striped trousers, black coat, Eton collar—I would gladly have exchanged places with my brother, German accent notwithstanding, who was to return in a few days' time to the homely night and day nurseries in Alexandria. After a dismal few hours in Bath, not eating the elaborate luncheon which my father ordered, we travelled on the Somerset and Dorset Joint Railway to the country station of Chilcompton. Here a one-horse shay, sent by the Head Master, awaited us, and we drove, my shining new trunk on the box, to the school. It was for all the world Tom Brown's introduction to Rugby.

The parting took place that same evening, and it was only when the three of us stood in the school quadrangle under the fading September sun that I knew what my parents meant to me. The rest of that day and the one following passed in a blur of discoveries, instructions, lists, lockers, unpacking, registering, receiving various sorts of equipment. The authorities wisely saw to it that we were kept busy. I, unused to the herd, had to be rounded up every now and then to have a medical examination with the other new boys or to be shown my place in church.

In later years I have been able without any effort at all to recapture the feel of my first night in a dormitory. It was not that anything particularly dreadful happened. It was rather that nothing happened, and that life seemed to stretch in front of me as an endless length of not happening. Life at home had been full, but life at home was over. Life from now on, I told myself as I lay between the stiff sheets and listened to the springs of the wire mattress, was empty. I was nine years old, and life was over. I had for weeks been preparing myself to miss familiar people and things, but it had been no preparation at all. The very stuff of homesickness is to feel that one has wasted one's chances while being at home. There might be a return, I told myself, but it would be no more than a geographical affair. The real thing would not be the same. I am not sure that I was not right.

For a boy who has never been away from his family for longer than lunchtime, the first term at a boarding school, with his parents on another continent, will be seen to have its drawbacks. For the first six weeks my effort was mostly directed towards not showing my feelings. This was according to my father's express injunctions. The remaining six weeks I spent trying to ignore the cold. In neither endeavour was I wholly successful. Experience has since taught me that occasions frequently occur in life when expression of feeling is not only permissible but called for. It has also taught me that the cold cannot be ignored.

But there were lesser obstacles to the smooth ordering of affairs. One of them was games. I found myself slow on the rugger field, awkward in the gymnasium, uncommitted in the rough-and-tumbles. Under my father's eye I had learned some of the principles governing sport, but few as regards games. In the classroom too I felt myself at a disadvantage. I did not hold it against Mr Carter that his tuition had been less professional than it might have been, but I chafed under the professionalism of my new masters. These, however, were only the first fumblings of the neophyte: both in the matter of games and work I found a level which, though never high, was not excessively demanding.

Another irritant was that for the first year or more I walked in fear of putting a foot wrong. Mine was just such a foot. The opportunities lay everywhere, and the penalties could be an embarrassment. Already at that date bullying was no longer thought of as a necessary adjunct to public school life, and though I am sure there was less of it at Downside than at most schools there was a certain amount of what was called 'plugging' which bore a resemblance. Something which people who have not been to a public school fail to understand is that malice and cruelty are very rarely behind acts of schoolboy oppression, and that privilege almost always is. I speak of half a century ago when it was still the privilege to plug. Neither then nor, I believe, at any other time would it be the privilege to perform acts of cruelty. It is the tendency in every age to blame the authorities for not taking effective steps to get rid of bullying. But when so much of the public school system is held together by privilege of one sort or another it is difficult to see what measures the authorities can take. The authorities and tradition between them bestow privilege: it is then for the privileged to reform themselves. This in fact is what has largely come about. In my day it was assumed without undue sense of grievance that the privileged, not so much because they abused their privileges but quite simply because they held them, plugged. Nor did they plug indiscriminately. It so happened that by the time I reached a position of privilege in the school, plugging seemed to have gone out. But until then I was an apt subject for plugging, the ideal pluggee.

Critics who point to the unfairness which must exist in a way of life the terms of which are to some extent dictated by the boys themselves cannot be refuted. A lot of it is unfair. But nothing like as unfair as what everyone meets with later on. Perhaps it is here that an incidental value of the English system of education is proclaimed: the boy learns not to look for an exact equation between merit and reward. Such an attitude does not posit a blindfolding process, a refusal to ask questions if all they do is to cause trouble, a supine acceptance of the vicissitudes of fate. Nor is it an attitude tinged with cynicism. It is an attitude which steers between two mesmerisms, one at each extreme and both equally misleading.

Writing as one whose bearing cried out for the plug, I can say that in avoiding mistakes such as might merit the weight of rough justice I learned much which was useful and little which was harmful. Also, together with the boredom which replaced it, my wariness of transgressing schoolboy shibboleths led me to the cultivation of interests which might otherwise have been neglected. If I was ripe for repressive measures dealt out by the boys with a more or less even and not too malign hand, I was ripe too for the stimulating influences which the masters brought to bear. From Father Austin Corney, who was in charge of the Junior School, I received every encouragement. He allowed me to draw and model in a classroom which was normally kept locked during free time, and he commissioned me to paint pictures for his room. He saw to it, by getting me to listen to gramophone records, that I mixed with a crowd of fellow juniors whose musical tastes greatly varied. Thus culture and companionship were there for the asking.

Though I enjoyed these various activities up to a point, and certainly dreaded nothing, I was listless. I lived only for the holidays. It was as though I were a flake of imitation snow in a glass paperweight. The glass ball had been turned upside down and I was quietly floating in space. For the first time in my life, and without knowing it, I was bored stiff.

It is probable that one or other of the monks pointed out my mistake, but if he did I forget it. Certainly it was not Downside's fault that I did not settle down during the first year. Had I known how much the school would come to mean to me I would have given it more of a chance at the beginning, but instead I held firmly to the belief that I could never belong anywhere apart from my family. Nor was I wholly mistaken, for during the nine years of my time at Downside I was moulded more by the contacts made in the holidays and by my numerous relations than by what I found at school. I grew to be much devoted to Downside, and some of the relationships I formed there as a boy are lasting still, but if the sense of belonging is the test I must qualify for the times in between. Today I find myself wondering whether this is everyone's experience. To judge from the contemporaries of my schooldays whom I come across, I am inclined to think that in the majority of cases the power exercised by the school is more formative and lasting than that exercised by the home. In the case of close friends it is difficult to assess the relative pressures; where it is a question of meeting a man whose existence has been forgotten for forty years it is easier. Confronted with a virtual stranger whom I remember to have been at school with me, I almost always discover him to be more of an old Downside boy than a new sexagenarian. But perhaps he discovers the same thing about me.

For the first Christmas holidays I went to Berthe's, at Lower Belgrave Street, where my other unmarried aunt, Yolande, was more or less permanently installed. Uncle Marcel, generally regarded as the scapegrace member of the family, was also there. It was my first taste of London in wartime, my first Christmas in England. The association of the Lower Belgrave Street house with my mother's presence of the summer before, already such hundreds of years ago, caused acute moods of melancholy which each member of the household, in his or her way, tried to dispel. Marcel took me to musical comedies and revues, Yolande to exhibitions and museums, Berthe to High Masses and Benedictions. There were people in and out of the house all day long and there was always something going on, but I recognised the symptoms of loneliness which I had read about. It shamed me to be at the mercy of loneliness and boredom in the busy life of school and holidays in England when I had known nothing of the kind in the quieter, and often more solitary, life in Egypt.

If in this book more space is devoted to my father than to my mother it is only because my father is easier to write about. I am not conscious of Oedipal stirrings. It is my guess too that he is easier to read about. Though I respected my father increasingly as I grew older (more than perhaps these pages would imply) my affection went with undisguised preference to my mother. My father would have been shocked if it had not. In my youth I believed that I derived little from my father, but today I know that I was mistaken in this. I am catching myself out all the time. The difference is that when I see my father reproducing himself in me I laugh, but when I see my mother acting through my thought I grow serious. This may or may not explain why I missed my mother so profoundly at Christmas in 1914.

Before going back to school for the Lent term I was taken by Yolande to Brighton to stay for two nights with yet another aunt, Beatrice, who had a large and rather forbidding house in First Avenue. Aunt Beatrice was the one who was married to the colonel whose military standing had seemed to me, a few years back, so far more exciting than my father's. Uncle Richard had now retired from the army and was doing what he had always said he wanted to do. Namely nothing. Though he never admitted it I suspect that he was bored even stiffer than I was. 'Poor Richard,' everyone said, 'he should have stayed on with his soldiering.' And there he was in Brighton. And a war going on.

This visit to Brighton was made, as I see now, with the Easter holidays in mind: I would have to be farmed out somewhere, and it was thought well to try out my hosts' response to me and mine to them. There was a daughter, Marian, aged fifteen, who was at a Sacred Heart school, and it was important, since her holidays coincided with mine, to see how we got on. I remember little of this experiment except the journey to Brighton and back. In 1915 the heating on most railway lines, perhaps on all, consisted of metal foot warmers. On long journeys these clonking rectangular tins, about three foot long and one broad with a handle at either end, were exchanged for hotter ones at intervals along the line. On the way to Brighton, having the compartment to ourselves, we sat on the footwarmers. The first thing we did on arriving at our destination was to buy two hotwater-bottles each for use on the return journey.

Two days later on the way back by a late train—the trial stay having evidently justified itself because it was arranged that I should go to Brighton at Easter—we reached Victoria while an air-raid was in progress. Lower Belgrave Street is no distance from Victoria, so we decided, clutching our hotwater-bottles, to walk. A policeman who held a hand over the lamp at his belt so as not to give away the position to the enemy, warned us to take cover if we heard falling shrapnel. The moment we left the station yard we heard shrapnel. Yolande, who can always be counted upon to remain calm but whom few would choose for an emergency, thought the best place to shelter would be against the railings under some trees, leafless at this time of the year, where the equestrian statue of Marshal Foch now stands. It was not, she explained obscurely, like lightning. In those days even small boys wore bowler hats, and though I mistrusted the trees as shelter I felt cosy and secure in my bowler hat. It was a cloudless night and we stood looking up at the sky and waiting for the zeppelin, which every now and then we could see in the beam of a searchlight, to go away. It looked very pretty, like one of the Christmas decorations which hung on the tree in my aunt's house a few streets away. It seemed, at that great height, hardly to be moving at all. Elegant and unconcerned, dropping an occasional leisurely bomb. After a particularly assertive burst of shrapnel I gallantly offered Yolande my bowler hat.

'No thank you, dear, but I think we should say a little prayer to the Three Holy Kings.'

'Why to them especially?'

'I don't know, darling, except that I'm sure they wouldn't like to be in this at all.'

What with the war going on, the almost daily entertainments to which Marcel was taking me, the pressing thought of going back to school, I was at this time less preoccupied by questions of social inequality than I had been for the past two years. Blacked out and rationed London showed fewer contrasts than London of the Lancaster Gate days. Everyone was huddled over the same few knobs of coal, scraping the same sardine tin. In the theatres, whatever seats they occupied, the men all wore uniform and none of the women wore evening dress.

Where one aggravation dies down, another flares up: far from being in abeyance my concern with reaching man's estate was receiving new impetus. Separation from my parents made me want desperately to skip the intervening months or, as was now becoming likely, years. I could think of school only in terms of getting it behind me. For reasons no doubt of romance I longed to be old enough to fight in France. Tommy van Zeller was at the front, sloshing about and getting mentioned in dispatches. Various relatives on the other side of the family, my mother's, who had passed through Lower Belgrave Street were either shooting (with sports rifles) in the trenches or nursing in hospitals or helping people to escape to England. There were stories of my almost mythical, and certainly patriotic, Belgian cousins who moved about disguised as peasants, punctured the tyres of German cars, pushed haughty Uhlan officers into canals, left sticks of dynamite in the cabs of observation balloons. While even here in England my uncle Richard whom I had seen so recently, and who had looked so much less dashing in Brighton than I had remembered him as looking only a few years before, was, it was now alleged, going off to some secret destination in the north to stand sentry outside a munition factory. Perhaps having shaken the mothballs from his uniform and polished his Sam Browne, poor Richard would begin to look dashing again. Uncle Maurice was under virtual house arrest in Brussels. Marcel was up to something in Intelligence, and nearly all the people we knew were either translating, decoding, or spy-tracing at the War Office. No wonder I was impatient to move on. I who was taking piano lessons from a middle-aged man in a winged collar.

Long ago I had asked, thinking it might have something to do with carving, to be put down for the carpentry class at school. My father, sensing against all previous knowledge of me a possible affinity to his own flair for accurate measurement, agreed with alacrity to this expensive and time-consuming extra. I soon discovered however that carpentry, being as far removed from carving as the drill-book is from poetry, was not for me. But the wood came in useful, and I made a practice of coming away with chisels hidden under my waistcoat which I would return faithfully at the next class. The class-time I would devote to resharpening the chisels. Thus, in deceit, are talents fostered. But if it represented a too liberal understanding of the parable, it at least got me through the Lent and summer terms. I was still unanchored. It was during one or other of these terms that I read for the second time *Tom Brown's Schooldays*, and decided that it was more true to life than I had thought.

My tenth birthday fell early in the Easter holidays and was accordingly spent at my aunt's house in First Avenue, Brighton. A birthday party was given to celebrate the occasion. I knew none of the children who were invited, and I doubt if Marian, being five years older, did either. In the middle of the almost silent celebration, and as a surprise to his family as well as to everyone else, the warrior arrived. Uncle Richard had been given a few days' leave from what was jocularly referred to as his sentry go. (The exact nature of his appointment was never made absolutely clear.) Both uncle and aunt were the kindest of souls, and each on this occasion showed it. They saw how the party was going. Marian, though no less kind, was seized by a fit of shyness, so contributed little. My aunt, quite against her usual habit and I am sure still more against her inclination, gave spirited impersonations of stage celebrities who belonged to an earlier generation and of whom none of the guests had ever heard. When this was finished, my uncle had all the lights put out except one and made funny shadows on the wall. Without props of any kind, not even a pipe, his fingers gave us, in silhouette, rabbits, pelicans, wolves, a Chelsea pensioner, Mr Gladstone. The guests stared but were unmoved. One or two smiled and looked round for more to eat. At the end nobody knew whether or not to applaud. Those who began to clap their hands thought better of it. When the lights went up we all trooped into the next room. The moment I had satisfied my duties in saying goodbye and showing the last guest out of the house I burst into tears.

Two years ago, in the autumn of 1962, I was giving a retreat at the Sacred Heart convent in Hove, and since time allowed between the discourses I went to have a look at First Avenue. Even if I had not remembered the number, I could have found my aunt's house blindfold. Indeed it would have been better had I been blindfold. Painted on a board by the side of the front door were the words 'Summer Flatlets, Furnished and Self-contained, To Let', and in smaller lettering on a line below 'Greatly Reduced Rates October to March'. From the steps I could not see far enough into the front rooms to note the changes. Anyway the big Chinese bowl of *potpourri*, and the dark red velvet curtains between which it had stood, had gone. The house, for all the talk of being self-contained, had a shamefaced look. It was the same expression I had seen on the faces of the merrymakers forty-seven years before.

With the summer term came initiation into the mysteries of cricket. To my surprise I found the game mildly pleasant. It was calmer, less involving than rugger. The violence of rugger I did not object to so much as the pace and the noise; cricket promised time off, demanded no physical engagement. Adjacency has always deterred me, and I can think of nothing worse than being forced to wrestle. That my father seems to have overlooked wrestling is to me matter for the profoundest gratitude. The cricket played by junior boys at Downside was well suited to my unenthusiastic disposition: it did not impose or intrude. Knowing it would please him, I wrote home to my father saying how easily I was taking to the game, and in no time I received a message from him at the end of one of my mother's letters: would I not like some coaching during the summer holidays?

That summer I spent the whole seven weeks of the school holiday at my aunt's in Ireland. My father must have forgotten Cork when he suggested my getting coached in cricket. It was only a year since I had been here before, with my mother and brother, but so much had happened in the interval that it was like returning to a previous incarnation. At Rita's the War was not the constant topic of conversation, there was not the same concern about money as there was at Lower Belgrave Street, there was none of the conscientious effort to make me feel at home as there was at Beatrice's in Brighton. I did not have to be entertained. There were Mildred and her younger brother William, the cousins, to laugh with, quarrel with, share secrets and prejudices with. It was an enjoyable interlude.

On one of our excursions to Queenstown, as it was then still called, where my uncle played golf and the rest of us swam, I was embarrassed to meet among a crowd of children and young people, a fellow Downside boy. He was two or three years my senior, and only recently at school had plugged me with vigour. I met him again on subsequent visits, and a more amiable person would be hard to find. This struck me as peculiar.

One of the things which I noticed about the relatives belonging to my own generation both in Ireland and England—there were three more cousins, the Gerards, whom I used to meet a good deal in London—was that they were all more religious than I was. Particularly I was made aware of this in Ireland where several of the household went voluntarily to Mass during the week and regularly to confession. I cannot say that I was greatly disturbed by my poor performance, but the greater devotion which I saw in others certainly made me more apt, when the time came, for a stir. So on returning to Downside for the Michaelmas term I attended more carefully to what was told to us about God, the Church, the sacraments. I had not noticed it during my first year, because I did not much listen to the weekly addresses which Father Leander Ramsay delivered to the junior boys in the study-room, but now I began to value the way in which religion was presented. I had not been hostile or unconforming before. Nor, with the exception of the wobble already alluded to in trying to square the unqualified demand with the prevailing interpretation, had I been sceptical. But now I discovered in Father Leander's Sunday morning discourses a new incentive. I wished I had kept my ears open the year before. On Sunday evenings Father Austin read and commented upon the Old Testament, and at these sessions too I stayed fully awake. In addition there were three short catechism classes a week, but I felt about these much what I felt about the relation of carpentry to carving. Looking back I can see how wisely the authorities handled this side of the small boy's education. Though both are necessary, indoctrination at this stage would appear to be less important, if my own experience is anything to go by, than disposition. The various religious influences to which I was exposed may not have been the kind to produce a theologian but as for steering me towards religious realisation they could not have been more happily devised.

In December of this second year at school I got pneumonia, and, without knowing it, for I was delirious, received the last sacraments. My parents were informed by cable; the two aunts, Berthe and Yolande, who were within easier reach than the others, came for what were expected to be last farewells; I was prayed for by communities of nuns with whom Berthe kept in unsleeping touch; and a boy of my year in the school sent up a note asking if he might have my camera in the event of my death. The presence of two aunts, both crying, in one room did not strike me, during periods of consciousness, as unusual. The significance of a night nurse, of a doctor who was not the school doctor, of whisperings and frequent spongings eluded me. Only on one point was my mind perfectly clear: that I had arrived somewhere and that nothing now mattered.

There was no question here of a mystical experience. It was

nothing more than the perception, brought about by a number of factors natural and spiritual, of a reality which up till now had appeared blurred. With perception came conviction, security, peace. The influences had been preparing the disposition, and now the disposition had closed on what was presented. Where flu or a slight fever has a way of cluttering up the mind with a hundred irrelevances, making it difficult to distinguish between what is important and what is not, a critical illness seems to have the opposite effect: the vital things are seen in simple terms and the rest drop away. I would like to claim for certain that the grace of the last sacraments brought me the awareness which I needed at this time. Perhaps it did. Whatever the means chosen I can count the effect produced by this illness and all connected with it as one of the most fortunate circumstances of my life.

So I spent the Christmas of 1915 in bed at Downside. The Dawn Mass was said for me in the sickroom, and I received Holy Communion with only my head showing and as though from a roll of cotton wool. A number of monks paid me visits, and I was made a great fuss of by masters and their families. Crowning the consideration shown to me was the news, given in person by the Head Master, that the school could do without my attendance for the Lent term. If this presented a problem for those responsible for planning my holidays I was not to know it. As I would have myself chosen had it been left to me, the prolonged convalescence was to take place in Ireland.

At Rita's I recovered quickly. I did not let on about this to Downside in case I should be recalled. From Downside they sent me textbooks, files of notes, and a forbidding document headed 'Syllabus'. There was every excuse for the solicitude: I was missing classwork and would have a job to keep up when I got back. It was arranged that I should join Mildred in the private tuition which she was receiving daily from a Miss Ford of happy memory. Honour was thus satisfied, but honour is not everything. Before, however, the shortcomings of this temporary tuition were pointed out to me there were facets of life which could be explored and enjoyed without a reflex thought.

After what I liked to think of as my 'conversion' I looked at Ireland with a different eye. I saw the old familiar and rather ugly

Cork churches as though for the first time, and saw them as being exactly right. They reminded me of the churches we used to go to in Alexandria: the same smells, the same dirty water in the holy water stoups, the same candles standing crooked on the altar, the same flowers thrust anyhow into brass vases by hands which would for ever remain ignorant of Constance Spry, the same sense of the place being used as an extension of the living-room. Cork churches, like those in latitudes farther south, looked lived in. Church here was not just for Sundays. Or even just for Mass. To the poor in Cork it was for sitting down in, for yawning in, for meeting people in. It was home. Cork in 1916 had many poor. Boys and girls went barefoot in the streets. Women wore shawls and clogs. Men with coats buttoned up to the neck were often without shirts. Everyone looked either soaked to the skin or drying out. Many were hungry. For them the churches were a place of refuge, a place where one belonged, a place where one could kneel on the muddy boards and pray, a place where nobody would mind if one stretched full length on the sticky varnished and uncomfortable benches and went to sleep. I once saw an old woman sitting on the step of a side altar eating her lunch. Bread and margarine off a piece of crumpled newspaper. You would not have seen that in the Brompton Oratory. In Ireland it was taken for granted that the churches were made for man and not man for churches. It would be not uncommon to come upon a mother praying aloud in church while at the same time blowing a child's nose, rocking a baby, and with her free fingers screwing a candle into its socket before a shrine. Nor were the priests fussy. They came of the same broad tradition. Not straitlaced was one priest whose Mass I served early one morning when his church was empty but for a man crouching at his devotions in a back bench. As we approached the altar, the celebrant, in his vestments and carrying the chalice, called to me, 'Hi, hang on while I see who the boyo is at the back.' Having assured himself as to the worshipper's identity he walked back down the aisle and picked up an umbrella and raincoat which were lying on the floor near the communion rails. The umbrella he hooked over his arm, the coat he slung over his shoulder. Arrived at the altar steps he threw the coat on to the deacon's stool against the wall of the sanctuary and gave the umbrella to me to put on the credence table with the cruets. During all this, and while finding the place in the missal, he kept up a monologue which was presumably addressed to me and not to the Almighty. 'Mike the old rogue, and him not come near a church in months . . . sure I wouldn't trust him farther than I could push him . . . he'll not find much in here this morning . . . God forgive me if he's come to make his Easter duties . . . *In nomine Patris et Filii et Spiritus Sancti, introibo ad altare Dei. . . .*'

I do not remember that the sight of poverty in the towns and villages of County Cork, certainly in striking contrast with the comfort enjoyed within gunshot, brought on a return of the old misgivings. Perhaps I had resigned myself to never finding, either in the Church or anywhere else, a solution to what appeared to be an explicitly gospel problem. Or perhaps the sense of security in the scheme of God's providence which had come to me with my illness had made me see that social problems were his before they were mine, and that if he had handled my own affairs so satisfactorily he could be relied upon to handle in his own time and, as satisfactorily, the affairs of the world. All I know is that my religious gropings were now not so much social as personal and ascetic.

The steps which I took in giving a new orientation to my life were, as has been the case since when I have tried to give outward expression to an inward impulse, the wrong ones. The immediate occasion was provided by Lent. I made out for myself a rule of life, designed to be kept up when the penitential season was over, which it was impossible for me to observe. There were to be special prayers, special fasts, special times for reading holy books, for silence and meditation. Both Berthe and Rita practised daily meditation, and if they could do it so could I. Meditation came more readily to one aunt than to the other. Berthe used to emerge from it with a seraphic look. Rita, who spent twenty minutes a day in it between tea and dinner during which she did not come to the telephone, felt the strain.

Filled with holy resolution, and combining it with an accepted schoolboy tendency, I built a hut. Here among the bushes beyond the tennis court I planned to pray, read, and do penance. It pleased me to be seen from the house going off with my books and with a frown of sacred preoccupation upon my face. So vivid is the memory of this experiment that I could today walk straight to the spot among the laurels where my hermit's cell lay hidden. The sound of dripping leaves and the smell of damp mould need no recalling. The experiment must have lasted long enough for me to feel pleasantly cut off from the outside world. It was a venture which in different forms I was to repeat in later life, and always with the same effect. Evidently I like to live in a goldfish bowl, floating about at my own pace. It seems I am happier seeing life through thick glass and refracted by the water. Anyway it was not because I tired of it that I abandoned my retreat at Carrigduv. The reason was even less worthy: it was because I crumpled up under ridicule.

Cousin Mildred, to whose eye all of us stood transparent, started introducing me to her friends as 'our potted little Father of the Desert'. Most of her friends were girls of fifteen and sixteen. Had they been boys, and had they plugged me, I might have resisted. It would have added to my status as hermit the lustre of persecution and the crown of martyrdom. But to hear my cousin as she pranced through the undergrowth which surrounded my pegged-out enclosure, calling to a party of giggling girls 'there he is, he's quite tame' was more than I could bear. Reluctantly, and long before Lent was over, I gathered together my lives of the saints, my homemade statues of certain anchorites towards whom I felt an affinity, my fifteen decade rosary made of beads which had come from the Garden of Olives, and joined the others indoors. The laurels had parted for the last time.

There was another development, connected both with religion and with the impatient desire to grow up, which manifested itself during this four months' sojourn in Ireland. Aware now, because I had been told of it, how close I had been to death, I began to wonder why I had not died. Everything had come right at the last minute: the next minute would have been the time to go. It seemed to me that a chance had been missed. In this way I came to conceive a wish for death which superseded, and in intensity vastly outmatched, the wish to grow up. The attraction has remained with me ever since. It must be insisted that I was not unhappy at the time of which I write. There was nothing morbid about it. There is nothing morbid about it now. But over the past forty-five years I do not think it has been out of my mind for as long as a single day. Earlier I had seen in growing up the means to emancipation; in 1916 I saw in death the means to a more important emancipation. Nobody has been able to talk me out of it, or to persuade me that so to think and so to hope can be in any way wrong. Idle for people to tell me that life is something good: I know. Idle to tell me that life is God's gift and must be lived fully, positively: I know. I am not, I think, a sombre person. I doubt if my friends think of me as a melancholic. It is just that I do not much like living. Certainly at no time in my adult life have I so enjoyed being alive as not infinitely to prefer the prospect of being dead. A spiritual adviser once told me that to look forward to death in this way supposed some constitutional flaw. If flaw it is, I can at least be thankful to it for having carried me over the most difficult times of my life.

Rita's house, Carrigduv, lay well outside the city, and though the whole family would have preferred a house in England—which was what they eventually got—Jack's business required residence near the Cork office. Uncle Jack was a corn merchant and a lovable man. But it seems that even a flourishing corn exchange in Ireland can be hit by a European war. So far as my grandmother's legacies were concerned, moreover, the prophets of doom had spoken only the truth: the Germans were sitting on every penny. Jack proclaimed a reign of retrenchment and austerity; Rita with tears in her eyes fingered her pearls, Mildred said she had no wish to go to a finishing school after all. And life at Carrigduv went on exactly as it had always done. The only difference was that, without getting rid of the Daimler which we had all so much admired, they bought another car. The new car was supposed to spare the Daimler and save petrol. It was called a B.S.A., though what the letters stood for I do not know, and, like the Daimler itself, had to be wound up by means of a cranking handle before it could start. It was as high off the road as the Daimler but there was no partition separating the occupants of the back seats from those in front. Consequently there was no speaking tube. But since the Daimler was used every bit as much as the B.S.A., there was no justification for resentment. I was still able to decry the leather-lined arm-rests and the moulded Viking shields from which they hung. Both cars were driven by the one-time coachman, MacDermot, who, unlike Ellwood in similar circumstances, had found himself able to make the change from horse to motor.

Shrewd, taciturn, moved by unexpected hates, fiercely loyal to the family but no respecter of persons, gifted with a feeling for language, MacDermot (or just MacD) was for us the subject of frequent discussion. MacD possessed especially two qualities which, in his profession, ran contrary to one another. He knew everything about a car, and had a genius for getting lost. But more interesting to me was his characteristic brand of humour. He enjoyed private jokes of his own, obscure and carefully tailored to some need or fancy, which left the hearer uncertain as to whether they were meant to be recognised as jokes or, for his greater enjoyment, ignored as irrelevances. MacD pretended during the years when I knew him, and I spent long and many visits at Carrigduv, that he could not understand a word I said. When I spoke to him he would touch his chauffeur's cap and look enquiringly at someone else. If nobody else were present to interpret, he would put a hand behind his ear and say in a loud voice as though I were deaf 'Slow-ly, slow-ly'. When he spoke to me, which was not often, he did so through a third party or else spaced out his words as though addressing a foreigner. Coming as I did from the other side of the channel I could hardly be counted as anything else. 'Master Claud will be interested,' he said once—speaking over his shoulder to those sitting in the back of the B.S.A. while I, the Master Claud in question, was seated next to him in front—'Master Claud will be interested to take note of our grand Irish breweries. Will one of ye back there explain to him, if ye please, the kind sweet way in which the dear Lord gave porter to the Irish people while denying to the English the understanding of ut? Ah, 'tis one of the happiest mysteries of our Faith.'

Men and women, poor in terms of earthly possession but rich in character and eccentricity, seemed instinctively drawn to the household of Jack and Rita. There was Mrs Murray who lived at the lodge at the end of the drive and who closed the gates when she saw a car coming. She looked after the hens, to each of which she gave the name of an Irish saint. 'St Clodagh has stopped laying again, and it's the devil inside of her . . . if St Ita won't be leaving them little ones of hers alone, sure I'll wring the neck off her.' Mrs Murray wore a man's cloth cap indoors and out, and it was said that she smoked a clay pipe over her bowl of black tea in the privacy of her kitchen.

There was Mr O'Keefe the gardener, who did precious little gardening but who was always busy with a dozen other things. One of the things which came before gardening was attaching little wooden brackets to trees so that the birds could eat their crumbs without getting their feet wet. It took him half the morning to distribute crumbs on the many brackets dotted about the grounds disfiguring the trees. In the afternoon he had to make a tour of inspection to assure himself that the morning's work had not been wasted. I once asked him why, since he was clearly more fond of birds than flowers, he had become a gardener. 'Ye've put your finger right on the great decision I had to make,' he replied, 'and the answer is that people would not be paying me to live up trees. It's me livelihood I have to think about, you understand. Me feet are in the garden beds while me heart is with them birds up in the sky.' And there we can leave Mr O'Keefe, with his feet in the weeds.

Then back to Downside for the summer term. At least I had missed out hockey, and with cricket my spirits rose. Indeed it all turned out easier than I had expected. The masters, though more institutional than the bicycly Miss Ford of Cork, were lenient. The boy who had hoped to come in for my camera accepted my return from the jaws of death without rancour. None of my friends noticed the new interest which I took in religion. Nor did I try to impress them with evidences of sanctification. I took care to avoid being a potted little Father of the Desert. The monks for their part, having hitherto treated me as a pathetic waif, began to take me as seriously as any junior boy can be taken who spends all his free time drawing and making likenesses of people in plasticine. I might be eccentric but I conformed. My reading progressed all the better for the direction it received in class and out; I was now reading Conrad, Barrie, Conan Doyle. I could see the point of education.

All this was before education was worrying about cubic space per boy in classroom and dormitory, about strontium A, about basic creative potentials and happy natural environments. In 1916 we were probably overcrowded, we undoubtedly froze in the dormitories and suffocated in the dayrooms; we did not see a film from the beginning of the term till the end; it was long before the day of the radio. But if the magic formula were offered me I would not exchange the uncomfortable 1914-1924 decade with any of the decades of educational advancement which came later. Even if the tuition then provided at Downside was not all that it might have been, was not what it certainly is now, there were some excellent masters on a staff depleted by military service. It was the boy's fault if he did not get into a good form. For my part I chose not to overburden myself with work, but the library was a good one and there was advice to be had. Mr Carter would have approved. Therein lay the beauty of Downside education: as an establishment it taught, it tolerated, it did not, fortunately for people like me, too strictly insist. Today, they tell me, it insists. In those days neither masters nor boys minded if you occupied yourself in painting pictures, digging up fossils, writing for the autographs of film stars, developing muscles in the gymnasium or expensive tastes in the study of Fortnum and Mason catalogues. If while watching a match from a bench on the cricket field you read Sapper or Homer or Thomas à Kempis you would not be thought any more odd than if you read nothing at all and watched the game.

Since I did not mean to sacrifice my dominant interests to the curriculum, I suffered academically. When I came to leave the school in 1923 I had gained only two certificates: the School Certificate and the Life-saving Certificate. The Oxford and Cambridge School Certificate Examination no longer exists. Those who sat for it were mostly of inferior intelligence, having in all probability failed (as I had done) to pass what was called, and rightly, the Lower Certificate. Successful candidates of the Lower Certificate were more often than not entered straight away, skipping the School Certificate, for the Higher Certificate. This Higher Certificate was no joke at all, and though I sat for it eventually I did not come within nodding distance of a pass.

My father, not understanding the subtlety of these distinctions, and learning in Egypt by cable that I had secured as late as 1922 my School Certificate, called for champagne. In my letter thanking him for his message of congratulation—only on two occasions did he write to me during my time at school and this was not one of them—I did not tell him that I had been among the oldest of those taking the papers, and that had I not passed I would have been given eight with the cane by Father Sigebert Trafford, who was then Head Master.

Like the School Certificate, the Life-saving Certificate—which I secured without difficulty, having learned to swim in Alexandria at an early age—is no longer awarded at Downside. Instructions in life-saving were discontinued in 1917, since when we have presumably given up saving lives.

There were others in the Junior School with whom I kept up in later life, but the four, George Bellord, James Reynolds, Tristram Hillier, Maurice Turnbull, each representative of a different approach to school life and to growing up, I knew best. Experience would show that the time for drifting from one set to another is between the ages of twelve to sixteen. I was to find in my own last year or two at Downside that the circle was composed of the boys whom I had known and liked in the Junior School. This is reassuring, for I would not care to be judged by the person I was in between.

The Junior School friends whom I used to meet in the holidays when in London were Alick Dru and Bernard Lane. They could not have been more different from one another. The fastidious man of the world, sure of his opinions, sweeping in denunciation: Alick. The lazy extrovert, pleasure-loving and indifferent to the claims of culture: Bernard. The three of us were roughly the same age, about twelve, when we went out together in our straw boaters for summer and bowler hats for winter. One day we saw a film which led to an interesting discussion afterwards. I remember neither the title of the film nor the names of those who were in it. I do not even remember much about the plot except that it had to do with a young man of humble origins, who, having become exceedingly wealthy, returned to his mother who lay dying. It was not a film I would have chosen to see, and watching it in the company of the sophisticated Alick robbed it of what merit it possessed. Why it has remained in my memory at all is because at one point in the interview between mother and son the old lady's lips could be seen to frame a highly significant pronouncement. The next moment, sure enough, was flashed across the screen: 'My poor, poor boy . . . how can it profit you to gain the whole wide world if you suffer the loss of your own soul?' We picked up our hats and, somewhere in the neighbourhood of Sloane Square, had tea.

'It's a funny thing,' said Alick, 'that even the best quotations don't work if they are repeated too often or too obviously. Take Shakespeare.'

'I liked the film,' said Bernard, 'but I would have liked it better if it had given more about how the chap splashed his cash about. It hardly touched on the wild life he led.'

'Even if it had,' said Alick, 'there was nothing to show that he *did* lose his soul and go to hell. That sort of story does a lot of harm. Don't you see it cheapens the whole idea of being either very good or very bad?'

Myself I did not quite see, and I doubt if Bernard did either. But Alick could not be allowed to have the last word in every argument, so I came out in favour of the film. I said that whatever we thought about the presentation, the melodramatic treatment of a sentimental story, the theme itself held good. I did not of course use these terms, but however I worded the thesis I was rightly understood by both my friends to mean that the old lady was so absolutely right that it was impossible to attack either the position or the purpose of the film.

'Then if you feel like that about it,' said Alick, getting once again his last word, 'you jolly well ought to go off and be a monk the *minute* you leave school.'

By this time my mother and brother were back in England, having crossed the Mediterranean under trying conditions. She wrote daily to my father and he to her. During my holidays we alternated between Berthe's in Lower Belgrave Street and Rita's in Ireland. It was like a Cox and Box, only with the figures of War and Peace. Fortunately for my mother, or she would have died of impatience and boredom, London was full of her friends.

She went out almost as much as she did in Egypt, but the only thing she really wanted was to be with my father. His letters, such as I was given to see, were so charged with his personality that I wished he would sometimes write to me. Occasionally I would get a message addressed to me by name. 'So you have recovered: we all thought you were a goner.' After a particularly bad report: 'who is this blasted chap who puts down your lack of concentration to *frequent readjustments to home life and setting*? What does the wretched man expect? If he's getting in a dig at us, just punch him on the jaw.'

While we were in London it was Yolande and not my mother who tried to improve my mind. Now that I was older there was less reading aloud, but the visits to places of interest and cultural advancement continued. She was in fact immensely helpful, and I can never be grateful enough. It was she who kept me stirred when I showed signs of going slack. Knowing little herself about the visual arts but having succeeded with me in the field of literature, she led me gently to look at pictures, statues, mosaics, tapestries, furniture. Together we would linger in the Tate, the National Gallery, the British Museum. Adoringly, much too adoringly, she would sit next to me for an hour in disciplined silence while I made detailed drawings of Rodin's bronzes in the Victoria and Albert Museum, while I broke pastel after pastel in my impatience to get down the colours of the Hampton Court gardens, while I splashed about with water paints copying Egyptian figures and Assyrian bulls, Babylonian friezes and, without anticlimax, Victorian trains. Over a charcoal of Watts's *Physical Energy* in the Park we had one of our very rare quarrels: she urging that we sit on the bench for which no payment was demanded, I insisting upon the hired chairs which could be moved so as to ensure to get the best light. I can remind myself today that but for the devotion of one to whom sculpture meant nothing I would probably have dropped carving altogether. Berthe's house had enough on its hands without blocks of wood and stone, so since I could not pursue my three-dimensional dreams at Downside I would have had nothing to go on if Yolande had not kept me hard at work copying on paper. Part industry, part recreation: it enabled me to get quickly what I wanted from reproductions. Years later, and without the use of pencil and paper, I learned from photographs of sculpture by Mestrovic and Barlach what I had no opportunity of learning from these masters' originals. Never since the Lower Belgrave days have I been able to study other people's carvings at such close quarters.

In lighter key, Yolande was guide and companion at such entertainments as pierrot shows on the beach at Broadstairs, Punch and Judy shows in the gardens at Brighton, open-air productions of Shakespeare's comedies which we found so dull that we handed in our tickets after the first two. Once, but this was after I had left school, we tried to cheer ourselves up in a dreary hotel by drinking champagne out of toothglasses while sitting on a bedroom floor. Yolande was a help in many departments, and still is.

Berthe was a help too, but in a different way. She was more the aunt, less the contemporary. Also she was at this time under such strain herself, social and spiritual, that she seemed no longer able to reach out to me at my own very elementary level as she had done in the Lancaster Gate days. Her help now lay in the force of her example: daily Mass at the Cathedral, uncomplaining endurance of constant pain, acceptance of frustration in every one of her many good works. 'She's so wonderful,' everyone said of her, 'it's a mystery how she manages to do it all at her age.' Later on, when she had calmed down, people said of her, 'Berthe is such an understanding person.'

Rita was more like my mother. Smart, full of charm, ever on the verge of elation or dejection. Demonstrative in affection, extravagant with money as in conversation, Beatrice did not mix either as much or as well as the other aunts. Locked in her Brighton fortress she was in a world of her own, a world not much shared by her sisters and perhaps not enough sympathised with. Beatrice's strong suit was her beauty, of which she had more than the rest of the family put together. Possibly that was not enough. All in all, and aunt for aunt, I would have matched my mother's sisters with any in the country.

In 1917, when we were in Ireland during the school holidays, my father developed typhoid. My mother was distracted with anxiety. Cables took too long; there were no overseas telephones.

It was difficult enough to telephone to people in Ireland, let alone to Egypt. My father had always been scornful of having water boiled, milk pasteurised, precautions taken against germs, so nobody should have been greatly surprised. We learned that he was in a military hospital, which turned out to be, of all places in the world, the Lindemanns' old house. Whether or not he came near to being a goner, he was granted a period of home leave so came over as fast as wartime transport allowed. He had not seen me for nearly four years and could not make me out at all. I had gone back to school by the time he landed so we met in the unpropitious surroundings of the Guest House which smelled perpetually of gas. He looked very smart in his uniform and I was glad of the chance to show him off in front of my friends.

If I was proud of him, he was I think—and perhaps for the last time in his life—a little proud of me. He was glad that I had worked my way to the top of things in the Junior School and was what was called a League Captain. His pleasure was increased when he learned from Father Austin that next term I would be Head Boy and Captain of Cricket. So secret was this information that I did not know it myself, but I was grateful afterwards to Father Austin for imparting it for it secured me a tip of the wildest magnitude. At our parting it was as much as I could do not to cry, League Captain and all, and a week later it was learned that leave had been extended. I was given permission to join the family in London for the final two days, so we had to go through the goodbyes a second time.

That was the point at which the father–son relationship should have faded away, leaving only agreeable memories. Thereafter, to my great regret today, we gradually declined in mutual favour. After so long an interval it is impossible to assign reasons, but if it is possible to assign blame I take it. By the time we next met, after the war, I was at the most difficult age and showed an unfilial attitude on almost everything that came up. On those occasions in later years when the rift was spanned, and these occasions were not too infrequent, the first move came invariably from him. But it remained a thing of misunderstanding: on his side unable to recapture the sense of affectionate ownership, on mine the sense of dependence and hero-worship. Perhaps paternity involves just this.

On the last day of that term, interrupting my packing for next morning's journey to Ireland, Father Austin told me what he had already told my father. The prospect of becoming Captain of Cricket I viewed without misgiving: there were only ten other people to bother about (eleven if you count the scorer) and they happened to be mostly friends of mine. Also I liked the game, and it interested me to meet other teams and to be in a position to do the honours. But to be Head Boy, placed over eighty juniors, was quite another story. I explained that I was not bossy enough. 'You'll soon get into that,' said Father Austin, 'they all do.' I pointed out that I was not high enough in form to be Head Boy. 'You would be if you worked harder,' said Father Austin. I showed I did not like the idea, but in the end gave in and agreed not to tell anyone about the appointment. Might I tell my brother when I got home tomorrow? Yes, that would be quite in order. How old was he? Eight.

When I broke the news of the exalted positions which I was shortly to take up, I was surprised to find that my brother remained unmoved. Despite his unawareness of the implications, my brother was an apt learner; I began grooming him for school life. He was destined for Downside in a year's time, and by then I would have gone on to the Upper School. Later in our respective school careers I came to be somewhat jealous of him, but at the stage of which I write we got on extremely well. While our cousins, Mildred and William, were otherwise engaged, he and I used to go in the car with MacD to pick up a parcel in Cork or meet a train. One day, while on our way back from such an expedition, a brewer's cart ran into the side of the B.S.A. We felt a sharp jolt, there was a shower of glass, and a horse's head came through the window startled and snorting. The rest of the horse beat the cobbles with hoofs which threw off sparks, and was obviously hoping to get in a good kick or two at the car.

'What's that doing in here?' my brother asked with an imperious look which reminded me of my grandmother.

'It's a horse, Master Geoffrey,' answered MacD, 'just a horse.'

'In case,' said my brother turning to me, 'I thought it was an elephant.'

This was the last of our holidays in Ireland because when the war was over Rita persuaded Jack to do what she had always wanted him to do. He sold Carrigduv and moved the family to Surrey where they settled finally at Nutcombe House near Hindhead. By then another new era and begun. Though some of the most enjoyable of my Upper School holidays were to be spent at Nutcombe, I still feel more drawn to the memory of wartime Cork. To me Cork means rain-soaked shawls worn over the head, iron-rimmed wheels rattling over tramlines and cobblestones, creaking side-cars and bucketing governess-carts, church bells and the thump of beer barrels as they are lowered to wood and stone. Especially do I remember the docks with their mixture of smells, with their half-tone colours, with their recognisably Irish noises. If the prevailing Cork smell is hops, the dockside smell adds fish to it. The smell in turn evokes the sight of seagulls wheeling in the grey sky, alighting briefly on the oily water and mounting again with diamonds dropping from their legs, then weaving to a graceful halt on the wharf. I see crates, baskets, puddles, mud. In Cork Harbour more slapping goes on than anywhere else I know. Men slap each other's backs, lean over and slap the sides of boats, slap capstans, slap rolling barrels of beer. There was less slapping at Hindhead in Surrey.

Now in my last year of the Junior School I should, according to the book, have enjoyed every moment. I had looked forward to the time when seniority should come with its laurel. After a week of it I asked Father Austin to let me step down from being Head Boy. Father Austin refused to consider it. After a second week I repeated the request. Father Austin could not have been kinder: he told me that if I felt the same at half-term I would be allowed to retire into private life. So at half-term I was able to hand the job over to a particular friend of mine, Antony Du Port, with whom I am still in intermittent touch, though I was required to keep on the leadership of the Cricket Eleven and the League. I had no regrets. Indeed I never do regret getting out of things for which I believe myself to be unqualified. My father was indignant when he heard of what I had done; my mother understood perfectly. Several times since this 1918 episode I have slid out of responsibility. This was just what my father said would happen if I once began. I am unrepentant: I am glad I did.

If the death wish, of which I have written above, denotes a flaw in my constitution, the retirement wish is equally a gift to the psychiatrists. Whatever else emerges from this trivial incident it shows I had already come to think of myself as a muddler—almost as though this were an occupation which could be entered upon a passport—and as one whose ambitions and competitive instincts were not the same as other people's.

CHAPTER SIX

The Upper School

Boys leaving the Junior School proceeded to the Upper School by what was then called the Middle School. It corresponded to what is today the Junior House so can be classified as part of the public school proper. The senior side of the school, then, claimed me at the age of thirteen. The first-year boys lived a relatively sheltered life, then came a year of fagging, and after this they enjoyed whatever freedoms were going until new responsibilities fell upon them with the restrictions imposed by privilege and authority. The newcomer to a public school does not know it, but if he takes his duties seriously he will be under a heavier yoke at the end of his four or five years than he was at the beginning. In the meantime he aspires to being a prefect regardless.

The ages of fourteen, fifteen, and sixteen are, according to many who have studied the subject, the trickiest in the life of the human male. They are the jumping-off years. Certainly in my own case the outcome was not one on which even the closest observer would have been wise to make a bet. The Junior School had been the appropriate environment for me over a period of four years, and now, with my religious fluctuations still pendulum active, I was in a world as disturbing as I liked to make it. I had another five years to go, and the Upper School as seen in fag's-eye perspective both attracted and repelled.

I remember this period less well than I remember any other. Perhaps the mind charitably forgets what the will would like forgotten. I know that I took up with a raffish set and that I kept away from the monks as well as from the friends I had made in the Junior School. I attracted attention and acquired a reputation for saying the harsh cynical thing. I was loud. On the academic side I took care to secure a settled position, letting it be understood that I was too dull to warrant an intelligent master's effort.

Accepted as a stupid boy, I was free to turn much of my timetable to whatever interest lay uppermost at the moment. I imagine that shiny magazines made a substantial claim.

A factor which contributed to the new mood I was acquiring was the new mood which was asserting itself everywhere. The war was now over and in the ensuing peace England was not at its best. It was the same thing after World War II. But though I went over to the Philistines for a time, I kept one foot—or at least my toolbag—in the home camp. I was hard at it with painting and modelling. Though art has never been for me primarily an escape, it has always been the first thing I have turned to when I wanted to escape. At this unfortunate 1918-1920 stage I was on the run, escaping from myself. I was escaping from reality, from my monastic vocation of which I was becoming more and more aware, from the tradition in which I had been brought up at home. But it was not altogether black: I was going regularly to the sacraments which I knew to be the saving strength, and I was working hard at other creative activities besides those of painting and carving. I wrote short stories and poems, which I used to send home to Yolande for criticism and for the correction of their spelling. I also acted in the school plays for which I painted the posters and helped with the painting of the scenery. I had no objection to work so long as it was not in the classroom. What I particularly did not want was to think. I had tried thinking too soon, and it had given me nothing but trouble. Since working out the problems of life in my head had failed, the best thing to do was to forget about poverty, disease, injustice and to start investigating the possible substitutes: reality could be left to those actually engaged. I was yet to learn that whatever conclusions are arrived at, they only create further problems. Solutions invite further speculation, and it is right that they should or everything would stop. It is the substitution and not the speculation that is the trap.

My brother was now at Downside, and though we did not often meet during the term, because he was in the Junior School, I saw a lot of him during the holidays. As an indication of my confused state of mind I began to resent his success with the rest of the family. Though he was ten years old against my fifteen, he struck me as being more settled and assured than I was, more wise in the affairs of society, more cool in his assessments of life.

Comparing our relative attainments I wondered how long it would be before people would begin to notice that I was my brother's pace-setter and that he was overtaking me. This self-depreciation was not the fruit of a beautiful humility which was to find its full expression later on in the religious life. There existed good grounds for seeing myself as the inferior. My father's judgment would not in the ordinary way have excited me: in judging the younger son to be the 'sounder' of the two it did. Boys and girls of fifteen tend not only to kill the things they love but also to go on loving the things they have killed. Having killed parental esteem, I knew still that no amount of aunts could do duty for one father. I might for a time get away with it so far as the aunts were concerned, but however scornfully I tried to discount his opinions I had to admit that my father was not subject to my spells. If he was already accepted as my father's choice, my brother was now in a fair way to being everyone else's. Then where would I be?

Accordingly it was probably to compensate that I broke out in so many directions. My childhood had been spent in weaving fantasies about myself, and now I was straining every nerve to preserve some of them. It was because I did not want to see the primary fancy tested that I applied myself in weaving new ones. But it is poor sport hiding among fantasies. There is about egotism this paradox, that though wrapped up in itself it stands exposed. If self-sufficiency resulted from selfishness there might be some point in it.

Today, in this psychiatric age, almost all adult aberrations are attributed to some early insecurity. Let it pass. Materially speaking I had not known insecurity. A different kind of insecurity threatened, and I was rebelling against it. At all cost, even at the cost of that special brand of reticence which I had been brought up to believe was the hallmark of breeding, I must appear secure. I must be in the stream, splashing among the best. The waters of the post-war stream sparkled, ran swiftly, roared. It put a strain on a boy of fifteen to be a man of the world.

I look back without pleasure at the tight-waisted suits, at the effort made to wear one's hair stuck flat against the skull in imitation of Mr Nelson Keyes and Mr Jack Hulbert, at the patent-leather shoes. With still less pleasure do I see myself hanging about the bars of London theatres. I do not think I enjoyed it much, but the image had to be kept up. The great thing was to be mistaken for a man.

I should add, though in any case it will become clearer later in the book, that my mood of fraternal jealousy was shortlived. It was probably not even suspected. And if it was, it would have given no concern. When shortly afterwards we travelled to Egypt and elsewhere, I was the one in charge and he was the dependent younger brother. Though this arrangement suited well enough, I knew that if a crisis developed I would not be much use in it and that he might be. In after years, when the tiresome necessity of saving face became less acute, I could be frankly incompetent and was able to rely upon a willingness which relieved me of the duty of signing papers, arranging for the sale of family property, seeing solicitors. But while we were still at school the fictions had to be maintained.

It was towards the end of what were for me the uncertain years that religion came once again to the rescue. It came first by means of a person and then by means of a book. I date the change from a retreat given at Downside in 1920 by Father Bede Jarrett the Dominican. The spiritual impulse was not like any I had received before, either in illness or from listening to Dom Leander's discourses or through the printed pages of the Gospel. Nor was I well disposed. A retreat-giver of whom I had never heard, and to whose retreat I had determined to give only a token attendance, was not going to influence me if I could help it. Yet influence me he did, and before the opening discourse was over I had been caught. Having long ago decided that consulting retreat-givers was a sign of inferiority I ran for the first place in the queue. Throughout the three days I was dodging in and out of Father Bede's room, defying rules of prior claim.

Father Bede heard me out as I told him what he must have heard a hundred times before: decline of standards, consciousness of a religious vocation, desire for death, compulsive ostentation, reaction against parents. A commonplace story enough. To me it seemed important. He did not attempt to sort me out: this came later. Instead he introduced me to some boys higher up in the school whom he had known since they were children. He was taking a risk but it turned out to be a wise one. It was as though he had said: 'You want to be grand, to live on Olympus. All right, I shall show you some rare and respectable Olympians. They may prove to you that it is worth while being grand only if you back it up with something better than grandeur.' I had never spoken to these important people, and if I was flattered by the introduction I was at least sensible enough to see the meaning of it. In the formation of new orientations this was the first lesson.

Other lessons followed. Without ever appearing to preach, and still less to condemn, Father Bede drew weaknesses into the open, and, by giving them destination, made them into strengths. A feature noticeable in his dealings with young people was his reluctance to prescribe this and forbid that. He disliked regimentation, he did not want to take over from the Holy Spirit, he believed that where the Christian ideal was clearly seen it would be followed. He himself saw the ideal so clearly that in responding to him his following responded to the ideal. It puzzled him to find that the ideal was not always as shining to others as it was to him.

Had I responded more to my father at this stage I might have admired Father Bede less. As it turned out, finding my ideal of manhood personified in Father Bede I was ready, prodded to it by his idealistic understanding of the father–son relationship, to accord to my father a not too ungenerous second place. I could have said with Plutarch that 'the virtues of a good man served me as a glass in which I might reflect my own life'; I could have added to the statement, 'and they also taught me to respect those who had most claim upon my loyalty'.

I cannot claim a dramatic conversion. After a while I found that exhibitionism had lost its attraction, and that to smoke and drink at my age was a mark of vulgarity. I shed my disreputable friends, who were not sorry to see me go because I was growing tedious to them, and took up again with my old ones. I even, as a penance, did some work in class. The reports which went home to my parents took a turn for the better. Not a complete turn: the masters were taking no chances. During the holidays I found favour, and the question of fraternal competition troubled me not at all.

Since he exercised such a significant influence at the time when I most needed it, some additional paragraphs must be given to Father Bede. For it was not in the religious field alone that I learned from him. The quality of his mind and his literary range made their impact so that soon I was beginning to appreciate Belloc, Chesterton, Baring, Gill: all of whom I had written off earlier as being what today would be called square. He got me to read the contemporary, or almost contemporary, poets: Elroy Flecker, Robert Bridges, John Masefield, Rupert Brooke, Lawrence Housman, Lord Alfred Douglas, Siegfried Sassoon, Wilfred Owen. He encouraged me to write essays, urging me to study style in the writings of Max Beerbohm and Walter de la Mare. To some of these literary figures he introduced me in person but since I dislike the kind of autobiography which records handshakes with the great, I am giving here, and only because it related to my job, one such encounter and no more.

In the summer of 1921, on August 14 to be exact, Father Bede took me on my first visit to Oxford. With him as a guide I was captivated. Coming away from Worcester College we saw a middle-aged man walking ahead of us whose appearance was in contrast to the surroundings. The collar of a grey flannel shirt showed over the back of his coat. The coat was longer and looser than that normally worn. His unpressed trousers, made of rough material, were rolled well above the ankle showing thick knitted stockings which fell in folds to the big easy-fitting studded boots. He was bearded and wore no hat.

'Guess who this is,' said Father Bede as we caught up with the pilgrim from Tolstoi's Russia. They hailed one another as friends, and Father Bede drew me forward saying, 'here is a young man who ought to interest you: he is trying to decide whether to be a monk or a sculptor when he leaves school.'

'Yes,' said the man after a long pause.

'Do you think,' asked Father Bede, keeping the conversation light, 'that he has the look of a sculptor?'

'No.'

'Oh,' I burst out eagerly, the sweet truth dawning on me at last, 'you must be Mr Eric Gill.'

'I must,' said Mr Gill, turning to mount the steps of the Randolph. To Father Bede he said, 'I'm lunching here, alas.'

That was the last I saw of the sculptor for some years and by then he had mellowed. In the interval Father Bede had sent Gill some photographs of my carving which elicited from him two carefully worded and exquisitely inscribed letters of technical advice. Six months later I sent him some newer photographs which were meant to show the master how faithfully I had carried out his suggestions. I had produced the inevitable neo-Gill with which England was to be littered for a generation. On a final postcard, received a few days later, Gill urged me to give up carving altogether.

It is gratifying to find that Gill's essays on art are coming into fashion again today. The young people with whom I used to mix in the twenties—even those who had no connection with cutting stone—used to read Gill's books with avidity. I remember thinking what a pity it was he spent so much time on writing which he could have been giving to carving stone.

Father Bede died at three in the afternoon on March 17, 1934. For fourteen years he had given me his help, confidence, affection. After leaving school I would travel considerable distances to meet him at a religious house where he was giving a retreat, at a parish where he was preaching, even at a station where he was changing trains. When I joined the community at Downside I saw less of him, but there were opportunities of meeting him: he was often asked to speak to the school, and on several occasions gave retreats to the monks. To no other man do I owe as much spiritually as I owe to Father Bede, and for few others have I felt as much affection.

If I was fortunate in finding the right person I was fortunate also in finding the right book. *The Practice of the Presence of God* by Brother Laurence, a Carmelite lay brother who lived most of his life in Paris during the seventeenth century, was lent to me by one of the monks at Downside as I was going to bed after a late rehearsal for a comedy in which I was playing a minor part. I was now high enough in the school to enjoy the luxury of a room to myself, and though there was a rule about putting out lights at a certain hour I read the little book right through before I had so much as undressed. 'This,' I said to myself, 'is going to make all the difference.' It did not make all the difference, because nothing like that ever does, but it made a good deal of difference.

With such a wealth of assistance, personal from Father Bede and theoretical from Brother Laurence, I might have been expected to press on without mishap. Not so. Once again my tendency to make false deductions from authentic premises led me to extravagance. Feeling the attraction to penance and holy poverty I made some ill-judged resolutions. I was self-indulgent and I had accumulated a lot of things which were not necessary. I had never known what it meant to do without whatever I happened at the moment to want. There was reason to take action, but asking nobody's advice, and lacking the safeguard of obedience, I took the wrong action. Instead of doing penance constructively, by charity and self-effacement, I reduced my eating to what must have been nearly starvation level and took to sleeping on the floor. On the point of poverty I did my best to observe literally the saying of Socrates: 'He is closest to God who makes use of the fewest things'. I gave away a number of suits, almost all my books, a bag of golf clubs, and a pair of silver-backed brushes.

Then, after a month or two, the reaction set in. It was inevitable that it should, and I am glad now that it did. Humiliation is good for the soul; gestures of renunciation may well not be. I was forced now, in defeat, to see the inwardness of both penance and poverty. I saw how Father Bede's accessibility was far more penitential than my ascetic practices, and that the dependence upon God's providence which was the theme of Brother Laurence's book called for a deeper detachment than that of getting rid of those things which I was now finding myself obliged to replace. Religion to me still amounted to what *I* did, how *I* denied myself, where *I* decided to conduct my next campaign. I wanted to assure myself that the great adventure was under way. I thought that by striking an attitude I would guarantee perseverance. I was to learn that it does not work in this way. Dramatisation carries the seed of reaction.

Since Socrates had let me down—I was buying back my hair-brushes—I tried St Francis on the subject of poverty. So far as I could judge from a reading of his life, the Christian saint and the Greek philosopher preached much the same doctrine. Once again there appeared to be a formula which solved all, yet when applied by most people solved nothing. Did it solve everything for St Francis? Or was it the love of God which solved everything for him, solving problems of poverty and comfort as it went along? Was there among the Greeks of classical times, among the Desert Fathers of Christian times, among Indian and Chinese holy men of our own times, the same sense of division? Feeling that no amount of apologetic talk could explain away a fundamental dichotomy, I went on living comfortably while at the same time feeling guilty. Always fatal in my case, I was back again at thinking.

Experience has shown me since that each man has one particular problem which presents itself to him at intervals throughout his life—sometimes in forms so different as not to be immediately recognisable for the problem it is—and that given even the best will in the world he never solves it. Without the best will in the world he puts off even trying to solve it. The tendency is either to look into some undefined future, where it is hoped that the problem will solve itself, or else to point to a specifically projected change in surrounding circumstances which can be expected to bring about an answer. It is as though someone, God perhaps, were playing ducks and drakes over the surface of one's life story. The flat stone hits the water, bounces into the air, then hits the water again. Here the illustration fails because in ducks and drakes the stone finally sinks and is lost.

Increasing my uneasiness as to how ascetic theory and practice might be reconciled was an incident which took place during the Easter holidays of 1922. For some years I had been staying off and on with a family who were extremely kind to me and whose way of life rose and fell with the stock market. When in funds they took an enormous house in the country, and for three months entertained handsomely. But as if suspecting the turn of the wheel which favoured them so singularly on occasion, they never engaged to rent these houses for longer than three months at a go. When not in funds this family went to ground, and one did not see them at all until some happy speculation put them on their feet again. Though I came to be very fond of the family, collectively and individually, I am not giving their name because in the end they came to grief and stayed there.

One of the sons, who may here be called Rodney, was particularly a friend of mine. Not as intimate as some of my friends—because for one thing I could never count on finding him during the holidays—he knew my ways and made allowances for them. The incident alluded to was connected with a golfing week which we spent at a rather too splendid hotel where there was a Hungarian band to which a few couples danced in the afternoons after tea. We had been urged by Rodney's mother to call on a retired naval officer, an admiral no less, who had taken a house near Poole. 'You will like him,' Rodney's mother had said, 'he's rum.' So, giving up a day's golf, we drove out in a hired car to meet the rum admiral. We arrived, without warning, before luncheon.

No sailor I have ever met had about him so much of the sea. His voice was like waves breaking on a beach of shingle, his face was like a salt-encrusted walnut. We mistook him at first for a seaman servant. He wore an open white shirt, riding breeches, fawn stockings, and a farmer's heavy boots. His arms were tattooed to the elbow, his hair and beard were cut close, he stood well over six foot, he held himself as straight as a mast. He must have been nearer seventy than sixty. When we introduced ourselves he was carrying two buckets. These he put down and asked if we had come to buy a horse. Rodney's mother had not told us that the rum admiral bred horses which he trained and groomed himself. We explained that our visit was purely social, and that we had no desire to buy a horse. He looked at our hired car and said, 'No, I suppose not.'

During luncheon, which was cooked by himself and served in a spotless dining-room, we learned that not only did the rum admiral keep no servant but drank no wine, ate no meat, did not smoke. From March till November he bathed every day in the sea, and during the same period slept in a hammock on a covered verandah at the back of the house. He was not boasting when he told us these facts about himself; he was answering our questions.

'Is it because of religion?' I asked.

'I do not believe in God,' he said.

When we had finished washing up in the kitchen which had been designed by himself and fitted with what his hands had made, we were taken by our host to see the horses. There was nothing of the show stud farm about either the stable or the enclosing paddock, but I doubt if the ponies had a very easy time. Each loosebox was what the bridge had been, and I half expected to see a megaphone hanging where there was a saddle. When the tour was over and we had finished asking questions, it was time for us to go back to the hotel, which I think was called Branksome Towers, and where I am sure at that moment half a dozen London-born musicians were getting into their Hungarian costumes.

'Do you know the secret of breeding thoroughbreds?' the rum admiral asked us as his leathery hand gripped each of ours in turn. Politely we admitted that we did not. 'Then I'll tell you. They mustn't be allowed to get soft.' The final word was emphasised and came spurting through clenched teeth. In our pressed city clothes, with our gloves and our hats, we climbed into the taxi and drove away. The last we saw of the veteran sailor was the outline of his head and shoulders above the wall and against the background of the sea.

'Mother's always right about people,' said Rodney.

During the drive back I thought hard and did not speak. Rodney and I knew one another well enough not to need conversation. A late tea, advertised by the management as *Thé Dansant from 4 to 6*, stirred us to argument.

'That blasted old man,' I said, 'knew we could be thoroughbreds if we tried.'

'But he saw we're too flabby to try,' said Rodney.

Across the strains of tzigane strings came the comfortable civilised clatter of little cups, little saucers, little spoons. Into the toasted buns, paper-thin slices of bread and butter, cream cakes, pot of China tea, came, as though launched from a torpedo-tube, the echo of the admiral's farewell.

'He was perfectly right,' I said, 'because our kind of life is useless. Don't you see, Rodney, that we are becoming utterly effete? Why on earth don't we do what he's done? Because if we leave it too long we'll become completely smothered.'

Rodney's answer ran something like this: 'You are always going on about the evils of luxury and worldliness. But I notice you enjoy these things just as much as I do. For myself, I never feel the least urge to renounce my comforts. This sort of hotel for instance suits me perfectly. I am consistent in hanging on to expensive pleasures for just as long as I can. In our family we are always having to give them up after a bit whether we like it or not. But you are different. You are made restless by the very things which make me feel at peace with the world. Perhaps the difference between you and me is that I pretend I don't mind letting go of what money can buy and you pretend you don't enjoy it. Both of us are hypocrites, but your kind of hypocrisy is worse.'

I told the story of the admiral to Father Bede. How was it, I asked him, that I had seen logically and practically exemplified in an agnostic what I had failed to see in the Catholics who had made up my world since infancy? Why had not he, Father Bede, put me on to the ascetic life? Father Bede's answer, though characteristic, was not altogether conclusive. He said that the danger of asceticism lay in exaggeration, regimentation, and the mistaking of the means for the end. He suspected that the admiral's austerity was no more than habit: he had been hard on himself in his ship so he went on being hard on himself on land. 'Why I have never talked to you about asceticism,' he concluded, 'is partly because I think you are the kind of person who might make a fetish of it and partly because I never like preaching what I don't practise.' I had to make what I could of that. In effect I was left where I was before, where Rodney had said I was: in a fog of inconsistency. I decided that I had better leave the whole subject for the time being, confident that once I became a monk the conflict would find its appropriate answer. A harmony, I promised myself, would fall out of the skies one day.

For the summer holidays of that year, 1922, my brother and I travelled out to Egypt together to join my parents. It was the first time we had made the journey on our own, and a number of precautions arranged beforehand saw to it that we wanted for nothing. In Paris we were met by a M. Gautier whose services had been engaged to conduct us round the Louvre and show us the Eiffel Tower. My brother declared that he had seen both before. M. Gautier doubted the truth of this statement and so did I, but we agreed between the three of us to substitute a leisurely meal where there was a band for a rushed tour where there were only pickpockets. M. Gautier pretended at first to be disappointed at not being able to justify himself as a guide, but admitted to me during the course of the meal, for which he had ordered wine out of what we had saved on taxis and entrance tickets, that he was in fact much relieved. Ours was his first assignment. We drank to his success as a guide and were very jolly. As he waved us goodbye he said he would show us Versailles on our way back in September. 'I've seen it,' said my brother.

In Marseilles we were met by somebody else, this time not from an agency. He was a dapper little man who looked as though he had come straight out of an early French film. He even walked quickly. He had been sent by some friends of my mother who lived near Marseilles and who were themselves supposed to be meeting us. I knew these friends, the Landers, but after two minutes of their emissary's company I was glad that the original arrangement had fallen through. The friend, who gave us his name as he described a brisk cinematic circle with his straw hat but which my brother and I instantly forgot, smoked cigarette after cigarette from a long amber holder and wore a high hard collar with a bow tie. He also wore white duck trousers, a boldly striped blazer, blue socks, parti-covered brown and white shoes, rings on both hands, and pince-nez suspended by a broad black silk ribbon from a button on the lapel of his blazer. He talked so rapidly in a mixture of French and English that it was difficult to follow what he said. After a while I gave up trying to listen, and even perhaps ceased to hear, so that only the swift movement of his lips remains as a memory—a memory further conducing to the idea of the silent film.

While we were waiting to collect our luggage and then seeing that it was sent on to the boat, I gathered, and my brother gathered too, that it was this gentleman's intention to hail a *fiacre* and take us up the hill to Notre Dame de la Garde overlooking the sea. I observed how my brother's face fell at the suggestion. We could see the hill from the station. We could also see the *fiacres*, with their white cotton shades and sleeping horses, lined up outside in the blazing sun. Our friend led the way, flickering in the glare and swinging his cane with Gallican swagger.

'We'll get out of it somehow,' I whispered to my brother, 'even if I have to tell him you have been taken suddenly ill.'

'But I *have* been taken suddenly ill.'

I looked at him closely and decided he spoke the truth. His face was so white that I had no difficulty in persuading our new friend to change his plans.

'In that case we shall sit in the shade of a café, eh? And watch the ladies go by.' It was sheer Max Linder.

I agreed to sit for a few minutes while we thought out the next move. My brother looked on the verge of collapse. Our new friend chose a streetside table under an awning, and ordered coffee. As he sat down he hitched up his trousers to reveal long underpants above the sock. I looked at my brother but he was past caring. I noticed also that our host mopped his head with the greatest care, and that this was because his hair was gathered from temple to temple over a bald head. Since we had the best part of a day to fill in, and since sightseeing was now out of the question, the obvious thing was to get a room in an hotel where my brother could lie down. In all this our *cicerone* could not have been more helpful. He saw us in and promised to be at the boat-side to say goodbye. I knew that if I were to be left with a dead brother on my hands in a strange city, there would at least be someone who would explain matters to the hotel management and the civil authorities. So while my brother was being violently sick, I had a bath (no easy thing to have in any but the best hotels in France at that date) and went on working at a short story I was writing about a consumptive artist down on his luck in San Francisco. When I was beginning to think we would miss the boat if he went on being ill much longer, my brother, showing a hardiness with which he had not hitherto been associated, walked uncertainly to the entrance of the hotel and hailed a cab. It was the first of the migraines which have troubled him ever since.

There, at the foot of the gangway, was the now familiar figure with rings and pince-nez flashing in the sun. A box of chocolates, its lid gay with raised gilt lettering and an enormous silk bow, was thrust under my arm. 'He will have to be careful, this Geoffrey,' he cautioned, 'when he reaches the Orient.' To a Frenchman the Orient is anything from the heel of Italy in one direction and the southern coast of Crete in another. A hooter sounded and we said goodbye. From the deck we waved, and watched him walking briskly along the quay—and back to the silver screen. On our return journey in September Mr and Mrs Lander came in person, so, to our sorrow, we had seen the last reel.

Of all our sea voyages, the one in 1922 was the most enjoyable. On board was a touring theatrical company bound for India, and which might have provided the material for Mr Priestley's *Good Companions*. There was the lugubrious comedian who had special food served in his cabin; there was the harassed manager who had lost all faith in human nature; there was the juvenile lead who gave himself airs; and there was the beautiful girl who created confusion among the ship's officers. My brother and I made friends with all of them.

Also making for Alexandria were boys and girls who, like ourselves, were joining their parents for the summer holidays. They came from different schools, and spent a lot of their time making comparisons and talking school shop. Some even went over their exam papers together. I took no part in this. Once ashore we did not meet again. But for as long as the ship was throbbing through the Mediterranean we played, danced, and swam together. Those of us who were Catholics gathered in the shadow of a lifeboat on Sunday to read the Mass from a Daily Missal. One of the things which pleased me most about that passage to Egypt was being thought older than I was. I did not let on that I was sixteen and a half. I must have been a young sixteen and a half at that, because I remember that I wore a new cream-coloured tropical suit which seemed to me so beautiful that when not otherwise engaged I would change, hang it on the cabin door, and gaze at it from my bunk.

My father came to meet us at Port Said. We had hoped that he would take to our theatrical friends, and perhaps ask some of them to dinner at the Hotel Regina where we were to spend the night before going on to Alexandria, but instead he refused to meet them. This is the sole instance of such unwillingness that I can remember. 'They look a lot of sloppy chaps to me,' he said, removing his eyeglass, 'stinking of greasepaint.' Since the boat was docked for the night and most of the company were dining at the Regina anyway, the situation was uncomfortable. A dance-band played in what was ineptly named the Winter-garden until two in the morning, thereby impressing me with a sense of deep depravity. My brother was more offended at hearing people pronounce Regina as rhyming with 'liner'.

In spite of my contracting dysentery in the first half and getting sunstroke in the second, this was the most pleasant of all my eight summer holidays. The first thing I did on arrival at the house was to visit my onetime workshop. More dust had collected over the eight years, and the place looked smaller as such places always do, but I was glad to find that it had not been used for anything else. My father was delighted that the discovery should give me so much pleasure, and at once had a new lock fitted to the door so that I could go on where I had left off. He went out of his way, reminding me of the old rule about privacy and providing me with new tubes of paint to replace those which had gone hard, to show me that here was a refuge, I could use as I liked.

A hundred things which I had thought I had forgotten came back to me. Memory is like that: touch it off with a match and flames jump from everywhere. Everything about Egypt became suddenly as familiar as my toothbrush and sponge. The particular way Egyptians walk, the noise of the lemonade-seller's cymbals, the noonday gun heard over the water, the amber beads with their red or black tassel, the playful ringing sound of coloured glass and chased metal and dangling charms, the smell of musk and incense and the burning of old clothes, the dry chirp of small animals at night, the flick of lizards in the sand: these things had been in my head all along and I had not known it.

For the first two weeks it was as though England, school, self-analysis had never been. The only people I missed were the Lindemanns and Ali. I do not know what had become of Ali. I went out on sailing expeditions and had the skin burned off my back by the sun. I went riding with my father, rowing with my brother, gambling with my mother at the races and pelota courts. There were picnics, dances, moonlight swimming parties. There was polo to watch at the Sporting Club in the afternoons and a military tattoo in the evenings. How I found time to fit in dysentery and a sunstroke I cannot imagine.

But there was in fact time for everything, even for religion and the arts. The churches of Alexandria, after experience of churches in Europe, appealed to me more than ever. I looked out for familiar shrines, familiar bearded faces, familiar departures from strict ceremonial usage. I visited the Franciscan friary where I had been prepared for the sacraments, and was remembered by some of the friars. Religion was altogether jollier than in England.

I cannot claim to have done much in the way of studying the visual arts. One oil painting and some caricatures in water colour. Literary activity, however, as soon as dysentery ruled out everything else and confined me to bed, flourished as never before. The impulse here was given, unexpectedly it might seem, by my father. Having accused me first of shamming, and having then discovered from the doctor that my complaint was genuine, he had come to feel that some sort of recompense should be made. Not only did he admit to me that he 'had made a bad boss shot' in his initial judgment but in an effort to compensate he brought me books and a gramophone. The gramophone, a wind-up affair with a rasping delivery and a horn like the giant convulvus which accompanies the central stem in *Jack and the Beanstalk*, did not interest me. But the books did. These included *Three Men in a Boat* by Jerome K. Jerome, *Elizabeth and her German Garden*, written anonymously, and short stories by W. W. Jacobs, O. Henry, Stephen Leacock. It may be recalled that I was myself engaged upon the composition of a short story, so the last three works on the list set me off on a course of writing and rewriting. I enjoyed my dysentery more than almost any other ailment since.

An additional asset to the time of affliction lay in the softening of my father's whole bearing towards me, a softening of which I was quick to take advantage. Looking as unwell as I could, I told him of my desire to become a monk when the time of my schooling was over. I could see that the news was not welcome. My mother told me afterwards just how unwelcome it had been. But had I made my wish known at any other time there would have been an explosion. Control, it seems, was secured only by my mother's pointing to the instability of my character and by the confident belief that my intentions would have completely changed by this time next year. She must have persuaded herself that what she said was true because when I returned to the subject a year later, and again a year after that, she expressed surprise.

In this connection, and by way of illustrating my attraction for some sort of complete dedication, I told my father about the old admiral whom I had met in the Easter holidays and whom I had so much admired. It turned out that they knew one another. 'The dear old boy used to be a member of my club in Piccadilly,' he told me, 'before he took up all this silly nonsense. In the Service they thought him as cracked as a coot.'

Alexandria at this time was still talking about Colonel Lawrence. The other great name was that of Lord Allenby. My father had had dealings with Lawrence during the war and said of him, 'he may be a genius, but he doesn't know the meaning of official channels'. Of Allenby his admiration was unqualified. It happened that the Field Marshal was in Alexandria during August 1922, so when my father suggested that I might like to attend a boxing match between the Army and the Air Force at which Allenby would be present, I readily agreed. My father was to judge the contest, and would be able to get me a ringside seat. Better still, he got me a seat immediately behind the guest of the evening, so I was able to study the famous soldier at close quarters and even to overhear his conversation. I understood him to be less interested in boxing than in any other sport. In 1911 or 1912 I had watched Lord Kitchener distribute roses to a regiment of the Brigade of Guards on St George's Day on a polo ground at the Sporting Club. I had been a distant spectator on that occasion. Today I was peering into an equally historic general's ears. As we were coming away, a certain Major Vereker who was a friend of my father and at that time Allenby's A.D.C. came up to us and said, 'I wonder if you know where I can get hold of a pogo-stick? The Field Marshal wants to have a go.' The pogo-stick was then in fashion. My father said he kept one at the office, and that he used it to get his weight down. So we went off in the car and delivered the pogo-stick at the Field Marshal's Headquarters. 'He'll skid on the tiles with the damn thing,' said my father on the way home, 'and I'll be courtmartialed. Say goodbye to your poor old father.'

At breakfast next morning my father recounted the evening's events, saying how pleased with himself he was for being able to get me a place so close to the man of the hour.

'Think of it, Nick. Your son could have stuck a postage stamp on the back of the feller's neck.'

'What a dreadful thing to have done,' said my mother absently.

'I didn't say it *had* happened. I said it *could* have happened.'

'Even so, darling.'

Also with military associations another incident of this Egyptian summer is, if only because of the further light it sheds upon my father, worth recording. He had been invited to some big official dinner, and had arranged that I should be admitted afterwards—with the coffee. His idea was that I would in later life be able to boast about it in the way that he was able to boast about the important figures who were his fellow guests at the civic and diplomatic dinners which he had attended as a young man in Hamburg. He had told me where this dinner was to take place but had neglected to put me through the procedure. Perhaps he assumed that I knew about these things already. In the cab I wondered how I was to present myself, where I should sit, with whom I should shake hands, at what rank I was to drop 'Mr' in favour of the appropriate military or naval title . . . or was I always safe with 'Sir'?

Dismissing the cab, I was so bothered by questions of etiquette as to consider retreat: might it not be better to go home again than to risk a whole range of social blunders? It was only the thought of how my father would view the act of cowardice that drove me forward. As I came up the drive to the Mess, which was a big marquee set up on a lawn in front of the barracks, I felt, in spite of the dinner jacket which I was wearing for the first time, not at all grown up. By the light of waving flares which threw wild shadows across the white canvas of the marquee I could see a tall man in blues kicking the tent-pegs with an impatient dress boot. He was smoking a cigar and wearing an eyeglass. Unmistakably my father.

'I thought you might feel a bit of an ass coming on your own like this,' he explained. He had evidently been waiting some time, fiddling with the guy-ropes and looking at his watch. I told him I had nearly bolted. 'Lucky for you,' he said, 'you didn't.'

In the car afterwards on the way home I expressed surprise that two senior French officers and one British colonel, all three clanking with medals had made themselves look foolish by taking too much to drink. He told me that it seldom happened at this sort of formal banquet, and then added: 'I wouldn't have minded it if it had been just those bally Frogs . . . it was the other feller, the English chap, I couldn't understand.'

It meant a wrench for all four of us when the time came for my brother and myself to leave for England for the Michaelmas term. How my brother spent it I do not know, but for me the last day was spent mostly in the workshop, clearing up the mess and collecting associations. I lingered wistfully, knowing that I had not used it as much this summer as I had promised myself I would. I felt vaguely apologetic. I cleaned the palette with turpentine, washed the brushes, packed the paints. Everything hurt—even the gramophone which played Italian grand opera with the voice of Donald Duck. Was it any good keeping the records which were already beginning to curl because of the damp? By next year they would be elliptical, and so would be the music coming from them. My father said that the place would be waiting for me next year, and that he would not have it done up in the meantime. He promised not to have the skylight wiped clean. As I locked up I would have been even more depressed had I known I was not to come back again.

My mother had planned not to come with us to Port Said but at the last moment changed her mind. Irresolution became in later years her normal habit, but at this stage she did not often change her mind. In the train our chief concern was to avoid other families with trunks labelled for England. Everyone was being sociable but ourselves. On the journey from Alexandria to Port Said I ate mangoes incessantly in an effort to keep up my spirits. I also wrote a letter to Father Bede which he showed me several years later, stained with mango juice.

My parents saw us into our cabin and told us they would not be on the wharf to wave but would leave at once, before the boat started. 'No fun for anyone, blubbing in public,' my father explained. But they were there all the same, my mother in floods and my father predictably dry-eyed but shamefaced. All I remember about the voyage is writing letters endlessly. Even my tropical suit afforded small consolation now.

The winter term, coming on top of the Alexandrian interlude, started inauspiciously. But it was my last year and I was a School

Prefect. Enjoying a plurality of offices I was entitled to a plurality of fags, so the never very arduous course of school life was eased for me. Though I did not play in either the First Fifteen or the First Eleven—unless the team in each case was ravaged by an epidemic—I think I represented my house in everything except chess. This sounds more of an achievement than in fact it was, the houses then being numerically smaller than they later became. Labelled an artist, and not good for much else besides art, I was granted a measure of independence not granted to others. True I had to do Corps, which meant parading twice a week, but by this time I had through no merit of mine risen to such high military rank as hardly to feel the weight of the imposition. All in all I had little cause for complaint. I came more and more to live in my room, which was littered with canvases and paints, attending few classes and no concerts or debates.

The Head Master, Father Sigebert Trafford, knew I was employing my leisure in a way likely in the long run to secure the best returns. He did what my father had done in giving me a place of my own where I could set my own pace and evolve my own technique. It was a kindness on the Head Master's part which I valued all the more in after years when I learned what demands were already being made of education in the way of examination results. He saw that while scholastically I would have nothing to show for my last year I would both work harder and be happier away from the crowd and unsupervised. Ten years later Abbot Chapman was to show the same consideration in allowing me the use of a disused stoneshed which amounted to a large-scale replica of the old harness-room in Alexandria. Twenty years after that again, in 1952, the kindness was repeated by Abbot Butler, and once more I was given a workshop to myself. It would seem that I have always received the preferential treatment accorded to isolationists only in the most charitable of human societies. If ever I come under an authority which forces the odd-man-out to become the odd-man-in I shall have a hard time.

So it came about that during my last year at Downside I was editing and illustrating, and almost exclusively contributing articles to, a privately printed magazine which survived long enough to put three issues on a reluctant local market. Together with a boy of greater literary pretensions I was writing a novel designed to counter Mr Alec Waugh's *Loom of Youth*, which had come out a few years before and had made a great stir. This undertaking was never finished: Mr Waugh got his free field. The essays and short stories were still in hot production. The consumptive down on his luck in San Francisco had been polished up yet again and sent on a round of publishers. In the end the story was accepted by a magazine called *Round the World in Eighty Pages*, which was run by two undergraduates and was devoted, it said on the front page, to 'far-flung fiction and indigenous culture'. Just the thing for me. The front page further stated, but in very small print, that material submitted would not receive payment.

I was taking lessons in drawing and painting from a Mr Goosens, who came out from Bath and when not giving regular art classes, which I attended, taught me in my room. Because of practical difficulties I was not doing much in the way of carving or modelling. For light relief I drew a series of caricatures of Downside and other celebrities. This practice had begun while I was in the Junior School and had made a drawing of Edmund Bishop, the liturgist. It now extended to anyone who came to give a lecture, recital, or concert. Indeed to anyone who came at all. In this way I made a drawing of Father Knox who for some reason was visiting the school. I did not meet him, but had the satisfaction of being asked to sign this the first of many drawings I have made of him. Ronald Knox was to play a large part in my life later on.

One of the advantages of being a School Prefect was being able to get away once in the term from Friday evening until Monday morning. For this *exeat* I went each time to Oxford where I had a number of friends among those who had recently left Downside and also among old boys of other schools. After my first visit with Father Bede, which is still associated in my mind with Oxford more closely than any other, and up to the time I became a monk, I enjoyed the attractions of Oxford whenever I could. Though never joining the university—without maths I could not have got in, and without the money to do it in the high tradition of horses and champagne I did not want to—I took part, off and on, in various aspects of its life. At first this embarrassed me, making me feel I was an interloper, but not, I am glad to say, for long. Sometimes I lodged as the guest of a college and sometimes in an hotel.

For the Christmas holidays my brother and I went to Rita's at Nutcombe. It was all very splendid but the old order was passing. Gone were the aged Irish servants, whiskered whether male or female, who seemed to have been inherited with the furniture and were as rooted as the trees in the grounds. Taking their places were young women who wore lipstick on their afternoons off and who left after three months. MacD was no longer at the wheel. Perfidious Albion was not for him. Instead there was a more accommodating and much younger Irishman called Mooney whose Iberian good looks, often found among the Irish of the south, recommended him to many. 'Faster, Mooney, faster,' my aunt used to urge through the speaking-tube. Whenever a recurrent nightmare took me along Downside's endless corridors in something which might have been either a steam-roller or a fire-engine with the brakes on, I would hear the echo of Rita's 'faster, Mooney, faster'.

The intention of becoming a monk well before my mind, I made particular point at this time of keeping to rule as regards religion. Since Rita possessed a store of spiritual books there was no difficulty in finding fuel for what I liked to think was a steady flame. Ample provision was made too in other directions. On Sundays the whole household went to Mass either at Haslemere where Father Mostyn, himself an old Downside boy, used then to rent a room for it on the first floor of an inn, or else to the stone church at Grayshott where Father Harvey was thought to be dying but where in fact he remained on as parish priest for a further thirty-eight years. On Tuesdays my aunt and I, and anyone else who wanted to come, went to Mass at a private chapel belonging to a Lady Bellew who was a friend of Rita. Of the three I liked the inn best, not only because of its New Testament association but also because while serving at the altar I could hear Saturday night's litter being cleared away: ninepins, glasses, bottles. I liked comparing the shove-halfpenny board immediately below with the collection plate, the bar counter with the temporary altar, the dart board with the Fra Angelico print between the candles.

On this Christmas (1922) we went to Midnight Mass at

Grayshott, and I remember being so carried away that I walked back the three or four miles in the moonlight with the frost crackling under my feet. I wanted nothing more than to become a monk. I told myself that my parents' dislike of the idea would evaporate, that I had only two more terms at school, that by this time next year I would be a novice, that I would then spend the rest of my life in a sweet haze of religious ecstasy. With everything running so smoothly it was now high time, in the providence of God, for a slosh in the face.

The setback came by means of a party given a few days later by some people who entertained a good deal. Not at that time a party-goer, I was persuaded to accept: it was an attempt to counter the surplus of girls. I was the required age, sixteen, and on the way back from the party I reflected upon conversations I had had with my male contemporaries at school and in the holidays. I saw now what all the fuss was about. Suddenly I did not want to be a monk any more.

Unsettled, I wrote to Father Bede about this new attraction, compared with which the old one to the religious life was nothing at all, and to my surprise got a letter back expressing nothing but delight and satisfaction. The gist of his argument was put in the form of a simple question: if people had nothing to give up for God, how could they be said to give anything to him? The letter did not reassure me. I did not want to give anything up. A project which was conditioned by self-sacrifice was consequently ruled out. When I put this to him in a second letter I received back from Father Bede a long and serious explanation of the relationship between human and divine love. I must take his word for it, he said, that without some sort of engagement of the affections behind him a man could not hope to serve God faithfully. An experience of one activity, he said, was a vital preparation for the experience of the other. I had to take his word for it because there was nothing else I could do.

On returning to Downside for the Lent term I did not confide my problems of the heart to my friends any more than I had confided the secret of my supposed vocation to the religious life. It was not discretion which kept me silent on either issue: it was simply that I did not feel drawn to confide in anyone. It might have been better had I told my secrets more readily. I found in later life that the people who talk too much about themselves are easier to help than those who talk too little.

Prone to pulling strands out of my psyche and then tying them into knots, I am not always able to get on without external aid. The Lent term that year was not the happiest. The external aid came towards the end of it and in the shape of a retreat. I dropped all problems and instead made the experiment, which I should have made years ago, of prayer. Hitherto I had dabbled. I had taken up *The Practice of the Presence of God* as a book to study and not as a faith to live by. During the 1923 retreat I read the book again, and this time tried to carry out what it taught. To my astonishment it worked. Confidence in my monastic vocation was restored, not to be disturbed again.

For the Easter holidays my brother and I split up. He went to Rita's at Nutcombe for the whole three weeks; I went for the first week to stay with my Downside friend James Reynolds, and for the rest of the time to Durrants Hotel in London where Yolande had established herself for the time being. The visit to Levens Hall in Westmorland, which the Reynolds family had taken for some years, was the first of a number of such visits which later brightened my lot when I moved north. I had stayed with James before, a few years earlier when the family lived at Dove Park, but this time I was less shy so enjoyed it more. While at Levens I celebrated my seventeenth birthday. It was ten years since the birthday picnic at the fort. I had another fort to wait for now.

The reason for Yolande's presence at Durrants was that Berthe had closed 45 Lower Belgrave Street which she was now trying to get rid of and was running a hostel in the most dreary of London's rougher neighbourhoods. I found Yolande the better for her change of residence. Berthe I found worse. Yolande and I visited Berthe often, both now and during the years following which darkened her life until she moved into a convent and lived happily until her death in 1949. Everyone visited Berthe: friends from the Lancaster Gate days, long-retired servants, drug addicts borrowing money, a novelist, a barrister, a duchess, a never-ending stream of priests. Sometimes people were there when we arrived, and then it was all right. If it were just the family the visits tended to be upsetting. One of what the family called her 'little states' forever threatened. This meant tears of temper and nervous exhaustion.

Nobody objected to Berthe's good works but everybody deplored their effects. The hostel was good works with a vengeance. Particularly was my father critical of her obstinacy, a characteristic which he shared with my aunt, declaring after each visit that it was time she gave up 'pigging it in that filthy slum'. Where she lived was not a slum but nor was it London's Tatlerland, and I remember how earnestly he tried to restrain his feelings as we sat in front of the hissing gas fire in Berthe's bed-sitting room. When exercising control of a violent emotion my father had a habit, which I always looked out for, of waggling his toes. His shoes would show a gentle ripple as though the keys of a piano were being played under a blanket.

While at Durrants I saw a good deal of Father John Talbot, of the London Oratory, whom I had come to know a year or two earlier. Among my few clerical friends he ranked second only to Father Bede, so that when I was ordained priest seven years later, Father Bede being then out of England, he acted as my assistant priest. Whenever I was in London between 1922 and 1934 the Brompton Oratory would be a place of call. Father John brought to my often extravagant religious views a sanity which I would have discounted had it come from anyone else.

With the final summer term almost upon me it was time to look round for a religious order which would take me. I judged, mistakenly as it turned out, that my parents would relent and allow me to start before the end of the year. So it would be as well to make plans. I knew my qualifications to be less than promising: one single examination to my credit—unless the life-saving certificate be counted, which, though it might recommend me to a missionary congregation, was not likely to be of much help in securing my entry into a monastic order. Inclination drew me towards the stricter orders: the Carthusians especially, and the Cistercians. It seemed to me that my leaning towards worldliness could be held in check only by an observance which demanded a complete break. I shrank from the idea of teaching (what could I teach anyway?) and felt no attraction whatever towards work in a parish.

During the last week of the holidays, after praying about it in the church of St James, Spanish Place, which is next door to Durrants Hotel, I decided to consult three people, and three people only, on the choice of an order. A Dominican, an Oratorian, and a Benedictine. Like the beginning of a funny story. The representatives were to be respectively Father Bede Jarrett, Father John Talbot, Dom Anselm Rutherford. The findings could not have been more clear. Independently of one another and giving much the same reasons, they came out with the same advice: try Downside first. Each of these experienced counsellors allowed that I might feel impelled in years to come, after a period of trial, to change over to the Carthusians or Cistercians. From the way they said it I knew what little significance they attached to my dream of an enclosed life. Each of them was equally clear about my misgivings as regards teaching and parochial work: these doubts would be resolved one way or the other long before I was required to take vows.

Before making formal application to the Abbot of Downside for admission, I thought it well to make final representations to my three advisers. I put to Father Bede the idea of becoming a Dominican lay brother. I would then not have to teach or act as parish priest. No, he answered, if I became a Dominican, it would be because I wanted to follow him, and this was no good way into the religious life. To Father John I suggested that the answer might lie in becoming a lay brother among the Servites. I could not, I said, become an Oratorian. Father John's answer could have come from nobody but him: 'Anyway I know jolly well *I* couldn't join an order which needed seven saints to get the thing started.' To Dom Anselm I outlined a project of travelling in Italy, where there was a greater variety of orders to choose from, until I hit upon the one to which I was best suited. He said it was a harebrained idea.

In retrospect I think that my three friends would have been wiser had they urged me to try the Carthusians or the Cistercians and get it over. I would either have left in the first week and then settled down in the Benedictine novitiate at Downside with the knowledge that a ghost had been laid, or else I would have stayed on and lived happily ever afterwards. As it turned out I tried the Carthusians ten years later, ten years of great unsettlement.

That three people who knew me inside out should think alike carried weight. Anyway the issue was closed, I told myself during my last term, and I did not have to bother about it any more. But since there was no sign of my parents withdrawing their objection there was also no point in my applying to Abbot Ramsay for admission to the novitiate. Two boys in my own house, Caverel, were known to be taking the habit in the coming September. I gave to Edward Nelson and Robert Brooks my envious good wishes.

I was sorry to leave school. It had had its bad moments but I had become increasingly attached to Downside and to the monks. Until the time came for the term to break up I wondered if the lines from *The Tempest* applied: 'And, like this insubstantial pageant faded, leave not a rack behind.' Pageant it may have been, and by comparison even insubstantial, but it was leaving something behind, something which was not all wrack.

CHAPTER SEVEN

The Wait

Though the time between leaving the school at Downside and joining the monastery lasted only fourteen months my impatience to get it over made the interval seem longer. Writing about it now, and finding so much that took place during it, makes the time seem longer still. The two months at the beginning and the two months at the end were spent mostly in London. For the ten months in the middle I was in Liverpool, apprenticed to a Greek firm of cotton brokers, and had it not been for the kindness of the Reynolds family, who rescued me at intervals during my exile, I would have thrown in my hand and come back to London before the stipulated span was up. So even this middle period, which loomed so black when I was thrust into it, had its days of grateful light. The Liverpool idea was part of my father's plan that I should see something of the world before entering the monastery —so that with any luck I would change my mind—and part of his wish to see me discovering a talent for making money. Forlorn hope on both counts, and the grounds of our unfortunate differences. What he had not thought of was that the kind of world which I would see from an office in the city during the day and from rooms in the suburbs during the night was not likely to further his first purpose. As to his second hope it shows how little he knew of his elder son.

The Liverpool interlude, beginning in September 1923 and ending in July 1924, can be treated on its own in the earlier section of this chapter, and the two London interludes in the later. Fidelity to the chronological sequence would mean taking the story on journeys which would be confusing to follow. It is easier to adjust the mind to changes of scene than to the process of going backwards and forwards between the same scenes.

In Liverpool I lodged in Prince's Road, where my windows looked out immediately upon Prince's Park. The walls of the room were of so bright a blue as to distract from the view of the Park. In the bathroom was a geyser which instead of being enamelled like most of its kind was of copper, its discolorations showing shades which never ceased to excite my interest. On the landing outside my door was a parrot which squawked, scratched its gravel tray, and ran its beak very quickly along the bars of its cage like a harpist tuning up. There was also a large thin dog with an unsteady eye, a white coat with black dots like blotting paper, and an appetite which belied its frame. Last among the pets was a cat which had a love only for Mrs Archer, its owner and my landlady.

Mrs Archer was a Scotswoman, recommended to me by the Reynoldses who had a house in Abercrombie Square which they used when not at Levens, and the kindest of landladies. Towards me she showed a motherly solicitude from the start, doing all my mending and gently reproving me when I showed lack of consideration. Mrs Archer was greatly given to the well-worn phrase, and it pleased me to hear her say in the Scots pronunciation such things as, 'ye never ken what ye can do till ye try . . . there's but twenty-four hours in the day . . . it'll be all the same in a hundred years.' Some of her favourite expressions may have started out as epigrams but by the time they reached her they had, like Mrs Archer herself, come down in the world. 'An ounce of help is worth a pound of pity'—had this ever sounded very glittering?

In the cotton office where I worked, if this is not too strong a word, there were some agreeable young men and some efficient older ones. One of the partners was a friend of my father, or I would never have got in at all, but him I rarely saw. He gave me lunch in the first week, and again in the last, but between us a chasm yawned. In the lower echelons of the firm we devoted our best energies to racing the tops of inkpots along the length of a sloping counter and signalling to people who worked in the building opposite. Another occupation was seeing if we could drop puffs of cotton on to the heads of passers-by selected by a third party. Life was not so very much different from what I had known in the Junior School.

Warned during the months before coming to Liverpool that I

would meet, outside in the world, a very different kind of person from what I had been used to I went prepared. My elders both at home and at school had warned me of mankind's cruel, deceitful, rapacious ways. I had led a sheltered life hitherto, and this was something which I needed to know. So it was that emerging from this sheltered life into the great world of sin I found people unexpectedly likeable. In *The Plague* Camus was to write about 'man's bestiality to man', and how the perennial struggle leads to pestilence, misuse of human powers, threat of extermination. The same idea of man's essential corruption was to run through much of Mr Golding's more recent work. Today the theme is a popular one. Yet in spite of the injustice, victimisation, indifference to human suffering which society forces to the surface every now and then, for every one exterminator there must be millions in the world who would not willingly hurt an animal let alone a fellow human being. Many debased in spite of themselves; few making a policy of corruption. I would have thought for instance, to bring it into the context of this book, that I am the kind of person at whom anyone with a disagreeable disposition would want to take a swipe. Very few have.

I was fortunate in having friends and relatives who came to visit me while I was in Liverpool. It was like being in hospital. There was Yolande, of course, who stayed in an hotel near Prince's Gate and took me twice to see A. A. Milne's *Truth About the Blaydes* at the Playhouse, where Hugh Williams, not much older than I was, had already made a name for himself in repertory. Yolande encouraged me to go more often to the Playhouse Theatre, and this in fact I did—to my great advantage in the work I was then doing in my free time, which was producing plays at a welfare settlement.

Father Bede, preaching in Manchester, came over for the day and expressed horror at the blueness of the wallpaper. Another visitor was my brother, now aged thirteen and in the Upper School at Downside, who joined me for three days during his Easter holidays. So as to be able to invite him I had put money on a horse and won. It was the only time I have betted on a race which I did not see. We spent our winnings with an easy conscience. Though my father provided me with a generous allowance he had probably not calculated on my improvidence. Also I imagine he believed I was drawing a salary from his Greek friends at the office, which I was not. During my brother's stay we went to see Lewis Stone in *Scaramouche*. It was still the day of the silent film.

Of the film world, but presenting himself in person, was a Downside friend, Tom Ronald. He was working then for Hepworth's, a film company which went out of business shortly afterwards, and we lunched together at the Adelphi with the cast of *Coming Through the Rye*, the star being Alma Taylor. Tom Ronald left the cinema in the end for broadcasting, where he remains, I think, to this day. Also on business, and also to the Adelphi, came Hugo Lindemann, hot from Germany and in the middle of a new fortune. Of all my visitors Hugo Lindemann was the most exciting. We had not met since before the war, and by now Helmuth was as grown up as I was and Lisa only a little less. He had brought photographs, and I was all questions. Memories shone. It was like coming suddenly on silver coins scattered in the wet grass. When I mentioned afterwards to Jack Reynolds (James's elder brother) that I had been having luncheon with a certain Hugo Lindemann I was surprised to learn that where Lindemann walked men trembled.

A Downside friend who at that time was working in the north of England and who came often to Liverpool was Gerald Dormer Dillon. Gerald's circle was for ever expanding, and within it I mixed with a number of people whom I would not otherwise have come across. It was a charming quality in Gerald that he viewed each friend of his, whatever the evidence for it, as a genius in his particular field. We were all destined for high office. What he had in mind for me I do not know. Probably a cardinal's hat. One day as we were coming down the narrow stairs from the chambers of a young barrister who had been at Balliol with him, he said in the prophetic voice which delighted me each time he used it: 'You realise of course that David will eventually be Lord Chancellor of England.' I told him not to be absurd. He was right. With his barrister friend, David Maxwell Fyfe, Gerald and I used to dine with some other friends of his, the Harrisons, who lived not far from me in Liverpool. David Fyfe married one of the daughters, and the son, Rex, became an actor. 'He will make his name on the stage,' said Gerald.

Another Liverpool barrister with whom I used to have meals at that time was Leo Gradwell. A Catholic, Stonyhurst and Balliol, he lectured me constantly about my lack of education. Was the deficiency, he asked himself, to be traced to home background, a poor Benedictine schooling, or native stupidity? I always thought Gradwell would become a priest. I told him he looked like a Jesuit, more precisely a Jesuit who had fled the Society, and that one day he would return to the rock from which he was hewn and become Rector of Stonyhurst. But my gift of prophecy must have been less acute than Gerald Dillon's for Leo Gradwell married.

Though these men with whom I associated in Liverpool—Gerald Dillon, David Maxwell Fyfe, Leo Gradwell, and Jack Reynolds—were only a few years older than I was, they seemed to me immeasureably more mature. I was envious of their balance, their knowledge of the world. I knew it was not Balliol that had given their assurance to the first three and Christ Church to the fourth. It was something which I was determined to discover and make my own. The old complex was proving itself active still.

From Friday night until Monday morning Liverpool saw me rarely. During the Oxford term I travelled overnight to join James Reynolds who was at Merton. South of the Midlands my spirits started to revive, and by the time the train reached Oxford I was ready to plunge with zest into whatever attractions were in season. If it were winter I would ride or play golf or sit in front of a fire and talk endlessly with my friends. If it were summer I would go on the river or bathe at Parson's Pleasure or bowl in the nets. In Liverpool there seemed to be little time for exercise. Since the evenings are the best time for prolonged talk there was little time for that either. Three evenings a week were spent at settlement work, and one at a meeting of the Apostleship of the Sea. The settlement undertaking was full of lively interest not only because it brought me in touch with working-class people from whom I had much to learn but also because on the theatrical side of it I was helped by William Armstrong, the producer of repertory at the Playhouse. If the Apostleship of the Sea afforded less scope it was not because the organisation lacked life but because I was judged to be too inexperienced for the more venturesome of its waterfront activities. Oxford two or three times a month blew away the somewhat parochial fog in which much of my Liverpool life was lived.

There was no lack of variety in my Oxford associations. George Bellord's sedate companions with whom I used to ride were very different from the convivial groups I met at Merton, Trinity, and B.N.C. I remember how five of us spent a night on the river in the summer of 1924, taking it in turns at the paddle and the punt-pole. In the morning, having not slept at all, we went to Mass at the Jesuit church of St Aloysius. I was the only one who did not go up to receive Holy Communion, and when we came out afterwards into the June sun, James turned to me and said, 'are you not in a state of grace, then?' I replied that I thought I had suddenly lost my faith. 'You will be all right after a cup of tea,' he said.

Between the Oxford terms, but not so frequently, I would leave the office the moment it closed on Friday afternoon and move north to join James at Levens. If Commem Week at Oxford, with college balls every evening, was for me the great event of the summer, Christmas at Levens, with Midnight Mass at Kendal, was the great event of the winter. I have the clearest recollection of the grounds under snow, of what must be one of the most beautiful houses in England overlooking the river which looked black in the moonlight against its white banks, of a shoot which took place on Boxing Day and at which I missed every bird to Sir James's annoyance, of falling off a horse at Levens Bridge to Jimmy's delight, and of parties both at Levens Hall and in the neighbourhood. After Liverpool and Oxford it was all the more pleasant to find oneself in the middle of a family again.

From the tale of visits to Oxford and Westmorland, it might be deduced that my time of exile in Liverpool was all frivolity and dalliance. Such an idea would be false. From Monday morning until Friday evening the cotton trade held me in thrall. If my future as a businessman was perhaps not taken very seriously in the office, where I was regarded more as a sort of gilded office-boy than anything else, I nevertheless applied myself in some departments. I learned to type. Though I still bring only two fingers to the machine I value this early training. I re-learned, and for a time mastered, long division. Outside office hours, I wrote poems which sometimes managed to get into a Liverpool paper, and I spent useful hours at the Walker Art Gallery. Lady Reynolds had given me for Christmas a leather-bound diary which was calculated to wind up its final entry on New Year's Eve five years later, 1928. Off and on I had been keeping a diary since before I went to school, as every serious self-centred boy must, but now I ranked its daily page as a literary duty. Lady Reynolds, who herself wrote poetry, recommended the practice more as a discipline than as an art form: she saw what my father had seen but which I did not see until later. Art of any sort must be a task as well as a release.

At last the time allotted to the testing of both my business ability and my monastic vocation came to an end. My father expressed himself satisfied. He sent me one of his rare letters from Egypt admitting that further experiment would be a waste of time. I was now free to shake off the dust of the wilderness and make tracks for London. I did not repine. I gave farewell parties to different groups with whom I had been associated at the office, resigned membership of the Sandon Club (which I had joined for art) and of the Racquets Club (which I had joined for squash and the *Illustrated London News*), gave Mrs Archer a copy of Miss Ella Wheeler Wilcox's collected verse ('Words can still make music,' I wrote in it, knowing Mrs Archer's addition to the pat, 'when the ear has ceased to hear'), had a last look at the copper geyser, and joined Yolande in London. Liverpool, I could reflect, had provided me with much amusement, and had shown me that I could mix with people unconnected with either my family or my school. This being so, I suppose my father was right: Liverpool had meant, whatever else, the outside world. I had no regrets.

When telling me to try my vocation at Downside before attempting something more strictly contemplative all three consultants made particular point of how I should behave in the meantime, not only towards my parents but towards the social environment which would be my waiting-room to the Downside novitiate. Father Bede and Father John thought that the decision to keep me out for a year was a wise one; Dom Anselm thought it was not. 'Let him come in and get it over,' was Dom Anselm's opinion. All three were agreed that I was not to strike religious attitudes while living in the world but should be as ordinary as possible. I think I interpreted this too liberally. Certainly I was not ostentatious in my religious practice, and particularly while in London I adapted myself readily to the ways of the world. Apart from daily Mass and reading a few spiritual books, which I found no great difficulty in doing either in London or Liverpool, I might have been a mildly fastidious Hottentot. The literature of the monastic life was not as abundant as it is now: had Father Merton's books appeared thirty years earlier I would have found a more stimulating incentive. Cardinal Gasquet's *Religio Religiosi* gave a statement of the case, but made the whole thing seem dull; Abbot Marmion's writings, so popular with most, were to me like biting on handfuls of fur; Newman's essays on Benedictine life were vivid and inspiring, but I suspected the romantic appeal. I bought a copy of the *Rule of St Benedict*, but, like the Ethiopian in the desert, I need a Philip to expound it to me. 'Of which century does this man speak: of our own or of some other?' The books I should have read, but nobody suggested them, were Abbot Cuthbert Butler's *Benedictine Monachism* and Abbot Delatte's *Commentary on the Rule*. Once I was in the monastery the reading problem was solved for me, because we were told whose books to read and whose to avoid, but for a layman in the twenties a lot of time could be wasted which today could be put to better spiritual use.

England in the twenties, viewed now in the social and not in the religious context, was recovering from the post-war mood. The vulgarity was not quite so blatant, the pace was slowing down. Young men of my age no longer wore claret-coloured suits, tight-waisted and with a link button; wide trousers and low-cut waistcoats were going out. The voice of the swanee whistle was no longer heard in the land. But though the immediate *sequelae belli* had worn off there was little evidence of the style and distinction which I could remember so clearly of the pre-war era. Culture, elegance, manners, reticence: these things had retreated into remote parts of the country. The towns, if they did not show heartbreaking figures of unemployment, showed a grey face of conformity.

When in London during this time I found myself moving in three circles, each distinct but having points of contact with the other two. There were the Chelsea people denoting art. These were very much what they are today. Nor do their haunts seem to have changed over the years. Then as now they were drawn particularly to Soho. Nothing could disguise the Englishness of their studios in Chelsea and Bloomsbury, but at the Latin call of Soho they would go off and drink *chianti*, walk arm-in-arm in the streets, lean out of windows and shout at one another in foreign accents. I remember a studio in the Bloomsbury outback where a number of young people were living and where there was so little money to spare that the still-life arrangements of fruit and vegetables were eaten for luncheon as soon as they had served their purpose. Everything in the house seemed to be peeling: the wallpaper, the paint on the doors and window-boxes, the linoleum on the floor, the gilt on the baroque looking-glasses, the varnish on the furniture. But every evening the formula would be the same: 'What about having supper somewhere in Soho?' I remember another studio, in the Chelsea hinterland this time, where I was persuaded to camp on the roof for the night because the moonlight on the Thames looked well from there. In this household someone would say towards evening: 'Why don't we go and have supper in Soho instead of staying in?'

Though each generation of Londoners tends to think of it as a place of advanced and emancipated ways, Soho is in fact a most conservative locality. Not only has it a stronger feeling for family life than would be found in other neighbourhoods, but even for traditional forms. On one of the many foraging expeditions just mentioned I was interested to see, painted under the name of a Soho clothier's, the words: 'With representatives in Paris, New York, and St Petersburg'. Passing that way only a few years ago, I noticed that the sign was still there. It may well be there today. Our man in St Petersburg. As further illustration of the theme there is the Catholic church in Warwick Street. I once asked the way to it, and was told: 'Yes, that would be the Bavarian Embassy: it's become a Roman Catholic church.' When, I wondered, had Bavaria's ambassador, accredited to the Court of St James, shut up shop in Warwick Street, Soho?

Not as bohemian as the restaurants in Soho but with still a

whiff of Montmartre lingering in its velvet upholstery was the Café Royal. Indeed in the twenties it was the temple, forum, areopagus, bar-room and banquet-hall of contemporary artistic life. Writers, journalists, musicians, painters. Here, holding court, sat Norman Douglas, now ebullient and now morose. Here, always at the same table, sat James Agate, square, looking like a groom, wearing gloves until the food arrived on the table. Roy Campbell was pointed out to me as a coming poet: he did not look like one. All I can remember about him is that he broke a long continental loaf across his knee and plunged the severed ends into the butter-dish, munching until he wanted more butter. Certainly there was something Homeric about this, and I thought of Greek athletes thrusting their torches into the brazier before they ran. One evening a man came in wearing a cloak, a broad black hat, a full tie, and a beard. Everyone in the room stood up and stayed standing until he had sat down and was roaring for wine. The trouble is I cannot remember who he was. Sickert? Augustus John? I must have asked, but the identity has gone from me. Whoever it was he made me feel I was in the Elysian fields with Degas, Renoir, Monet, Toulouse-Lautrec.

Impinging on the circle of café society was the theatrical circle. It spun at a different pace, but to me was quite as attractive. Not so reactionary, class-conscious, earnest and opinionated as the artists, theatre people struck me as easier to get on with. One did not have to argue all night about principles. I found great friendliness in the maligned world of the theatre. Perhaps because it got about that I intended becoming a monk, but more probably because the stage teaches people to be perceptive, nobody of this circle tried to draw me farther into worldliness than I was already. When at the end I came to do my round of goodbyes, not one of my friends 'in the profession' talked nonsense about the religious life being a waste. On the contrary they seemed to agree with my uncle Marcel, who had originally introduced me to backstage society, that it was the best thing I could do. One or two of them promised to visit me in the monastery. That these promises were not fulfilled caused me no dismay—it would have been embarrassing as a novice to be summoned to meet a party from the current musical comedy at the London Pavilion—but I was touched that the project should be even thought of.

With the third circle of friends I was in what my family considered to be a more appropriate element. It was composed mostly of Downside people and those whom, though Downside people, I had got to know at Oxford. If it was a more restricted circle than the other two as regards personnel, it was hardly more restricted in its activities. With these as companions I touched facets of life which I would have had no inclination to explore on my own. It involved expensive meals, attendance at dances, a nodding acquaintance with sport. The *mystique* of food has always passed me by, so it was only because of the conversation that the dinners held any appeal. Neither was my performance on the dance floor such as to give, to my partners or to myself, more than casual pleasure. With a detachment which had nothing to do with religion I watched cricket at Lords, played squash and golf, went on rowing expeditions which always seemed to end up at Skindles, and attended an occasional race meeting. These were occupations of which my father greatly approved. Against this tally of social engagements I must say that I have never ridden to hounds, been present at a Henley Regatta, or stood in the rain at Cowes. I did, however—though, in spite of long practice, very badly—still ride.

In those days a young man who admitted that he did not ride was looked upon with disfavour. He could say that he did not play bridge, shoot, fish, dance, play an instrument. But it would have been safer to admit that he could not read than that he could not ride. It was not, however, for reasons of status that I rode. I rode partly because I liked the Park in the early mornings and partly because Rodney, whose parents just then were rolling, provided a horse. Rodney would have preferred a later hour for our meetings, but I was firm about this because I wanted him to come with me to Mass afterwards at Farm Street. So with bowler hats almost down on our noses we used to canter along the Row, thudding over the brown-sugar surface, at a time when I knew the sun would be striking the dome of the Albert Hall. Sometimes we would meet squads of military out for a run from Knightsbridge Barracks. They ran in army boots, keeping perfect time, and when the order was given to change from the double to marching pace, steam rose from their white singlets into the morning air. Watching the precision of this exercise I reflected upon the resemblance which the guardsmen bore to the equally studied model which so lately had been their enemy upon the field. Wars lost or won, regiments of the same tradition seemed to go on doing the same things.

Not in boots that beat the road like riflebutts, but in rubber-soled gymshoes which padded comfortably along, a runner appeared one morning in the far distance, and he too was steaming. The approaching figure, in white shorts and shirt, turned out to be a Downside boy, a prefect belonging to a house which was neither Rodney's nor mine, who was getting into training for the coming term's rugger. We on horseback removed our bowlers, nodded gravely to the runner who puffed a nod back, and no word was spoken as we passed. I have thought since that, given the necessary transmutations, this would have happened differently in America.

On these sunrise rides Rodney was very much taken by a tall, goodlooking girl who, astride a formidable chestnut, shared the almost empty Park with us. More often than not we would see her again afterwards in the nave at Farm Street. For Mass she would put a skirt over her riding-breeches, and this amused us. Months later, when I was a novice, Rodney wrote to say he had found out more about her and that she was entering the Sacred Heart novitiate when she had finished whatever studies she was doing. So the next time I saw her, in 1947, was when she was a professed nun.

These rides were not only good exercise but also, though I did not appreciate this at the time, good copy. They provided some incidental material for a religious novel which, under the name of Hugh Venning, I wrote during the Second World War.

An occupation considered suitable at this period to young men who did not want to lag behind was that of making sorties from the west to the east end of London. The young man of fashion would put on a cloth cap, remove his collar, wear his oldest clothes, and assume what he conceived to be a Cockney accent. The favourite objective was Limehouse, and these adventures were thought to be, if not particularly dangerous, at least dashing. Though I never graduated to Limehouse, so am not strictly in a position to speak, I twice roamed round Camden Town at night and found the experiment unexciting. I went with a Downside friend and two Harrovians. Since we were seen through at once, it meant that in public houses we were expected to pay for what people drank and in dance-halls we had to listen to the refined voices adopted for the occasion by our partners.

Even considered as a study of east–west metropolitan discrimination, these ventures were a failure. The young women to be met in Camden Town appeared to be just as agreeable or disagreeable, just as intelligent or unintelligent, as those whom we were meeting every day. The only difference that I could see was that débutantes* did not have chilblains or complain about their poor feet. The dance palaces of Camden Town, although decorated with coloured paper and clusters of balloons, were one up on their west-end counterparts in the matter of heating.

With the same three friends I used sometimes to visit a music-hall which must long ago have been either suppressed or bombed; or perhaps has simply fallen to bits. It was on the far side of the river, somewhere near Blackfriars Bridge. A distinctive feature was that on paying their entrance fee, which was the same for all, patrons took a folded chair from a diminishing number leaning against the back wall, and sat where they chose. From time to time during the performance, patrons would interrupt and there would be scuffles. We, the diehards, took the chairs vacated by errant members of the audience and put our feet on them. Such was the scale of ejection at this music-hall that the audience was rarely the same at the final curtain as it had been at the opening number. Our party always stayed on to the end. I wonder now why.

In the same empirical spirit, and also vaguely hopeful of being able to recoup financially, I tried my hand as a pavement artist. The enterprise lasted three days and brought in less than ten shillings. My next engagement was as a bartender in Guildford. But this was a question of honour, for I owed money to the landlord of the inn. After a few evenings the debt was paid off, and I returned to the capital. Frolics of this kind did not please my father. He was puzzled and mortified. He saw my behaviour as showing ingratitude to him personally. 'I've given you a good education, an allowance larger than I can afford, a godfather who

* The term 'flapper' had gone out by this time, and the equally atrocious 'deb' had not yet come in.

has a seat in the House of Lords—and then you play about on the pavement and wipe glasses behind a bar.' I did not blame him for his view; justice was on his side. At the same time I knew that he might equally have taken the opposite view. With him the borderline was so elusive that nobody but my mother could tell where it was. At this time particularly, before becoming a monk, I could do little right. Whenever I managed to get a few lines printed in a provincial paper, earning thereby a pittance which I could show as evidence of my expensive education and untiring industry, I was told that writing poetry was a mug's game and that writers of any sort were a pretty rotten lot. So down the slopes of Parnassus rolled neither golden coins nor the thunder of applause. Thinking I would be on firmer ground in the matter of painting, I tried to sell some oil paintings which I had done at school under the influence of the kindly Mr Goosens. My father put a stop to the attempt on the score that he, who had painted all his life, had never stooped to receiving money for his work. A more cheerful note was struck when I told him I had been offered a small regular salary in return for a weekly cartoon. In rejecting the proposal he said that if the drawings turned out to be bad he would feel ashamed, and if they were good everyone would think they were his.

Not enjoying the easy wealth of some of my companions, I was debarred from many of the entertainments and social activities current in the London of that time. But even so, standing respectfully and without envy in my appointed station, I managed pleasantly enough. Helping me to rub along were not only the three friends who had conducted me on a tour of what they believed to be London's underworld but a number of other friends who claimed to have ready access to London's overworld. Even seen at a distance, while paddling as it were in the shallows offshore, this overworld made considerable appeal. A little inland, deep in the heart of Boat Race Night, lay the Cavendish. In the twenties it was one of several rallying points where the *jeunesse dorée* would assemble. Here the young men of England's future would bank up the fires of privilege against the coming storm. And they could not have had a better place for it. Nor could anyone have championed their cause more loyally than Rosa Lewis, proprietress of the Cavendish Hotel. Rosa was then at the height of her power. She was more than a ruler, and certainly more than the proprietress of an hotel. She was a high-priestess to whose temple—an Edwardian temple where the furniture and fittings were, already in the twenties, fashionably out of date—came worshippers different from those whose spiritual centre was either the Café Royal on the one hand or Claridges on the other. At the Café Royal people used to draw pictures and write poems on the menu cards. There was none of that here. At Claridges there would be visiting Royalty occupying suites on the first floor and being given the same sort of deference as they would enjoy in their own courts. If Royalty came to the Cavendish it came unheralded and in a soft collar. It was probably Gerald Dillon who introduced me to Rosa Lewis and the Cavendish, and though I never became a regular visitor I saw enough to know that here was something rare and splendid, something which would be written about in later generations. Rosa, with her vague memory but acute business sense, survived, and apparently still in command of unlimited champagne, the Second World War. It is sad to think that the bathrooms with their rich complement of douches and the broad mahogany frames which gave access to the bath itself no longer exist.

In a few weeks' time, on September 17, I would be leaving London to try my vocation as a monk. The tumbrils were almost at the door of Durrants Hotel, but I was not afraid of the knife. I sold my dress clothes—indeed I sold almost everything except what I stood up in—and felt the glow of not owing money to anybody. I spent a lot of time with Yolande, who for so long had covered up my follies and encouraged me to look beyond the immediate mess. With her I called on Berthe for the last time. 'I do wish she'd leave that dreadful place,' she said as we came away, 'where the girls are always gassing themselves in locked rooms and making eyes at your father.' My father and mother were in fact at home in Egypt, so at least the major parting was spared us. The sun shone incessantly, and parties abounded. Careful self-discipline was needed to avoid dramatisation: at all cost I must not play up the grand renunciation—either in front of others or to myself. I was being torn inside (who would not be?)

but I knew that this was only a preparation for tearings which were to come. Also there was a certain sweetness, even without dramatisation, in the wretchedness of these goodbyes. More vividly than the dinners of farewell, at which there was much noise and things got broken, I remember a quiet tea in the smallest of teashops in the Burlington Arcade. It shows how unpredictably the memory operates, blurring the big scene looked forward to and etching deep the unrehearsed.

To see me off from Paddington were six of my friends, two girls and four boys. They wore gardenias. Today the smell of a gardenia will take me back with a sharp stab to Platform 1 at Paddington Station. Jack Carroll, arriving as always at the last minute, brought me Michael Arlen's *Green Hat* to read in the train. He said it had just come out, that he had sat up all night reading it, and that I would be interested because most of the characters in the story were drawn from people whom we knew. At that moment I had no desire to read about anyone not of the group in front of me.

'Don't come to see me for at least a year,' I begged them as the train started to move.

'You'll come out long before then,' growled Cyril Bull.

I had dinner on the train, treating myself to a pint of champagne (there were no mangoes) and a cigar. I was not a monk yet. From Bath I drove out to Downside. It was just ten years since I had arrived at Downside in the one-horse shay. This time I was alone and had no trunk. Having read somewhere that a monk should not possess more belongings than what he could carry on his back—and I was determined, once I started, to be that kind of monk—I had with me two suitcases. Everything else I had shed before starting. It was dark in the recessed Gothic porch of the monastery, and as I pressed a firm finger on the bell I said with Dante: 'Here beginneth the new life.'

CHAPTER EIGHT

The Early Years in the Monastery

But the new life did not begin as immediately as I had expected. I rang repeatedly but nobody came to the door. After trying two other entrances I dragged the suitcases to the bursar's office, which was still open, and eventually found my way, by the light of the bursar's torch, to the novitiate quarters on the top floor. I had forgotten that monks go to bed early. In the novitiate there were names on the doors of all except two cells, and my name was not among them. It was an inauspicious start. Lowering the suitcases as silently as I could on the bare boards, I knocked at the end door marked *Magister Novitiorum* and was told, in a muffled voice, to come in. Dom Richard Davey, who was to be responsible for my monastic training for the next three years, was sitting on his bed with his hood up squeezing toothpaste on to a brush. 'Hallo,' he said, 'I thought you weren't coming.' Still with his hood up, for this is the custom with us after Compline, he led me to one of the two empty cells, and, with a roguish look, whispered, 'Reggie hasn't turned up'. But in this he was mistaken, because at that moment we heard Reggie stumbling up the stairs. He was dragging two heavy suitcases.

Reginald Segrave-Daly had been two or three years senior to me in the school at Downside, and now, because he had come by Templecombe and not by Bath, was my junior. I was sorry about this, not so much for his sake but for mine. Feeling I might profit by the mistakes made by those above me on the list, I had hoped to be last. I had missed the position by half an hour. Together Reggie and I got our things into our respective cells, whispered a grateful goodnight to Dom Richard, pinned our names on the doors, and went to bed. But at some point Reggie must have felt the need for conversation because he came to my door where, with the gas turned down, we talked till late. When this was over

I lay in the dark, unable to sleep and waiting for the end of the world.

That, for months to come, was the only bad bit. And it was not as bad as the first night at school had been, or the first night in Liverpool. In the morning I was caught up by the novelty of the life, and this carried me over until the postulants' retreat which was to be in preparation for the clothing. I found I knew nothing, not even how to make a bed. For the first week I dusted the cell before sweeping it, believing that the dust had to fall on the floor before it was swept up. It took me a long time to get things done, and I was late for everything. One of the two novices who had been members of my house, and who were now ahead of me, was put on to instruct me in what would now be called cellcraft. From him I was introduced to scrubbing, polishing, emptying slops, cleaning windows. There was no running water in the cells, and I broke two china basins and one jug between the end of September and Christmas. I was told to use tin. My clumsiness continued for I broke gas-mantles innumerable and the glass funnels which fitted over them. Holy-water stoops fell to pieces under my hand.

There were six of us making the retreat. When it was over we would receive the habit and rank as novices. Four of us had been in the school at Downside, one had come from the school at Ealing, one was a convert. Of the six, three made final profession: Dom Oswald Sumner, Dom Matthew Kehoe (who later transferred to Ealing), and myself. Reggie, or Brother Maurice as he became, left after a few months. He had provided the liveliest entertainment. Brother Jerome survived late into the summer. The last to leave was Brother Theodore.

Contrary to expectation, for I had been warned, the retreat was for me a time of great peace. One or two of the others, I could see, were in the throes of crisis. I was grateful for my own calm. During the full six days, with an extra slice at either end, I made notes and gave myself to serious thought. I had never done anything so thoroughly before. From the notes of this retreat, which I kept until I went to try my vocation with the Carthusians in 1934, I see now that I was approaching monastic life along the wrong lines. I was resolved, putting it in writing, to forge ahead in following my own spiritual attractions. It was as though I were saying: 'I am prevented from joining the most severe orders in the Church, so I will force myself to severity here. I pledge myself to poverty, silence, penance, and if I lag behind in observing these things I shall be called to account by God.' Such was my attitude then and later. It was what I believed God wanted of me. In that retreat of initiation I was not preparing myself to receive, with the Benedictine habit, whatever the monastery might give me; I was preparing myself to hang on, come what might, to my conception of monasticism. My plan was so to cement my purpose as to rule out return or deviation. The dedication was there, ready made before the clothing ceremony, before the process of training had begun, before the mould to which I was expected to yield was properly seen. This of course meant that if I were to take the shape monastically and spiritually in the monastery of my future profession, I would have to allow this cast of my own to be broken. I would have to be re-set. How far I have submitted to this re-setting, how far it has been accomplished in spite of me, how far God intended it to be put in operation at all: these are questions to which I can expect to find answers only in the next life.

So whatever the difficulties with which I have had to contend over the years since my novitiate, they are difficulties which have come from inside me. My superiors have not made things difficult; my brethren have not made things difficult. Quite the contrary: the house of my profession has consistently put before me its ideals, consistently helped me to see the meaning of these ideals, consistently justified these ideals by their fruits. The margin of error and doubt lay in a preconception of my own. There is probably a margin of error and doubt in every vocation, but in my case I wonder if it had been so wide had I been ready to look more closely at the terms of the religious life as presented and paid less attention to the marginal comments.

It was as well that no such reflex thoughts troubled me during the retreat. We were given the habit on the feast of St Michael, September 29, and I was allowed to take the name for which I had asked. St Hubert had for a long time attracted me as a patron. There was a lesson to be learned from his obstinate pursuit of a particular satisfaction only to find the cross in the middle of it. As a spiritual Captain Ahab, plunging after a spiritual white whale, St Hubert typified the kind of singleness of purpose to which I aspired. I felt that if I hunted long enough, and stuck to the straight path through the forest, I too would find Christ between the antlers of the stag. The details of the chase could look after themselves. I was counting telegraph poles again.

A novice now, and eating up the literature of the ascetical life, I wondered what practical steps could be taken in the way of self denial. What could I give up? (Not what could I *give*, but what could I give *up*?) First to go were the photographs I had brought in with me, and then the letters. The only letters I kept were those from Father Bede. The poems I sent to Maurice Turnbull, the only one of our group who was still in the school and who alone among my friends would have known what they were all about. Drawings I sent to James Reynolds: they were mostly caricatures of himself and illustrations of holidays we had taken together in Wales, Shropshire, Oxfordshire, and Herefordshire. Also as fuel for the holocaust were some dance programmes with their little white pencils on a cord, some signed menu-cards, and seven yellowing gardenias. It cost me little to discontinue the diary, especially now when one novitiate day was not likely to differ much from another, but I deplored the destruction of Lady Reynold's morocco-bound five-year volume. Feeling lighter than I had ever felt before I addressed myself to the task of being a novice.

The weeks went all too quickly, and by the middle of December the routine life of the novitiate was second nature. Dom Richard advised me not to look too far ahead, so whenever the thought of having to teach in four or five years' time came to my mind I obediently pushed it aside. I did the same with the thought of possibly having to work on a Benedictine parish. I was taking life so much in my stride, adapting myself so easily to the novitiate setting, that I was perhaps leaving too much of my thinking to other people. I was pushing what lay ahead so far into the remote future as to render it virtually invisible. I was doing in the monastery what I had done in the world whenever an apparently insoluble problem came up. Something would happen eventually; the next stage would show. Profession would mark the next stage, and the priesthood would mark the stage after that. Until the stages came I must make myself snug while the making was good. Ducks and drakes.

So far as discipline went I did not chafe. While I would have relished something more extreme, I enjoyed the contrast with conditions I had known in the world. The rules of silence ensured a privacy such as I had not been able to count on the year before. The rules of the novitiate and the boundaries of the enclosure secured the withdrawal I had been looking for. The daily manual labour, though there was only an hour of it at a time, was no penance. What with work in the sacristy, attending conferences on the holy Rule, getting up the lessons for the next day's choir office, meeting three times for recreation, devoting two half hours to mental prayer and one to spiritual reading, serving a private Mass and taking turn in serving at the sung Mass, the day was a reasonably full one. It suited me.

If there were quarrels in the novitiate they could not have been serious or I would have remembered them. Certainly there were no such enmities and estrangements as are ascribed to men living in close proximity to one another. I may have been fortunate in my year because there was not one of our number with whom I would not willingly go through another novitiate today.

With Christmas came something of a setback. My first Advent in the monastery had opened new horizons: I began to see what the liturgy was all about. Midnight Mass in the Abbey, the three private Masses which that year I served in a domestic chapel which has since been abolished, transported me. But before the day was half over I had spent myself and there was a feel of anticlimax in the air. The wings had begun to melt, and Icarus was dropping fast.

It was a mild soft Christmas that year, in contrast to the crisp white Christmas at Levens of the year before, and I decided to pray my way back to the Christmas spirit by going for a solitary walk round the Long Shrubberies with a rosary and St Bernard's sermons on the Nativity. On the top field one of the monks was practising approach shots with a mashie. Christmas being what is called a 'community day', which means that the novices are allowed to speak to the professed, the monk hailed me with his golf club and told me to come over to talk to him. He had known me in the school. He told me as he bent over the ball and made preliminary swings that he had been waiting for a chance to speak to me. He had been watching me during the past weeks, he said, and had come to the conclusion that I was overdoing things, losing weight, taking life too seriously. 'What you need is to slack off a bit,' he told me. I was touched by this wholly unexpected solicitude, particularly since he had not been much in my confidence when I had come under him in the school, and did not know what to say. Tactfully he began talking to me about my friends, who were his friends as well, and asked me whether they had written to me for Christmas. I replied that they had, the dozen or so whom I knew best, but that I had not yet read their letters.

'Too busy with sacristy work? Surely even Christmas leaves you novices enough time to read your letters?'

'It isn't that. I would have had time.'

'Why not then?'

'I was afraid they might be distracting,' I admitted.

The monk put away the mashie, and in the kindest way possible told me that I was on altogether the wrong lines. He said that as a novice, he had felt the same but that now he knew better. We talked for a while until he sent me away to go on with my walk in the Long Shrubberies. 'And think over what I have told you,' he said in farewell, 'because we won't have a chance of talking till Easter.'

This conversation, grateful though I was to find sympathy where I had not looked for it, left me disturbed. I stayed outside, walking and asking myself questions, until it was time to go in for Vespers at five o'clock. By then it was dark and I had missed tea. Fortunately I had laid out the vestments in the sacristy immediately after luncheon so did not have that to worry about. I remember standing on the grass slope next to the rock garden and watching the lights go on first in the sacristy and then in the Abbey, and wondering if I belonged here after all.

Of the thirty to thirty-five Christmases I have spent at Downside, that first one stands out from the rest. It was not over yet, and because of the light it sheds I make no apology for continuing the account. It is our custom at Downside to move out of the monastery refectory during the Christmas and summer holidays, and to take our meals in the school dining hall. Here there is a log fire from Christmas Eve until the octave of the Epiphany, and instead of listening in silence to the reading of a book we talk throughout the meal. After dinner in the evening there is full community recreation which, for the novices, ends at nine o'clock. At nine, since Compline during the Christmas holidays is recited before dinner, the novices go to bed. Novitiate bounds are also relaxed during the holiday season.

The combined effects of the Christmas euphoria with the resulting aftermath, the afternoon's conversation on the cricket field, and the contents of the letters which I had now read, left my mind in a state of turmoil. With the letters still in my hand I chose to go up to the novitiate by way of the Petre Cloister and some stone steps leading off it. Only on the greater feasts are novices allowed in this part of the house, so there was a certain novelty about the route. Where the steps turn right there is an alabaster statue of St Benedict which stands nearly life size on a stone mount set against the wall. The figure possesses no sculptural merit whatever. For me it held numerous associations, and I had not seen it for some time. At the age of ten I had spent hours hanging about at this bend in the stairs, waiting for someone to come. Whenever someone was wanted from the monastery, whether to take a Junior School walk or organise a Junior School game or tell stories in a Junior School dayroom, a handful of small boys would be sent up to this spot where they rang a little hand-bell and waited. It was the frontier post beyond which the profundities of the monastery were not to be explored. I seemed always to be among those who were sent to ring the bell and wait. On one such mission, and during a longer wait than usual, we grew so restless that we climbed on to the top of St Benedict to see how many of us could be supported at once. Before the point was established, a boy called John Phillips (the one, as it happens, who had asked me to bequeath him my camera) rested his foot on St Benedict's hand, and an alabaster finger fell off. What were we to do with it? Were we to own up? Could it be stuck on again—by dead of night perhaps? While we were debating these questions we heard someone coming at last to answer our bell, and John Phillips adroitly hid the finger out of sight in the bend of St Benedict's arm. Nobody was told about the breakage, and there in a shallow recess behind the alabaster book the finger stayed.

On the Christmas Day of which I have been writing I looked to see if the bell and finger were still there. The bell had gone, but the finger was where we had left it ten years before. (It is still there today if anyone cares to look—a grey alabaster finger lying loose in the hollow of St Benedict's arm nearly fifty years after John Phillips knocked it off.) Other associations flooded my mind: coming past this same statue on my way to see Abbot Cuthbert Butler to whom I used to go to confession when my regular confessor was away, coming past it during times of retreat when the monastery was accessible without having to get permission, coming past it in jolly disarray during Rogation Day processions. It represented to me the whole Downside part of my life. It spoke for the past, did it speak also for the future? Seeing it now on Christmas Day, and knowing that it would be out of bounds tomorrow, I warmed towards this very inferior piece of statuary. I prayed in front of it, asking St Benedict to resolve my vocational problem for me. I asked not only that the conflict between love of the world and love of monasticism might cease but that the other conflict—namely between the rival attractions of solitude and severity on the one side and those offered by my devotion to Downside on the other—might reach a decision one way or the other. I asked for a lead which would show me how to serve my friends in the world without going back upon my renunciation of the world. I asked that between now and my profession I would be shown where I was meant to be. I asked for a good deal while I was about it. Though no assurance came, and though the alabaster figure recommended itself to my stone-cutter's eye no more than it had ever done, there was now yet another association with that seldom admired corner of Downside.

It was a little later, when the school reassembled after the Christmas holidays, that the proximity of the boys and of all that went with them began to trouble me. Up till now I had been so busy learning what to do as a novice, and finding satisfaction in the fulfilment of what had been so long awaited, that I had not found the presence of the school within hailing distance any great distraction. But now the whole question of my place in Benedictine education became more acute. The immediacy was brought home to me on February 2, the feast of the Purification.

At Downside the Candlemas procession, everyone holding a

lighted candle, moves round the cloisters. Following the cross and acolytes come first of all the boys, then the monks, then the celebrant and ministers. So it was that together with my fellow junior novice and I (Brother Maurice, *né* Reggie) I came close upon the heels of the two most senior boys in the school. These were Maurice Turnbull and Robert Arbuthnot—Robert as well as Maurice being a very particular friend of mine. By stretching out my candle I could have singed the hair of either of them. I was as close as I had been to the Field Marshal's ears in Egypt. While the Purification antiphons were going on and we wound our way from one cloister to another I was conscious of a dualism at work inside me which so boiled up as to make me wonder for a moment which part of the procession I was in. I felt that there was a significant difference between belonging to those who walked in front of me and belonging to those who walked behind me. I was caught in the middle between two environments. Spiritually I was in one, emotionally in another. It was like a bad dream, because I could not tell where the one ended and the other began. I knew only that for me there were two quite separate worlds, and that one or other must win in the end. Must, indeed, be winning now. I knew in which world I willed to be—namely among the monks who were just behind me in the procession—but was the will strong enough to override the pull of the emotions which drew me towards those in front?

This Candlemas procession came to be, during the months which followed, something of a symbol to me. It was one which carried particular urgency as the time for taking vows drew near: I must know in good time where I was in the procession, and where it was leading me.

Things were not made any easier by such glimpses and echoes of school life as inevitably came my way. The roar of laughter from a classroom well beyond novitiate bounds, light music played on gramophones in rooms whose doors had been open to me eighteen months ago, the sound of a band-practice, the cheering at a rugger match, the sight of teams on their way up to the field, the crowding in to Mass and Benediction, the group of rather cheeky boys whom I had known as fags who would bump into me on purpose in the church and then laugh and look away: all this made for matter of further self-searching.

It is a commonplace to observe that the human mind can want two opposite things at once. I wanted very much to be under the rule which forbad novices to speak to anyone not in the novitiate, and at the same time wanted to talk to people. Everything all round me told me that the school was an essential part of the life, that it was an extension of the community, that the boys belonged to the procession as much as the monks did. It was not even a question of one world impinging on another: they coincided. But until I could myself feel this, and not merely see it as an identification which others could feel, I knew I would never be at peace. Without the experience of such a harmony, I would always be a misfit.

While in America not long ago I was saying Mass at a convent where the community runs a large high-school for girls. Some few of the students are boarders, but the majority are day-girls. These, the 'day-hops', arrive noisily in cars and school buses just in time for the first class of the day which begins at a quarter to nine. I had said Mass at eight and was about to leave at a quarter to nine when I noticed a young nun rinsing out the cruets at the sacristy sink. Cars were still racing through the campus and skidding to a gritty stop at the school entrance. I could hear the car doors being closed with a rich *plunk,* the loud cries and shrill laughter, the hurrying of feet and the dropping of books. The young nun was hearing it too, and I watched her face as she looked out of the window. She was too preoccupied to know that I was there, that the tap was running, that the cruet needed no more drying. My guess was that she had been in the school a year or two before. I felt like telling her to keep her wits about her at the next Candlemas procession.

The next thing to think about was Lent. On Shrove Tuesday I was given permission to see my brother for an hour after supper. No carnival could have been more exciting. I think it was the first meeting with anyone from outside since September. The next meeting would be, since the school were to remain for Holy Week, at Easter. In the meantime the Church's penitential season, calling for a new orientation as far as I was concerned, was upon us. Those of us who were under twenty-one were not allowed to fast for Lent. I was twenty. It was probably a wise prohibition, but having fasted merrily the year before in Liverpool I was dismayed by it. Obedience, I was told, was more meritorious than the mortification of the appetite. Another thing which dismayed me was an alteration in the timetable, making five o'clock the hour for getting up instead of half-past four as hitherto. The same answer came: obedience to be preferred to getting up early. That was all right too: I was learning about the submission of the will being more important than anything else. To replace fasting and early rising I obtained permission to have a cold bath every morning before Matins. It nearly killed me each time. I would have preferred, in imitation of St Benedict, to cast myself without any clothes on into a bed of thistles—provided the thistles were heated—than into a cold bath. The mortification proved so suitable that I kept it up after Lent was over. I did not drop it until a year or so later when, during a drought, we were forbidden to have baths at all. When the drought was over I could not face another cold bath, and I have never had one since. Whenever I have tried to counter the tendency to softness, I have found support in the thought of my father's approval. Fasting he judged to be, like so much else, a mug's game, but anything which made one hardy would have gained his support. I did not write home about the cold bath. Or, if I did, I made no mention of having dropped it.

In the novitiate it was not easy to find penances for which permission would be given. When I did finally hit upon a penance which I thought would be apt, I discovered it was one for which no permission was necessary. Accordingly I gave up drawing and writing, which was a bad thing to do. Creative outlet at this stage might have helped. Without time or opportunity for carving, and being utterly unmusical (I have yet to meet a sculptor who is not), I was becoming a vegetable. Even if secular literature had been encouraged in the novitiate I would not have chosen at that time to read anything much lighter than the lives of the saints. Correspondence was reduced to the minimum, as indeed I wished it to be, and when visiting old Downside boys or others asked to see me I begged the novicemaster to withhold his permission. The exception here, and without misgivings, was Father Bede.

I learned after Christmas that Father Bede was to give the Holy Week retreat to the school, so from January onwards I looked forward to his visit. Dom Richard assured me that permission would be given to see as much of him as I liked, so I was confident that Father Bede would smooth away all my difficulties. When Holy Week came, bringing Father Bede early on the Wednesday so that we could meet at leisure before he got himself caught up in the business of the retreat, I found myself unable to explain what was going on inside me. I was dumb. It was not the cold baths, it was me. I could see that he was as disappointed as I was. For the first time in our relationship we were unable to find common ground. For my part I felt I had lost his friendship, that we were a hundred miles apart, that my last prop had been kicked from under me. He was leaving on Easter Sunday, so after the pontifical high Mass I came in to say good-bye. He interrupted his packing and looked at me squarely. I guessed he had made up his mind beforehand to speak, to have a last shot.

'You are not really settled yet, are you?' I did not have to reply. 'Well, don't go back until you are really sure you are not meant for it.'

'But I don't want to go *back*. If I go anywhere it will be to the Carthusians.'

'So that's still on. It certainly makes it more complicated. Perhaps I was wrong. Perhaps you should have tried them first. But I still feel it won't work. I'll pray for you.'

I could not tell whether he was relieved or not to know that I had no intention of going back to the world; it was clear that he did not like hearing how the original desire had persisted. Although this last exchange was the nearest we got to the old relationship, I have seldom felt so acutely alone as when he had gone. I learned later that when some of my friends asked him how I was getting on, he said, 'I don't know—except that all the lights have gone out'. Some of the lights might have come on again had I known that this was not the end of our friendship. I still had a long way to go in the spiritual life, and much of the journey was taken with him.

That evening, after Father Bede had gone, there was the usual Easter dinner. The year before I had come from Liverpool for

Holy Week, so had attended it as a layman. Today I was sitting at the novices' table, which is always placed a little apart, and was not greatly enjoying the meal. It was a relief when the novicemaster led us out immediately after the dinner—the idea being to avoid explanations about novitiate *purdah*—and I went to bed hungry. Next morning, Easter Monday, I asked the novicemaster if I might write to the Prior of Parkminster applying to join the Carthusians. Dom Richard was most understanding and kind, but urged strongly against interrupting the year's noviceship to go off on a scatterbrained search which could lead only to disappointment. He pointed out that there were five months still to go before I would be due for the first lot of vows, and that there was nothing to get excited about. In the meantime he would speak to the Abbot about my unsettled state of mind. So the letter to the Prior of Parkminster was not written for another eight years.

Dom Leander Ramsay, whose Sunday talks had so much helped me in the Junior School days, was now Abbot of Downside. Between Easter and the autumn chapter which was to vote upon my suitability as a candidate for profession in the Downside community, the Abbot saw me several times. I made a frank and full manifestation of conscience to him, explaining that if I could be sure of living under novitiate conditions for the rest of my life I would have no hesitations. So long as I was sheltered by the rules which kept the world at bay I could feel secure in my vocation. It was because I could not foresee what would happen to my monastic life when I left the novitiate that I hesitated. 'Nobody can foresee that,' said Abbot Ramsay; 'which is precisely why temporary vows were introduced.' In these interviews he neither advised nor attempted to dissuade. That, he said, was the novicemaster's job. On each occasion I came away stimulated—if only by the distinctive character of his utterances. 'Why the Carthusians specifically,' he asked me once, 'instead of the Little Brothers of Saint Sebastian?' I replied that I did not much mind what the order was so long as it promised an exact observance of the Rule, and that the question boiled itself down to a toss-up between the Carthusians and the Cistercians. Which did he suggest. 'Neither,' he said, and his mouth shut with the finality of a safe deposit.

Rather to my surprise the community passed me at the end of

the year for temporary profession. I had supposed that, learning of my state of mind from the novicemaster's report, they would throw me out. I did not invite any of my relatives or friends to the ceremony, not at all because I thought it quite on the cards that I would bolt at the last moment—I knew I would not—but because I felt that final profession in three years' time would be a more appropriate occasion for celebration. Abbot Ramsay received our vows, and since I had been smashing things throughout the novitiate year it was no surprise to anyone that in signing the document I broke the pen.

Among the letters of congratulation was one which consisted of the single sentence 'What time do you want to be fetched?' On the envelope was written 'Please forward if already left.' The letter came from one of those who had seen me off at Paddington a year before, and enclosed was a cutting from a London evening paper showing a photograph of me in a morning suit and grey top hat, allegedly at Ascot. Under the reproduction was a short gossip paragraph which flamboyantly announced my flight from the world of fashion and frivolity, and how I was now hidden behind a monastery's high walls, living upon a spare diet and devoting myself to menial tasks. This cutting stirred no desire whatever to resume the life of what the gossip writer would have described as that of the eligible young bachelor. For one thing I had never been to Ascot. Yet, unmistakably, there was I in my morning suit (now sold) and my father's grey top hat (now returned), and, as I concluded, the stands of Ascot in the background. Closer examination showed that a photograph of me, taken one Sunday morning in the Park as I now remembered, was superimposed upon a print of the racecourse at Ascot. Such was the veneration which the word 'Ascot' commanded; such too was the industry with which press photographers in the twenties went about their work. The sender of this token was the same who, a few years later and in order to calm my anxieties about his spiritual state, sent me a cable from Canada which read: 'Keep hair on stop am still in state of grace.'

The next three years, except towards the end when the old issues came up afresh with their demand for decision before final vows, were uneventful years. Though not bound to it when the novitiate year was over, I was careful to keep up daily manual labour: it was suitable work for a monk and games no longer appealed. Though also not bound to it, I held to my mistaken resolution about not drawing, writing, or carving: just how mistaken it was I learned from Father Bede when he came to give the community retreat in 1928. His stay in the monastery was longer this time, and we gradually got back to the old level. I did not tell him everything, because I felt he had a prejudice against solitude and the stricter orders, but I told him enough to show that the hankering was not dead. It surprised him to learn that I could take no great interest in the course of philosophy which I was required to take. He put it down to a defect in the teaching, but it was not that: the defect was in me, for I do not possess that kind of head. I told myself that when it came to replacing philosophy with theology I would be on more congenial ground. I told Father Bede this too, but he was of the opinion that if philosophy bored me, theology would bore me just as much. By the end of this 1928 retreat I knew that there were now three subjects which it would be better not to bring up with him any more: ecclesiastical studies, the death wish, primitive observance. It was a sad conclusion to arrive at, because at one time I had been able to discuss everything with him and no holds barred, but at least the shadows of the Easter visit had passed.

Having to take exams in a study which I knew to be necessary but towards which I felt no inclination was not much fun, but having to take games in the school was a lot less. Philosophy I could accept as the most appropriate of current penances, and slog at it accordingly, but rugger and cricket were another thing altogether. It was not the waste of time which I minded so much, because this was covered by obedience; nor the actual games themselves, because at the very inferior level at which I took them the players were mildly amusing; what I minded was having to face, sooner than I thought I would have to, the practical aspect of integrating school and monastery. As a gesture towards further adaptation I cut out from my reading anything which had to do with the Carthusians, the Cistercians, and all other splinter movements among the Benedictine following. I thought that by starving my mind of this kind of nourishment I might be in a better condition to make a detached judgment when the time came. Looking back, I do not think it made the slightest difference. St Bernard's works, being more patristic and spiritual than inflammatory as regards my particular problem, I continued to read. (For ten minutes a day I read St Bernard over a period of many years, and it is matter of regret to me now that I do not seem to be able to read him any more. When I try him today he gives the impression of having read too much Abbot Marmion.)

When theology followed philosophy I was no better off. Though the professors could not have been better, the lectures interested me not at all, and the essays which I was expected to submit once a week must have made weary reading. But the course of studies by now were more varied than it had been during the first two years, so I was able to devote my energy to scripture and church history which were to become life interests. Also, following the retreat from Father Bede, I was once again drawing, painting, writing verse.

In the summer before final profession I was appointed assistant guestmaster. This is a job not normally given to juniors in temporary vows, so I imagine the appointment was designed to test my vocation. Whether so designed or not, it did. That summer there seemed to be a constant stream of young men who had recently been sent down from Oxford or Cambridge for riotous living. They made interesting guests. I felt not only that I was too young, both in years and in the habit, to deal with their problems but also that they were just the kind of people to aggravate my own. More than ever I felt the need to sit in an enclave of silence where there would be nobody to beguile me with accounts of bump suppers and meetings of the Bullingdon.

A guest who came under my care at this time, and who repeated his visit later on, was Gilbert Harding. He was then writing a novel, extracts of which he would read aloud to his fellow guests and to me between supper and Compline. Compline on these evenings would be much distracted. To us who listened to Gilbert's gravel voice getting more than ordinary value out of his script, it seemed patently obvious that no publisher would risk the libel actions which publication would entail, but to the author himself it appeared unthinkable that those from whom the characters had been so unmistakably drawn could mind. Each evening we would be treated to a new display of fireworks, but, sure enough, the publishers turned out to be shy of the venture.

A guest of a different kind with whom I formed, while acting guestmaster, a friendship which was to last for thirty years and eleven months was Ronald Knox. It may be recalled that a drawing of mine had been given to him during my last term at school, and now, in 1927 and in a religious setting, we were meeting for the first time. For two weeks or more—Ronald, like Gilbert, was working on a book—we swam together and sat out in the sun talking for hours about literature, spirituality, people. When I had finished my exams I was left free to enjoy that hot summer, and since the guests were my province I felt no guilt in spending as much time with Ronald as he asked for.

His was a quite different charm from Father Bede's, but it drew me hardly less strongly. He knew Father Bede well, admiring him as much as I did. Father Bede, the preacher, knew how to use his charm. Father Knox, the scholar, knew how to hide it. For me Ronald's attraction lay in his reluctance to attract. While always friendly to people, he never went out of his way to make friends. His friendships made themselves or they were not made at all—were not worth making. It was this detachment, this take-it-or-leave-it of his, which made him seem always a little withdrawn. People mistook the quality for indifference, weariness with the affairs of others, boredom, preoccupation with himself, even for superiority. His manner, certainly, was casual. The manner could be misleading. Whatever remoteness there was, and towards the end of his life it showed more than at the time of which I write, it had little to do with the factors just mentioned. It sprang from a mixture of diffidence, self-depreciation, and a fear of imposing himself on people. If anyone had a right to feel superior it would have been Ronald. He saw the danger of superiority and avoided it. It made him all the quicker to see through the superiority of others. Reserve and delicacy of perception came to the rescue, serving as a natural defence in the use of his unquestionably superior gifts.

At first I myself found it hard to believe that some of the mannerisms—the languid droop, the halting voice with its drawn-out emphases, the dragging walk—were not put on. But as I came to know him better I could see that the whole Ronald performance was unconscious. For him to have acted a part, even if the part reflected himself, would have been quite out of character. If there is one thing above all that his friends will remember it is that he was never out of character. Until the day he died he was wholly, typically, uniquely Ronald. 'Nobody but Ronald would have said that', is a phrase I have heard often from two friends of his, Mrs Raymond Asquith and Lady Helen Asquith, who saw more of him towards the end of his life than the rest of us did. 'Who except Ronald would have ever dreamed of it?' The reference is usually to an act of thoughtfulness.

Thoughtfulness, reticence, the habit of acting consistently: these things come more or less naturally to men of sensibility. In Ronald such natural qualities were, one felt, given supernatural direction. Self-effacement which was as true as his must be born of humility. This is not to say that thirty years before his death Ronald showed the marks of a holiness which became evident later on. It is to say that there must all along have been something rare and special in him or the ideal of holiness would not have elicited the response it did. Father Bede was holy; one knew that. Only to watch Father Bede saying Mass was enough to clear up any doubt on that score. Abbot Ramsay was holy: again the signs were there. Ronald's particular brand of holiness was something which developed slowly, and which, even when developed, had to be looked for. In parenthesis it might be added that although Ronald thought he said his Mass badly, finding fault with himself for gliding over the rubrics and making mistakes in the prayers to be said, the way he did it was strangely moving. 'I love watching Ronnie *slithering* through Mass,' a little girl once told me. I remember how deeply I had been impressed by the sight of Abbot Ramsay praying in the Lady Chapel, bolt upright on his knees and statue still. I was hardly less impressed by the sight of Ronald lolling back in a chair in the nave with a copy of Caussade open on his lap and one arm over the back of the chair next to him. A fellow junior of mine said he thought Ronald was affected. Had Ronald assumed Abbot Ramsay's position when praying, or Father Bede's recollected drone while saying Mass, he would have shown affectation. The exact opposite was the truth: it was because he was *un*studied and not because he was studied that apparent affectations appeared. Like the clothes he wore, there was nothing about Ronald that was cut to shape.

When my mother met Ronald for the first time she told me afterwards: 'I can see what you like about him. He's different—especially from you.' She did not mean that she thought him an eccentric but that she found him rare in a way which she knew would particularly appeal to me: she knew that the contrast between the two of us was a factor in my admiration. There was no question of matching: in background and upbringing, in intellect and taste, in fields of religious interest, Ronald and I were poles apart. The balance was so uneven that I had no need to bluff or try to compete. With others my efforts not to lose face could be cramping, but freed from the strain in relation to Ronald I found myself becoming more natural and at ease with him than with almost anyone else. At this particular time in my life, when I was cut off from the friends of my own age whom I had known in the world, and when I seemed to be losing touch with those older than myself in religion, Ronald, who was ageless, made all the difference.

After thinking about it for some time, I decided not to tell him —yet anyway—about my vocational problems. While I had confidence in his judgment, I did not want to put him in a position where he would have to use it. Already I could see, and as I came to know him better I saw it more clearly, that personal confidences bothered him, and that the confidences which bothered him most were those which called for decisions. Nor did I think it was fair to extract an opinion from one who had no inside knowledge of the religious life. Also there were too many people as it was to advise me. So it was only after I had made my perpetual vows that I told him of the direction in which I appeared to be moving. Later still I spoke to him of my hopes and plans, but I was careful never to suggest that I wanted him to make my decisions for me. On those occasions in my life when I have chosen the easier way of putting on to others the responsibility of a decision I have regretted it afterwards. From my mistakes I have learned to form my own mind: it is no good letting other people form it for me.

If, as has been advanced above, the boy is at his worst between the ages of fourteen and sixteen, then perhaps the monk is at his worst between the ages of twenty-one and twenty-five. I was now twenty-two. Without making embarrassing disclosures I can give as the main source of trouble a false conception of the common life. With what I took to be religious zeal I wanted all the monastery to move as one man, to receive equal treatment, to aim at the same height. To some the idea of uniformity is repugnant, to others it promises manifold solutions. It certainly attracted me. I mistook regimentation for good order. By a paradox which greater experience would have warned me to expect, I discovered that in requiring everyone to be in step I was the one to be out of step myself. It is a pity that I had not read what Aristotle had written about true equality consisting in 'the treatment of unequal things unequally'.

It would seem that there is really no substitute for the blessing of making thumping mistakes. Hearing sermons, reading books, receiving advice in correspondence and in the confessional: the significant message can be misread or simply not heard. There is less chance of misreading the significant lesson of mistakes. My mistakes were yet to teach me how to steer a course between what I aspired to and what would have been wrong for me to bow to. I am not at all sure that I have got it right yet. But I know that in the meantime, precisely by being the one out of step, I have often found things harder than I need have done. In these early years especially, I saw what appeared to be an inescapable inconsistency about my life, about my choices, about my evaluations, and if this distressed me, meeting it all the time at close range, it must have puzzled (to say the least) my brethren who came across it now and then at a distance. I think that at this period I was happiest, in spite of the singularity of it, when I was at manual labour in the cabbage and potato fields, away from guests, studies, and the tensions caused by contacts with the school. Since I did my digging on my own, I was able to benefit by the combined effect of silence, isolation, impact with the soil. During those hours anyway, I was very nearly at peace.

It is the custom in the English Benedictine Congregation that before taking final vows the candidates for profession spend ten days at home with their families. In order to be present for this holiday my mother came over from Egypt, where my parents were still living, and it was arranged that we should spend the first five days at Nutcome with Rita, and the last five days at Durrants Hotel in London. My doubts about the wisdom of taking vows were accentuated by the recent introduction of some minor relaxations in the monastery, and I arrived at my aunt's house fever-hot with worry. I prayed for a miracle which would show me what to do. Round every corner I expected to see The Sign Which Would Show All. On the second evening of my visit a man came to dinner who had been to Downside as a boy, and who had not a good word to say about the place. He was an elderly man, and in any case it would have been uncivil on my part to start a fight in the middle of dinner with a fellow guest, but his criticisms so roused my Downside loyalties as to make it clear to me before the meal was over that I would be doing right in a few weeks' time to pledge myself for good to the community which I had just heard attacked. Was not this the Sign Which Sealed? Next day I went over to Farnborough Abbey where one of the monks was a friend of mine, and where I was able to attend the office in choir. There was no school at Farnborough, and the monks did not leave the enclosure. If it represented a sign in the contrary sense, I tried not to let this visit influence me.

And so it went on throughout the whole ten days of the holiday. I told my mother nothing, but she could see. One day during the time when we were in London—we had left Rita's without having mentioned the subject of vows—I was praying at St James's, Spanish Place, when my mother came in to look for me and take me off to lunch. 'I didn't recognise you,' she whispered, 'you look so *old*.' Ten years earlier this would have been a great consolation. As I got up from my knees I pointed to the text which was worked into the metal of the communion rail in front of us. It was a line from the Benediction hymn, and read *Bella premunt hostilia*. 'Translate,' my mother said. I did, and we went out.

It was a relief to get back to Downside after the psychological ping-pong of the holiday. I could see now that to expect a sign which would point the way was sheer superstition. The issue had to be decided by myself and not by magic, but at the same time I felt I was not yet ready to decide it. Dom Richard had been master of novices while I had been in the novitiate so it was to him that I turned for consultation. I suggested that my profession be delayed for a few months and that in the meantime a trial be made either at Parkminster with the Carthusians or in Leicestershire with the Cistercians. I felt I could not go ahead with the millstone of the stricter life hanging round my neck and blocking out the view of the playing fields and classrooms. Dom Richard said he was against delayed professions. Then might I go to Oxford for the day and talk to Father Bede? Dom Richard said, again quite rightly, that this was a domestic matter and that we ought to settle it ourselves. He would like me instead to state the case to a senior monk working in the school who had known me since I was nine. This monk, Dom Richard said, would confirm his own opinion as to the authenticity of my Downside vocation. Though I did not welcome the idea of opening up all over again, I did as I was told. 'I am so glad you have come,' said this senior monk, 'because I have voted against you at every stage, and I think you should go. It was not my business to tell you, but since you have asked me I think you should apply to Parkminster or Mount St Bernard and get on with it.' Dom Richard, suitably flabbergasted, held to his opinion.

Before anyone else had time to take a hand in it, I did what I should have done all along: I took all responsibility upon myself and applied for profession. The chapter accepted my petition and that was that. Abbot Ramsay received my vows, and James Reynolds came for the ceremony. Since my mother felt unable to face the ordeal the rest of the family stayed away too. There exists a pious belief that whatever is prayed for by the newly professed monk lying prostrate on the pall during the litanies is invariably granted. I prayed—selfishly of course, but I think without self-pity—to die. When the ceremony was over I was greeted by the community with a warmth which made everything worth while.

I was at peace. It might turn out later to have been a mistake, but this was not something for me to worry about now. I had done what I believed to be the best thing, what I believed to be the will of God. I could leave it at that. If this was what profession was like, what must it be like to get married?

On the first Sunday of Advent in that year, 1928, I was given the subdiaconate, so there was now the priesthood to look forward to. As well as taking junior games I was taking junior forms for religious instruction, and the idea of ordination acted as a counterweight. That I should still think of needing counterweights to school work might be unfortunate, but there it was. Ecclesiastical studies, with their three examinations a year, took up most of the time not devoted to preparing classes, so it was a closed period as regards creative work. I preferred to keep to manual labour rather than give the hour in the afternoon to art. There were no upsets, no distracting visits. It looked as though life might go on like this for ever, and if it had I would have been perfectly satisfied to let it.

In the autumn of the year following I was given the diaconate, the ceremony taking place at Belmont Abbey where Bishop Butt was ordaining several of the community. James Reynolds drove me from Downside in an enormous Hispano, and at a speed which enabled us to explore Gloucester Cathedral and Woodchester Priory on the way. He did not stay the night, so, as always after our now infrequent meetings, I was in desolate mood next morning. I need not have worried about being left without friends in a strange place, because while I was vesting in the sacristy before the long pontifical service, who should come up to me but Gilbert Harding. I did not know that he was teaching at Belmont, nor had he known that I was coming for the ordination. Having caught a glimpse of my head emerging from the crisp neck of the alb, he had left his herd of small boys to press past the hot and heaven-bent surge of *ordinandi*, and so reach my side. Without a smile or salutation of any sort he said: 'Be a chum to a chap, Hubert, and lend me five pounds.' I was too pleased and surprised to say anything. 'Perhaps you are right,' he went on, 'hardly the time and place. Meet me in the porch after this, and bear in mind that five shillings will do.'

We spent the afternoon walking hilariously round the grounds in the thin autumn sunshine. After this occasion we met again only two or three times. But each time hilariously. Once we met on a channel boat when I was on a pilgrimage to Lourdes and he on his way to look for a French cook in Calais. His death a few years ago meant a twofold loss, the greater being the loss of a friendship which did not have a chance to develop.

By 1929 I was teaching full time in the school, and since one of the subjects was art I was back again in creative work. The talents had rusted and the results were poor, but returning to the only work I was ever likely to be good at—my studies having proved that I would never make a philosopher or theologian—was agreeable. Since I had not been told to teach carving, which in any case I would not have known how to teach, I taught only drawing and painting. And very elementary drawing and painting at that. Later I was entrusted with a class which met twice a week and to which I was expected to give lectures on aesthetics. Though the boys who made up this class were not hungering for culture—they were mostly the athletic kind whose timetable showed a blank which needed to be filled—the effort to teach them something about the principles and history of art called for a lot of work which I have never regretted. I lectured, if this is not too grand a term, mostly on sculpture. Now that I was teaching regularly, and still acting as assistant guestmaster, I found that the forebodings which had beset me for years were not without foundation.

Manual labour was still my chief solace, taken in solitude and regardless of weather. Abbot Ramsay had died, and Dom John Chapman had been elected as his successor. Abbot Chapman considered manual labour to be a great waste of time for monks. He said that if he had done manual labour as a young monk he would never have had time to write books. He thought my ideas about manual labour, indeed my ideas about most things, were nonsense. So he decided that as soon as I was ordained priest I must go abroad for two or three years and do another course of theology. It would broaden my outlook and perhaps awaken intellectual interests which now were dormant. He chose Munich, with its university and a conveniently placed Benedictine college where I could be housed, as the scene for this experiment. Though the prospect of further studies did not excite me, I welcomed the proposal on two counts: first it would get me off teaching and taking games, second it would allow me to see what the monasteries in Germany were like. These were not the best motives, but they were the best I could manage. In any case I had not asked for the proposed arrangement, so the motive of submission could be taken to supersede less worthy motives. Abbot Chapman handled all the negotiations himself (he was an expert at this, and loved doing it) so it was settled with the university authorities and with the Benedictine superior of the Ottilienkolleg in Munich that I would arrive at the end of October in time for the start of the new term. How was I off for German, Abbot Chapman asked. I told him I had spoken it as a child but that I doubted if it would stand up now to the lectures, essays, and textbooks of university German. 'Then I will arrange for you to go to Maria Laach and Beuron earlier in October so that you will have time to pick up what you have forgotten. Fetch me those envelopes over there, and I will write now before I forget.'

Abbot Chapman was so pleased with the success of his negotiations that he decided to include Dom Adrian Morey, a junior like myself but a year senior in the habit, in the Munich scheme. Nothing could have suited both of us better, and Dom Adrian and I spent some entertaining hours over maps, guidebooks, railway timetables, and German dictionaries. He had little more German at that stage than I, but having been to Cambridge, where he had covered himself with glory, he possessed all the advantages. It was fortunate that we got on well or the close association of two fellow countrymen in a German community was likely to make for complications. But this was looking ahead. There was still, for me though not for Dom Adrian until the following year, the question of ordination.

Together with four of my brethren, two of whom are still alive, I was ordained priest on July 13, 1930. This time the ceremony took place at Downside, but for some reason I can remember neither the ceremony itself nor my own state of mind during it. Much clearer to me is the first Mass next day, the feast of St Bonaventure. Father John Talbot, as assistant priest more nervous than I as celebrant, asked that we should be surrounded at the altar by servers so that our mistakes would be less visible to those assembled behind us in the Lady Chapel. Thus, to my great distraction, we were attended by Maurice Turnbull, George Bellord, Lord Clonmore, and Jack Carroll. For a low Mass this probably constitutes a record. Among the congregation were, besides some more contemporaries of my own, and a number of the community, Yolande, Berthe, my mother and brother. Berthe and my mother cried throughout. James, to my sorrow, was not there. He was getting himself engaged to be married.

On October 1, 1930, began one of the most confused journeys I have ever had the pleasure to make. Since the mode of travel was left to me, and since as may be remembered I was drawn to the practice of religious poverty, I made it my aim to spend as little as possible in getting from London, via Bruges and the monastery of St André, to the Abbey of Maria Laach, near Koblenz, where I was expected on October 4. In order to avoid having meals on trains or in restaurants I took food with me from Downside (a paper bag for each day and carried in a rucksack) and counted on a generous distribution of public drinking fountains. Such few belongings as I felt I would need until my return to Downside fitted easily into two expanding suitcases. Scorning the clerical suit as unworthy of the monk on a journey, I travelled in a habit and flat hat. This costume is all right in a Catholic country but it is no fun at all before you get there. This was the last time I ever travelled in England wearing a habit. I took care to see that none of my brethren witnessed the wayfarer's departure from the monastery looking like a slice of medieval folklore. Dom Adrian, I should add, was travelling by a different route and on a different day: we planned to meet in Munich in a month's time.

Getting as far as Bruges was no trouble. The trouble began when I turned down the bus from Bruges and decided to cover the distance to the Abbey of St André on foot. Taking what I was assured to be a short cut I lost the way in a wood, and the walk took me nearly three hours instead of one. Several things happened before the monastery was reached: I had a nose-bleed, I was bitten in the leg and had my habit torn by a dog, and one of the two suitcases which I was carrying exceeded its mandate by expanding before the time. I had to pick up the clothes and washing things from the path and add them to the paper bags in the rucksack, walking the rest of the way with an empty suitcase in one hand and a heavy one in the other. With unusual foresight I had brought a torch with me or I might have spent the night wandering in the wood. By its light I recited Vespers—for the feast of the Guardian Angels appropriately enough—and finally arrived while the monks were at supper. The brother who opened the door, seeing the blood on my face and the torn habit, ran for the infirmarian and guestmaster. He thought I had been shot at in a hunt. The infirmarian brought me a wet sponge and some safety-pins; the guestmaster brought me cold ham, salad, home-made bread, cheese, and a jug of beer. I had something to learn from this if I were ever to return to the job of guestmaster at Downside.

But there was something more immediate to be learned from Dom Thomas of Canterbury, the guestmaster. It turned out that before becoming a monk he had been a diocesan priest, and that as a refugee from Belgium during the war had sheltered for some ten days at 45 Lower Belgrave Street as Berthe's guest. It was out of his great love of England that he had taken the name in religion of Thomas of Canterbury. I remembered him perfectly as Père Thibaut in a frock-coat and black cotton gloves. The frock-coat and gloves had gone, and there was a white beard instead. Addressing me as 'my little Claud'—introducing me later to the Abbot by this, my baptismal, name—he was full of questions.

'Your dear aunt Berthe still lives? Ah, I am glad. And her works of piety? Yes, yes, I am sure. And habiting, I hope, that so elegant house *bien chauffée* in Belgravia? I remember it well.'

Elegant and *bien chauffée*. It was not as I remembered it. No, I told him, Berthe had at last got rid of it to a Lord ffrench who was altering it out of all recognition.

'Indeed? The great Lord French . . . Ypres, Loos, Neuve Chapelle. How proud she must be.' It would take too long to explain.

On this the first of several visits to St André I made friends with one of the monks who was an artist, Dom Bruno Groenthal. He gave me one of his compositions, a drawing of St Lidwina in ecstacy, which I have in front of me as I write. The guestmaster sent me in a car to Bruges to catch my train: the drive took about twenty minutes against my three hours. Visiting Bruges years later I did not recognise the station from which I had set out on two arduous journeys in 1930. Then I saw the reason for this apparent lapse of memory: the old station, my station, was gently falling to bits among the weeds two or three hundred yards away, and I was standing in something completely new.

Since I was travelling cheap, third class in fact, the route was not direct nor the pace swift. The carriages were not divided into compartments so much as into pens. The wooden backs of the seats were exactly vertical, stretching to a height in line with the top of one's head. Above this line was space shared by all until it reached the metal roof and was interrupted only by iron racks for the luggage. My fellow travellers were extremely friendly, offering me food and drink from wicker baskets. Had I known how hospitable these Belgian peasants would be I would not have brought my paper bags. Everyone hailed everyone else, and the stops, which were many, were occasions of effusive welcome and farewell. When I climbed out at Brussels, stiff and sore, I feared I might be clasped by strong arms and kissed on both cheeks. It was the first time I had travelled in this sort of train, and was pleased to find that I had survived the first lap of the Munich odyssey. I can laugh now at my foolishness, but I sometimes wish I had preserved a little of it.

The only thing I regret about those days and nights of hard benches and hardening sandwiches is that during the long wait at Brussels I did not go to see my uncle and aunt, Maurice and Stephanie, who lived there. This was because of some idea that to do so would be a departure from the régime I had set myself. I remember standing outside the station, the suitcases at my side, wondering wistfully what the chances were that Maurice would come to this part of the city and buy a paper from the stand at the corner of the street. Probably about ten million to one against. A few years later I had occasion to visit Maurice (my aunt was dead by then) at his large, over-furnished and over-staffed house in the Avenue Louise. Never has a man enjoyed his comforts and position less. Early in his career he had married an heiress, Baroness Stephanie van Zeulen whose mother was a Rothschild, and throughout their long married life they were entirely devoted to one another. Had there been children they might have made more of their material, intellectual, and even spiritual advantages. As it was, there appeared on the surface to be a great waste. Leaning against the stone wall of Brussels Station I remembered how Maurice had told me stories in the evenings at Lancaster

Gate, and played rough games with me which got him into trouble with my grandmother. I remembered Stephanie's French accent, her slight moustache, her cameo brooch surrounded with seed pearls, and the unattractive way she did her hair which made it look like a motor tyre. Without any doubt at all, and régimes notwithstanding, I should have let them know at Avenue Louise that I was passing through.

On the German side the trains, even the kind which I was taking, were less primitive. But they were not Golden Arrow quality either. Mr Cyril Connolly has said of the Settebello, which does the three-hundred-and-ninety-mile run between Rome and Milan in just over six hours, that it 'is one of the most beautiful trains in the world, with unhurrying anapaests'. He would have described the choppier passages of the stopping train between Aachen and Andernach in different terms. Not risking the last stretch on foot this time, I took a bus from the station to the monastery. The route took us past a field, already in early October sugar-coated with frost, where a college gymnastic display was in progress. The bus stopped so that we could watch the two teams, stripped to the waist, as they sprang about in the cold air. When an interval was reached we all clapped and the bus moved on.

At Maria Laach a Father Otmar was carving a set of four figures, bigger than lifesize, so I was quite happy. Also working at the arts and crafts were some young monks who had come to Maria Laach from other monasteries to learn, and this made me less conspicuous as a stranger. During the ten days of my visit, besides what I picked up in the way of technical help, I learned some German and some valuable knowledge of continental monasticism. Abbot Chapman had been right: it was not time wasted.

Maria Laach gets its name from the lake on the edge of which the monastery is built. There could hardly be a more beautiful setting for a monastery. Once a month, when the weather allows, the community go out on the lake in rowing boats which hold from eight to a dozen passengers. The outing takes place immediately after Vespers, and lasts for about two hours. The brethren bring stringed instruments with them, and there is a lot of singing: ballads, hymns, *Lieder*. As it gets darker (and colder) the scene becomes increasingly Wagnerian. A feature of this monthly *Ausflug* is a special sort of doughnut for which tradition has exactly stipulated. It is the size of a grapefruit or baby melon, and comes aboard two deep in rows on wooden platters with a raised edge. The monks are hardened to dealing with doughnuts, but to a neophyte like myself, never a doughnut man anyway, there were obstacles. After nibbling primly at my heavy sticky lump I found an opportunity of lowering it overboard. I assumed it would sink like a cannon ball. Instead it bobbed up and down on the now moonlit surface of the water. As I was then taking my turn at rowing while the others sang, I was able to remove an oar from the rollocks and with this—after striking it to no purpose—pushed the doughnut into some reeds. But not before my activities were noticed. The boatload consisted of juniors like myself or perhaps I might have given offence. That German sensibilities were not hurt I found on the day I left when in the parcel handed to me for the journey was included, weighing about a ton, a doughnut.

From Maria Laach I went on to Beuron, another great Benedictine monastery. Though the journey was lively with adventure and absurdity, I must avoid the trap which lies in wait for the writer whenever he leaves his place of residence and takes to road or rail. I liked everything so much at Beuron that I prolonged my stay, reaching Munich only just in time to join Dom Adrian in registering at the university. The combined effect of a Bavarian winter, working all day to keep up with the studies, not enough fresh air, brought a return of a lung trouble which had started with pneumonia in 1915. After X-rays the doctor sent me back to England, instructing me to rest for three months and telling me that I would never again be able to get up for Matins in the mornings. On December 22, with more photographs of German sculpture than clothes in the two suitcases, I arrived at Downside. Within a fortnight of Christmas I was allowed to get up as usual at four, which, except for times in hospital and for a short while during my period as housemaster, I have been doing ever since. Dom Adrian stopped on in Munich and eventually received a doctorate. Later he was appointed Head Master of the Oratory School, an office which he holds today.

So as to allow for longer hours out of doors, I was not required to resume the classes to junior boys or to go on with the guest-mastering. My obligations in the school were confined to the talks on art twice a week, and outside the school the only job I had to worry about was serving a newly opened Mass centre at Temple Cloud, about eight miles from the monastery. At the art sessions I spoke mostly about Barlach and Mestrovic; Barlach's work I had come across in Germany, and this had put me on to Mestrovic whom I grew to admire even more. The Sunday duties at Temple Cloud involved confessions, Mass, sermon, and instruction to the children. These apostolic works were not laborious. They took place at Humphreston House which belonged to the Vaughan family, and, excepting when I bicycled over to visit the flock, motor transport was provided. To my surprise I found that preaching troubled me far less than taking classes. In fact not at all.

Under orders to get out in the open, and with my studies now behind me, I was able to spend more time than before in manual labour. Morning and afternoon I dug the soil. Abbot Chapman, still thinking that work in the fields was a waste of time, proposed that I should work out of doors at carving stone. Nothing could have suited me better. Since building operations were going on at that time there was plenty of material lying about in the stoneyard, and when the weather was bad I moved into the stoneshed and worked with the masons. I was thus able to get on with what I had wanted to do for years, and when the masons finally left I had the use of the stoneshed to myself. For this permission I can never be grateful enough to Abbot Chapman.

Resembling my father in this respect, Abbot Chapman was always in favour of securing professional training for those under his care. So when he judged that I had absorbed enough fresh air to keep me going, he arranged to have me enrolled at a technical college in Bath, where, in September 1932, I began attending classes which taught design, composition, flower painting, architectural and commercial drawing, and the handicrafts. It was hoped that with a diploma of some sort at the end of a year's course I might teach these subjects at Downside. It meant a train journey to Bath and back, missing the conventual Mass and Vespers each day, and an end to digging in the fields. It did not seem to me a very monastic arrangement, but once again there was the safeguard of obedience: I refused to speculate as to whether or not I was in the right box, and in any case it was only a temporary measure. A school drawing book under my arm, a packet of crayons in my pocket, a bunch of tired michaelmas daisies in my hand, I used to reach the monastery with only just enough time to have supper and do my homework before bed.

Though I think I was conscientious enough in submitting diagrams which illustrated the principles of perspective, drawings of cones and egg-cups which showed the way light and shade worked, tinted sketches which revealed the structure of beech-leaves and rose-petals, I cannot say that this side of the course excited me. The man who taught handicrafts was kind enough to let me skip the primary stages and pass straight on to direct carving. So I never had to master the mysteries of making book-markers of stamped and poker-worked leather, whitewood napkin rings with a mickey mouse design, clay ashtrays and pots whether glazed or left matt. The teacher of handicrafts was for some reason reluctant at first to let me work at stone, which was the only medium with which I was familiar, so I had to satisfy him by carving lumps of soap. Having satisfied him on soap I brought in a large cheese, and further satisfied him with a replica of a Romanesque capital. His objections broke down and thereafter I carved, for the short time that remained to me under his tuition, stone. Even the subjects to be carved were left to my choice so I abandoned the book of architectural decoration and produced shapes of my own. My taste must have been more in the direction of the abstract than it is now, for my instructor was clearly puzzled. In a half-term report on my work, submitted first to the principal of the college and then to Abbot Chapman, he recommended a closer study of stone-carving than would be possible for me to make at the school, and suggested the names of some places which might be tried. Unofficially he urged me to go back to Downside and bash away as hard as I could in any way I liked. This was wise counsel, and Abbot Chapman agreed to my dropping the course at the end of the term. I was sorry to say goodbye to my professor, but less sorry to say goodbye to my fellow students who were mostly boys and girls from neighbouring secondary schools. I seemed to have been the only one not taking 'commercial', and, now that I was leaving, it would be possible for the giggling flirtations to be resumed, for more of the rather indelicate jokes, for them to forget about the special voice they had used in front of me. 'The old feller is hopping it,' I heard one boy whisper to another while we were busy over our floral design. I realised I was getting on.

I was glad to be back at the stoneshed and working on my own. I had reached the age of twenty-seven, and looked forward to spending the rest of my life using my hands and keeping out of people's way. But the interlude was all too short. Although there was fortunately no talk of sending me anywhere for further artistic training, might it not be as well to put me on a parish for a few months? Perhaps I would find myself in apostolic work away from Downside in the north; I had plainly not found myself yet. Anyway the experience, it was believed, would be good for me. So I was sent to the Benedictine parish in Coach Road, Whitehaven, Cumberland.

Not counting the cold bath, Whitehaven was the toughest thing I had yet experienced. At least it was among members of my own community that I was to learn the pastoral sciences. Dom Ambrose Agius was then superior, and if I can look back now with pleasure to what seemed at the time to be a fruitless experiment, it is largely because of what he gave me in the way of help and example. Two other monks made up the resident community from Downside, one of whom was smiling and unpredictable while the other was solemn, punctual, enclosed in holy occupations of his own. Monks on supply from the less distant monasteries came and went. To me was given the hospital, which meant a more than ordinary number of sick-calls, and an area of dockland where domestic peace reigned rarely. The two made up a world in which my aunt Berthe would have felt perfectly at home. Visiting the sick while the ether still clung to their blankets was for her an everyday work of devotion, and if report was correct she was for ever having to remove people's heads in the nick of time from gas ovens. But for me all this was something of a revelation.

In addition to hospital wards and dockside dwellings I had schoolrooms also in my care: half an hour's religious doctrine each morning to children of nine to thirteen. My experience of teaching at Downside was no use to me here. A state-aided school in the north of England is, whatever people may say about children of the same age being all alike, a very different kettle of fish from a boarding school in the west country. Drawing a blank on catechism I moved hopefully to scripture; from scripture, which was now interesting me more than almost any other study but which apparently had no attraction for the young of Whitehaven, I passed on to church history. Church history, particularly the monastic side of church history, had never failed at Downside. It failed here. Anyone who has taught a dull class will know how until a certain glimpse has been caught by the blank sullen faces there is no communication, and how, when the moment of illumination has come, the faces will be washed of their sullenness and almost anything will get across. At the school where I taught in Whitehaven there was a woman who came in to clean ('charlady' is a term which seems to have gone out) whose name was Mrs Quinn. Everyone called her 'Mary'. I compromised by calling her 'Mary Quinn'. She was not a native of Cumberland, but came from over the border. She had a way with her, a mock-heroic way which endeared her to all. She was by far the most interesting person in the place. One day while I was taking class she came in to deliver a note. 'Aye, and a body waits ye below,' she said, 'and fare ye well now, Father.' Without feeling that I was showing any great brilliance, I replied, 'And farewell to you, Mary Quinn of Scots.' My credentials were assured. The faces in front of me thereafter took in catechism, scripture, church history, and talks about the current feasts of the Church. The classes which were junior in the school took their cue from the seniors. So comes the divine *kerigma* to the dawning intelligence.

Though much of the work at Whitehaven was enjoyable, and all of it presumably worth while, I found myself looking forward as seldom before to my parents' next visit to England. Yet when they came—and I was back at Downside by this time—I seemed to have grown away from them. From all the family, Yolande included. In regard to my friends there was the same sense of estrangement which could be neither accounted for nor remedied. I remember telling Father Bede, the last time we met, of my plans and hopes, and how I wished afterwards I had not. We were sitting in the gardens at Blackfriars, and I told him how for some years it had seemed possible that Downside might make a contemplative foundation and that if this idea fell through, as was now almost certain that it would, I meant to ask admission as a novice at Parkminster. I reminded him that this was what I had wanted to do nine years before, when I was still in the world, and that he had opposed it.

'I am still opposed to it,' he said, 'because I don't see that it will settle anything. You'll come away from the Carthusians after a bit, but that won't be the end of it. It may bring you peace for a while, but all your life you will be chasing the same mirage.' It was unfortunate that we should have ended on that note, but I suppose I can respect him all the more for being right. I applied last year, 1963, for admission to a Cistercian community in America. I was told with great charity that it would be unwise at my age to go ahead with it.

Abbot Chapman died in 1933, and from Abbot Hicks, who succeeded, I met with great understanding. Having taken the name of Bruno, he was perhaps more disposed than most to sympathise with my Carthusian aspirations. He knew that throughout my religious life I had been looking for something which I had not found, and he gave me every assurance that he would help me to find it. I had been sent into the school to teach, he pointed out, and this had only increased my desire for the more extreme forms of monasticism; I had been sent to work on a parish, and this had produced the same result. He undertook accordingly to write to the Prior of Parkminster, suggesting that I make a trial of their life.

So on February 11, the feast of our Lady of Lourdes, I left Downside believing that it would be for good. As I was walking through the cloister with my two suitcases I was stopped by the senior monk whom I have mentioned in connection with my profession. 'Off on a holiday?' he asked cheerfully—though he must have known my destination for he was a member of the council and would have learned the Abbot's mind on the matter. 'You ought to have done this years ago,' he added when I told him, 'you have never really been one of us.' This kindly send-off helped to neutralise Father Bede's gloomy prophecies.

My parents were back in Egypt again and Berthe was in Brussels with Maurice, so going through London I had only two farewell calls to make. After saying goodbye to Yolande I went to see Father John at the Brompton Oratory. I owed it to him to explain this venture which I was embarking upon and which he had opposed years before. While he bore no resentment, and even admitted that he should have let me go in the first place, Father John was not on this occasion helpful. So when George Bellord arrived in a car to take me away I was relieved.

George and I had confided in one another since Junior School days, and I would not have dreamed of asking anyone else to drive me on such a journey as this. Sussex in February looked bleak. We had tea in a café which had once been an Air Force hut, and which was still so proud of its origins as to have two aeroplane propellers nailed to its walls. There were photographs of men in the uniform of the Flying Corps, and of chorus-girls in silk waistcoats, tall cloth-covered laced boots, and hats tilted sideways. George and I looked glumly at these trophies of the war which the world had said would never be repeated.

'This is the last tea you'll get,' said George, 'so you might as well finish the strawberry jam.'

The last few miles were made in silence. It was getting dark by the time we arrived, and at the entrance to the monastery George knelt on the path and asked for my blessing.

CHAPTER NINE

The Middle Years

Here, with Dante all over again, began a new life. If extreme monasticism was what I wanted, I could get it now. If I was looking for solitude, discipline, physical hardship, separation from the world, I had nothing to complain about at Parkminster. For the first few months I was perfectly at home. I knew the peace of believing that I was exactly where God wanted me to be, and surely there can be no greater luxury than this. My sole regret was that I had delayed so long to take the step of coming. Then, after a series of weekly visits from the master of novices, the unwelcome knowledge began to dawn: I was not thought to be an apt subject for the Carthusian life. Looking back upon the experience today I can judge that I made exactly the same mistake in the novitiate at Parkminster as I had made in the novitiate at Downside: I had come in both instances with a clear idea of what I was looking for, and when the object supplied was not what I had expected I held on to the original conception. The only difference was that at Parkminster they found this out.

A brief outline of the Carthusian life may clarify. The Carthusian works, reads, and for the most part prays, in isolation. He lives in a four-roomed 'cell' which is provided with a covered cloister or *ambulacrum* and a walled-in garden about half the size of a tennis court. He joins his brethren in choir for certain offices, and in the refectory on Sundays and feast-days for the midday meal. He speaks twice in the week: during a short recreation lasting about twenty minutes and during a long walk outside the enclosure lasting about two hours. He does not eat meat, and for a considerable part of the year his diet excludes eggs, cheese, butter, and milk. On Fridays, unless a holiday of obligation falls on that day, he fasts on dry bread and water. He neither eats nor drinks before the main meal of the day which follows the Angelus, and his supper consists of a salad and the bread he has saved from the earlier meal. He sleeps on a narrow straw mattress, wearing a different habit from the one he has been wearing all day. There is no electric light or gas; oil lamps are used throughout. There are no baths or showers, and there is no running water in the cell; water is fetched from a fountain in the main cloister as the monk comes back to the cell from one of the offices in the church. He goes to bed early, breaking his sleep for three hours of prayer during the night and getting to bed again shortly after two. Prime, mental prayer, conventual Mass, and private Masses occupy him until after eight in the morning, and the rest of the day is cut up into periods of reading, study, manual labour in solitude, devotional exercises. So the life is eremitical, but with an element of association in community. It is liturgical as well as contemplative. It is ascetic while remaining essentially balanced.

Feeling I was in my element, I had little difficulty in adjusting to new perspectives. I learned to see prayer and work not as two things but as one. I learned to discount the importance of fatigue. Waiting in the *ambulacrum* for a bell to go, I sometimes found I had been asleep standing up—like a horse. Though hunger did not bother me, the cold remained a distraction which I never mastered. The church, cloisters, chapter-house, refectory and library were unheated. The only heating in the cell was an iron stove which depended upon one's powers of chopping wood. I have never in my life chopped so much wood.

It is part of the Carthusian system to interrogate the newcomer as to his preferences and prejudices relating to the life. In communities where daily intercourse is restricted, some such arrangement is found necessary or the authorities would be left to guess at the subject's state of mind. This questioning I took seriously, giving thought to the answers I returned. I told how I valued the silence, the prolonged periods of prayer, the solitude, and having penances given to me instead of having to choose them for myself. I told also how distracting I found the two recreations a week, and how I would feel more at ease were there no talking at all. If the eremitical life was worth living, it might as well be lived completely. My frankness in answering the questions put to me by the master of novices told against me. It was explained to me that the cenobitic ideal was as much part of the Carthusian vocation as the eremitical, and that though I might be well enough adapted to the solitary life I was lamentably short on the social or cenobitic side. I lacked the Carthusian balance. My case was put before the seniors, and in the kindest way possible I was told that my chances of perseverance were slim. At my request I was granted a few weeks' grace in which to try to learn the secret of this harmony. At the end of this time I had to admit that for me the scales were unevenly weighted and showed little sign of drawing level. It was a disappointment, and I wondered if I would ever be able to resolve the forces with which my life seemed inescapably beset. While in the world I was criticised for being too worldly. In the monastery I had been too monastic. And now I was having to leave the solitary life because I was too much of a hermit.

Though it spelled another personal failure and the extinguishing of a hope I had carried with me for more than a decade, the Carthusian venture taught me a good deal and I have never had any regrets about it. It gave me an appreciation not only for the Parkminster community but for the Downside community as well.

While I was there I learned, early in Lent, that my father was ill and not likely to recover. I realised now that it was too late to get back to the old relationship, and when he died a few weeks later my grief was deeper than I would have believed possible. I could imagine him saying to my mother: 'He's changed, Nick, and since he's been togged out in that monastic rig I haven't understood him a bit.' When Easter came—and Easter Sunday is observed by the Carthusians as a day of complete silence—I was homesick. I remembered the eggs, stained red and blue and yellow, which Josephine used to hide in the garden and on the balcony in Alexandria.

Messages of sympathy about my father's death were delivered at my *guichet*, and letters came also from Downside. However doubtful I might be as to which religious house I was meant to settle in, I was left in no doubt about the charity which existed in each of them.

Memories of this time are plentiful, and not all of them sombre. I remember how when exchanging cells—a practice designed to take place each year in the interests of detachment—an elderly

French monk lectured me on the need to keep the faculties ever fresh and alert. 'In our kind of life this is especially important,' he said, 'and for this reason I surround myself with the animated, with things that are growing and vital.' He led me to a shelf on which were displayed some potted ferns, a greying aspidistra, and a very hard small cactus. I remember a fellow member of the novitiate, who is today the superior of a Carthusian foundation, who knew by heart the lyrics of *Iolanthe* and *The Gondoliers*. I remember asking a brother what I was supposed to do with orange peel and asparagus stalks at the end of a meal. 'Eat them,' was the reply. I remember how, in coming down from a ladder in order to greet the Prior who was visiting my cell, I got my foot stuck in a bucket and had to go clanking after him as he walked through the little garden to the door. Prior Weld was a very shy man, making no reference to the bucket but looking the other way. On the day I left he came again to see me in the cell, and gave me two hairshirts and the discipline which I had used during my stay.

The Vicar, a Father Petre who had a name in the order for both piety and originality, came also to say goodbye. He gave me a medal of St Bruno which I dropped twice while he was talking to me. He then gave me an old envelope to put the medal in, saying obliquely, 'that will now be that'. Among those who obtained permission to call on me before the end were two of the junior professed who had been at school with me at Downside. There was another old Downside boy at Parkminster when I was there, but since he was at a different level we never met. With hardly more than twenty Englishmen in the order at that time, the Downside percentage stood high.

It happened that I came away on the day of King George V's jubilee. The streets were decorated, bands played, people at Victoria Station wore paper hats and blew hooters. Not having seen a paper all the time I had been away I wondered if we had just won a war.

The sadness of leaving Parkminster was softened by the generous way with which I was received back at Downside. There was no suggestion of I-told-you-so. The only explanation I could give to those who asked me what had gone wrong was the kind of explanation which people give after a car smash: I cannot think how it happened . . . I do not remember pressing the wrong pedal . . . I am sure I observed the traffic lights . . . it was all perfectly clear up to a certain point, but then the scene became confused and the next thing I knew was that I was out on the flat of my back.

With no longer a chimera to pursue I felt uncertain, without direction or destination. My safety lay in keeping clear of chimeras—of what Father Bede had called my 'mirages'. The wisest course, here in the house of my profession, was to lie low and avoid extremes. I must make it my business to fall in with whatever was asked of me. For me there has never been much attraction about sitting on the ground with folded hands listening to the grass growing. I did not have to sit for long.

Hardly had I got used to having meals with other people again, to sleeping the whole night through, to having a bath without resorting to a complicated disposition of basins, when I was sent to act as chaplain at Ladycross School which at that time was served from Downside. I came at the end of a long line of Downside chaplains, remaining for four terms and finding great satisfaction in the work. It meant teaching Christian Doctrine to rather more than a hundred boys ranging in age between seven and thirteen, preaching twice a week, and running one of two religious societies. During the school holidays, instead of being recalled to Downside, I was lent to Worth which was then still a dependent priory belonging to Downside.

In putting me at Ladycross, Abbot Hicks made it clear to the Head Master, Mr E. A. Roper, himself an old Downside boy, that I was cooling off after a sojourn with the Carthusians and would need to be left alone as much as possible to start with. Antony Roper understood perfectly, and I was required to attend only one school meal a day, to accept no social duties, to take no games. The conditions were faithfully observed and I can look back upon the Ladycross interlude as one of the least disturbed of my career.

Though the teaching irked me, I managed to turn the instructions almost into conferences on the spiritual life. It seemed to work both with my audiences and with me. The instructions were given in the chapel instead of in a classroom. It marks the only instance when as a pedagogue I have not waited the next class with something approaching terror. Without opportunity for carving I had time on my hands, which allowed me to go on with the practice which I had begun a year or two before of making notes on the Old Testament and the holy Rule. Both studies proved invaluable later on when I came to write about these subjects.

The Ropers and I became great friends. Before I had been at Ladycross very long they asked me to give spiritual conferences once a week in their private house for any of the staff who might care to come. From these conferences emerged the kind of unprofessional talk which I was to give in the retreats for which I was now getting requests. Retreat work had already been started at Worth, so during the holidays I was able to help out in this way. It was a work which was obviously worth while, and one which I felt to be not incompatible with St Benedict's Rule. So far as I was concerned it called neither for pulpit oratory, for which I knew I had no gift, nor for theological exposition, for which I knew I had even less. It meant no more than talking to people about prayer and the spiritual life. It was something I was doing every day with individuals, and now was asked to do with small groups of a dozen or so. It is a work which I have been glad to do ever since.

After leaving Parkminster I did not take up my diary for a few years, so the events of this time are remembered without sequence, but it must have been about now that Ronald Knox wrote to me from Oxford suggesting that we spend ten days at Caldey together and make our retreat there. Hitherto he had made his retreats each year either at Downside or at Worth, so I had been seeing him. But this invitation I felt to be a more special tribute. He said we could combine a holiday with holiness. 'I'm all for killing birds with stones,' he wrote. Off and on, whenever we had met, we had been going to confession to one another, so this retreat, I told myself, was not just an excuse for amusing ourselves. 'I wish you didn't always need reasons for doing things,' wrote Ronald in answer to my letter agreeing and asking him to look up trains, 'because in the end it means you have to invent them.'

Ronald liked nothing better than planning train journeys of

exquisite complexity. He arrived at Tenby on the right train, I arrived on the wrong one and nearly three hours late. If there was one thing he detested it was having dinner alone, so when I reached the Coburgh Hotel, where we were to spend the night, to find that he had had a meal by himself and was suffering from a streaming cold, I found him not in the best of humours. We had arranged to say our Masses next morning not at the parish church of St Teilo's but on the island of Caldey, in the abbey. I was looking forward to this little sea voyage, in the monastery motor-boat with Mass at the end of it. I told him how exhilarating it would be. 'I loathe saying Mass through a *crust* of salt,' said Ronald.

Shortly after four I went down to the quay to do my regulation half hour of mental prayer before Tenby started getting out of bed. I was not alone, however, for a man who appeared to be a sailor had got there before me. (Afterwards it turned out that he was not a sailor at all, but liked dressing up as one so as to impress the trippers.) He told me two things: first that the tide would delay our voyage to Caldey beyond the time we had expected, and second that the seagulls in that part had become so effete in recent years that they no longer bothered to fly to the three islands which lay offshore but waited for one of the pleasure boats to take them.

Ronald's cold was no better, and by the time we cast off in the monks' motor-boat he was as limp as I had ever seen him, leaning over the mouth of the hatch like a wet glove and sinking deeper and deeper into his collar. We reached the island making good time, said Mass, and all was well. It proved the most enjoyable retreat I have ever made.

In many ways it also proved enlightening. Though we had known each other for upwards of ten years we had not before lived at close quarters. We were the only guests, and as we were spoken to only by the guestmaster and the prior we had the place to ourselves. Except for the guestmaster, an Irishman from St Joseph's Abbey at Roscrae, the monks were mostly Belgian. Also on the island were Hilary Armstrong, who was lecturing at Cardiff University, and Roger Kynaston, who was an artist and an eccentric. The Armstrongs had taken rooms; the Kynastons had taken the lighthouse for the summer. Ronald knew, though he did not know they were going to be there, both families. The Kynaston children recited the full monastic grace in Latin before and after each meal. It is the only occasion on which I have heard the Latin grace said aloud at high tea. They also kept a donkey, presumably transported from the mainland, because for some reason cow's milk was held by the Kynastons in suspicion. Never before or since the Caldey retreat have I seen Ronald Knox, translator and author, riding a donkey.

It was very hot that summer, and Hilary Armstrong wore a tropical suit rather like the one I had taken to Egypt with me. Roger Kynaston, making no concessions to the heat, wore a round fur cap like a poacher's. The children too wore fur caps; they had made them themselves. Roger was older than Ronald, and had in his time been first of all a friend, and then an enemy, of Baron Corvo's. Ronald told me that at Oxford, and before he had become a Catholic, Roger used to give bridge parties in his rooms at which he used to preside wearing a biretta and a saffron silk cope from Spain. It was hard to see in this poacher with the homespun clothes, the tangled beard, the rough hands and big boots—the Kynaston of Eric Gill—the elegant dilettante who had sat as host in his baroque throne and yellow cope at Oxford, dealing out the cards and smoking a cigar while incense burned in a brazier behind him. But this, Ronald explained, was in the Corvo days. The Kynastons came later to see me at Downside ('What, the whole boiling lot of them?' Ronald asked when I told him of their visit), all with their poachers' caps.

While we were at Caldey, Ronald and I were each asked to give a conference to the community. Ronald spent a whole irritable day preparing what he was going to say, typing his script, polishing it, and finally reading it to me. It was a perfect piece of composition, as all his compositions were, and I had no suggestions to make. He was still not satisfied with it. 'You had better bat first,' he told me, 'I take so long to get my pads on.' So next morning I went to the wicket instead of him, allowing him more time. The duty fulfilled by both of us, I asked the guestmaster how the community had liked Ronald's talk. I would have been glad too of a word about my own. 'Ah, the meaning of it was nothing to them; it's trying to learn English they are.' I decided not to pass this on, but Ronald heard it himself from the guestmaster. 'And to think,' he said to me, 'I might have been reading them Father Bernard Vaughan.'

During our walks on the island, or sitting for hours overlooking one or other bay, he told me that he had not himself felt the attraction at any time to the monastic life. Observance as such did not greatly edify him, and ceremonial frankly bored him. He saw the point of separation from the world, of silence, of self-denial and religious poverty, but he felt that to put all one's eggs, as I was trying to do, into that basket was a mistake. I said I thought it was a question of vocation and not of choosing a basket, and that once the basket had been chosen by God, the more eggs you put in it the better. The danger about this, he argued, was coming to value your eggs more than God's basket. This or that interpretation of St Benedict's Rule was, he felt, immaterial. So long as the purpose of the Rule was secured, namely the love of God, why bother? For his part he did not envy, as I obviously did, our Cistercian hosts their greater opportunity of serving God. He was not at all sure that theirs *was* a greater opportunity. He was not one to sniff at a vocation which seemed to make less demand. 'The things I would make a great song about, if I were founding a religious order,' he said, 'would be frequent prayer and really deep spiritual reading. Fewer lives of St Joseph, and more Arintero and Garigou-Lagrange.' Then he added that even here he would claim it to be more perfect to put away the book and answer the door than to fulfil the half-hour obligation and keep someone waiting.

Possessed of a spirituality which dug deep below the external forms of religion, Ronald could afford to be flexible. I could not. What I learned of him from the Caldey retreat was that his flexibility came from strength and not from compromise with weakness. It came also from consideration for other people and for their differences, and not from a consideration for his own convenience. This is the more impressive because, as he was the first to admit, his own convenience mattered to him a good deal. I wish I could remember more of our discussions on Caldey Island. If I have forgotten much of Ronald's conversation, then and at other times, it is probably because his thought was so quick and so subtle, compounding a profusion of ideas which were both reasoned and intuitive to him but which were not so to me, that I found myself running out of mental accommodations with which to meet them and which would have helped to store them in my memory.

On our way back from Caldey, and changing trains at Bristol, Ronald introduced me to Mr Evelyn Waugh, who himself was changing trains. As we moved out of the station for the last stretch of his elaborately organised journey Ronald said, 'You hadn't met him before then?' I said I had seen him often years ago at Oxford and in the Cavendish but that I had never aspired. 'I know my place,' I said, 'which is not the same place as Evelyn Waugh's.'

'You had better not call him that. He likes to be called Mr Waugh.' For many years I acted on Ronald's warning until Mr Waugh started signing himself 'Evelyn', which I took to be letters patent. When he became a regular visitor to Downside, and particularly when he attended two of my retreats, I found in him much that I would not have looked for had I known him only from his books. It was because of his good offices that I first went to America, and for this if for nothing else I would be lastingly grateful. However much may come to be written about Ronald, nothing to my mind will ever equal the Waugh biography.

In the summer of 1937, having finished my time as chaplain at Ladycross, I was appointed Head Master of Worth. This opens a brief period about which I would much prefer to remain silent, indeed about which I would like to forget, but which honesty compels me to record. If rules govern the writing of biography, autobiography can hardly exempt itself.

Having indicated what I conceived to be the main disqualifications—namely my inability to teach, organise, handle accounts, draw up timetables which would work when put into operation, make convincing contributions at meetings of fellow head masters who would all have university degrees against which I would be able to match only my one School Certificate (and of course the Life Saving Certificate)—I left the matter in the hands of my superiors. In doing this I was trying to pursue the policy I had proposed to myself after leaving the Carthusians, the policy of falling in with whatever was asked of me however unlikely. I was told, by way of rebuttal, that an efficient secretariat would deal with finance and clerical work, that I need not teach unless I chose to, that I would easily be able to hold my own at the meetings of head masters by returning bluff for bluff, and that virtually all I had to do was to establish the kind of easy relations with the boys which I had managed without much difficulty to establish with the boys of Ladycross.

That things turned out quite differently from what was hoped can be nobody's fault but my own. I planned the way in which I would go about the work, and it so happened that it was the wrong plan. I judged that the deficiencies which I brought to the job could be made good only by increasing the spiritual pressure. I judged that I could best help those under my care by the indirect means of praying more and eating less. Since I knew I was no good for the work, I felt that the sensible thing was to get God to do it for me; and that the best way of getting Him to do it was to increase the pressure. The argument seemed unanswerable, but there must have been a flaw in it because before very long confusion reigned.

My time as Head Master of Worth Preparatory School did not last as long as my time at Parkminster, and in February 1938 I was taken to the Middlesex Hospital where I spent the next two months. The Worth community were very nice about it, and so was the Abbot of Downside, but I was unquestionably a disappointment. To myself too I was a disappointment. Two major failures within the space of three years.

The only memories which I cherish in connection with the sojourn in hospital are of an alcoholic patient and of some nurses on night duty. The alcoholic sang a song which contained the lines 'It ain't no fault of me poor ol' ma her tongue's as dry as the Sa-ha-ra'. The night nurses played cricket in the corridor to keep themselves awake, and so as not to disturb the patients they used a temperature chart as a bat and a rolled-up bandage as a ball.

When discharged in April, I was told to convalesce for three months, to get used to the idea of being an invalid for life, to rule out any idea of getting up early in the mornings. By the middle of May I was back to my normal timetable.

At intervals during my life, usually when things have not been going very well, a large family of young people has come along, taken me up, and made me one of themselves. According to the book this is supposed to be a trap for the monk or priest. It is assumed that he is drawn out of his environment by it, and comes to taste again the sweets of a domesticity which he has renounced. All I can say is that in my case the experience has each time made me more of a monk, more of a priest. Perhaps people like me need to learn about the supernatural from association with the natural, and more about the natural when seen against a background of the supernatural. I had been getting rather out of touch with the natural.

The Bernard Rochfords were one such family at the time of which I write. I knew them from Ladycross days, and now they were visiting me at Worth and Downside, coming to my retreats, joining me on pilgrimages to Lourdes, and making friends with my friends. They are in touch with me still. In later years I was to know the same kind of support from large households of children and on each occasion I was surprised to find myself not distracted at all but on the contrary shown more of religious reality.

In 1938, there was, both at Downside and at Worth, a reshuffle of personnel. I was recalled to Downside where I was able for a time to devote myself to preaching retreats and carving stone. I had done some wood-carving at Parkminster but nothing since then, and now I was able to get on in both materials. Though the Gill influence had lessened, there was little originality in what I was turning out. From Ernst Barlach and Carl Milles I was developing a lumpishness which would have shamed these sculptors had they known I was trying to capture their spirit. From Ivan Mestrovic's powerful but emotional work I was acquiring a style which reflected more of the emotional and less of the powerful. To have learned only sentiment from his work would have shamed Mestrovic into his grave. I remember showing to Gurth Addington, who was now a constant visitor to the stoneshed, a madonna which I had just carved and which I was now paying the unsculptural compliment of painting. 'Against what sort of background,' I asked him, 'do you think I should have this figure mounted?' 'A theatre organ,' he replied.

As further therapeutic treatment after the setbacks sustained at Parkminster and Worth, I went back to manual labour: pulling up cabbage stalks, clearing undergrowth and shrubberies, cutting down trees. It worked wonders. In a practical way the truth was confirmed that for introspective people like myself, beset by monastic problems, work with the hands is the only way. From childhood I had needed to forget myself, and I was finding in these manifold occupations a measure of escape. 'The most unbearable punishment for the human soul,' wrote Pascal, 'is to live with itself and think of itself.'

The pattern established, everything for a time unfolded smoothly and fitted neatly into it. My trials, I told myself, were at an end. If further obstacles awaited me I would know how to deal with them. So when it was proposed, in the general disorganisation and changes of office caused by the outbreak of the Second World War, that I should become a housemaster at Downside I was not greatly apprehensive. All over again I enumerated my deficiencies in regard to educational work, supporting the argument with the additional evidence of my failure at Worth. I was told that there was a war on, that nobody held it against me that I had misjudged the Worth venture, and that the housemaster's was not an office which required administrative ability. I was accordingly installed in the school with a room of my own and some sixty boys to look after. The eight years that I spent as housemaster were the unhappiest years of my life.

Up till now, even during the head-master episode, I had been able to keep a firm hand on my day. Indeed therein lay the error: it was *my* day. Education as it had presented itself to me at Worth—involving me knee-deep in staff meetings, report cards, boy scout parades, letters of complaint from parents, disciplinary crises, engagement of masters—was confined to itself. It was strictly education, much of which could be delegated and what was left could be dealt with at regular hours. Education as seen from the housemaster's desk means absorption. Though his administrative duties are localised, the housemaster's other obligations are comprehensive. Where a head master is able to stand back from the scene, a housemaster becomes part of it: he is assimilated into the system, into the lives of the boys, into the mesh of his house. For the first time in my religious career I felt that my life was not my own any more; it was slipping away from those controls which I had spent fifteen years in fashioning. Very good for me no doubt, but unsettling. Obedience was there to justify what was happening, even presumably to sanctify what was happening, but I did not like it. It was the sense of being unanchored to any sure area of monastic observance, as much as a want of competence in the actual running of the house, which kept me in a state of tension throughout the whole time I was employed in the school as housemaster.

That there were consolations attaching to the work I do not deny. For one thing it brought me in closer contact with human problems, with souls, than the other appointment had done. Weekly discourses in the old school chapel gave rise to rewarding interviews, and in some cases to lasting friendships. For another thing it got me into the way of piecemeal writing. Having to take five minutes here and five minutes there, and when even these intervals are likely to be interrupted, is good practice. Today I can write while on a bus or in a telephone booth.

So far as recreations went, there was much in the new job which appealed to the worldly side of me, and I welcomed the excuse to keep abreast of current interest and, especially now during wartime, news. But enjoying these things only added to my inner discomfort.

By now Abbot Trafford, who had been Head Master while I was in the school, was next superior after Abbot Hicks. Invited by the War Office in the early months of the War to supply as many monks as he could spare from the community to act as chaplains, Abbot Trafford called for volunteers. Along with the rest I gave in my name and sat back to await the publication of the list. Before the selection was made known, Abbot Trafford, surprised that I should have thought myself eligible for serving with the forces, called me to his room.

'I can hardly take this offer seriously,' he said with his most engaging smile, 'because you must know as well as I do that you are not in the least cut out for this sort of thing.'

'Oh? You may remember that I only just failed Cert A.'

'They wouldn't have passed you in a hundred years. You didn't even know the parts of a rifle.'

'I would take to the army as easily as anything.'

'Don't deceive yourself; you would be hopeless. What's at the back of it? Are you asking to be relieved of the housemaster thing?'

'No.'

'Look, you are doing what you can for these boys in the school, you are turning out a book or two a year, and you are giving retreats during the holidays. You are working for souls as it is, so what is it you hope to gain by going off to the wars?'

'Death.'

'So that's it,' the Abbot said with a return of his quick smile; 'well, I'm afraid I can't help you. Permission refused.'

Abbot Trafford and I have had our minor disagreements in the past fifty years but we have never failed to get on. Each of us understands what the other says, and this is an inestimable advantage.

The War. To my generation war meant *Thirty-nine Steps*, recruiting-posters showing Kitchener pointing straight at you and unequivocally demanding that you join him, black treacle instead of sugar with porridge, Edith Cavell's head and shoulders printed on celluloid buttons to be worn on the lapel, crêpe arm-bands, howitzers, zeppelins, black German helmets with metal spikes, shiny postcards of famous generals with medals, rumours of Russians with snow on their boots travelling through the Midlands in trains with the blinds down, Bruce Bairnsfather cartoons in the *Bystander*, Angels of Mons, George Robey, tanks which were easy to draw. It took a little time adjusting to the Second World War where they did not seem to want horses any more. This new warfare meant parachutes, *Roll out the Barrel*, Anderson shelters as well as deep ones, Vera Lynn, gas-masks, women's clothes cut square at the shoulder, Garrison Theatre with Jack Warner broadcasting from an abandoned church building in Bristol, Mr Noël Coward in khaki shorts holding a microphone, whale-meat, evacuees being disinfected and getting lost, powdered egg in tins, Lord Haw Haw, and tanks which were more difficult to draw. But we soon got used to it. If you were in London you would get used to the shrill bell of the ambulance which rang through your head like a silver drill, to the sigh of a falling bomb, to the hiss of water from the hoses, to the crack and cackle of anti-aircraft guns mounted in the Park, to the smell of smoke, to the sight of empty window frames, blackened walls, jagged sides of houses. If you were in the country you would get used to a milder variety of sensory impressions. During the holidays I was frequently, when either in hospital or giving retreats, in London. For the greater part of the war, I was at Downside attending to the affairs of the house.

Unforgettable were the nights, not many of them fortunately, spent in the vaults under the church while German bombers flew overhead on their way to Bristol and the depots and installations in the Cotswolds. These pyjama-and-dressing-gown hours in the improvised shelter would begin with a roll-call to which boys answered their names with 'Jawohl', 'Si, signor', 'Ici, mon père'. Then there would be games of cards, and some suitably muted music. At the first wail of the all-clear everyone would go back again to bed, trailing rugs and pillows along the corridors. Unforgettable too were the Masses at temporary altars in a blacked-out cloister, and at Christmas the Midnight Mass in the Abbey with just enough of the blue-shaded light left on to prevent the ministers from bumping into one another. Unforgettable the German prisoners who came in lorries during the Christmas holidays and sang *Heilige Nacht*, to the disapproval of the liturgical purists, during the High Mass.

The manual labour which I had cherished before the war as a monastic exercise, as something almost sacred to be carried out in silence and remote from observation, became now, with the threat of invasion adding to the threat of bombing, a noisy, social, unrecollected, jolly business of filling sandbags. Under supervision from me and coming in relays throughout the day, teams of boys would appear in strange clothes whenever a bell rang and start filling innumerable sacks with rich red Somersetshire earth, wheel them off and pile them up in front of ground-floor windows and outside the crypt. A few months later our sandbags, by this time sprouting weeds and wild flowers, were taken down and replaced, professionally, by concrete blocks which were believed to give better protection. Such are the uncertainties of war.

Not wanting to lose touch with mother earth, and feeling I should bring my house into this, I got together voluntary gangs of boys to help me in what was called 'digging for victory'. The boys got tired of digging and waiting for victory, as though victory were to come up like a turnip, and I was left to finish the field by myself. I should have been glad of the chance of digging on my own again, whether for victory or peace of mind, but for some reason the spell was broken. I suppose I was distracted by too many cares. The more I was an executive the less I felt a monk. I decided to drop manual labour and sculpture for the duration of the war.

I have purposely lagged behind, until it can be dealt with in one piece, on the Knox record. In order to bring it up to date I must go back to the years immediately before the war. Father Knox had become Monsignor Knox, but more significant changes were in the air. When Ronald was still Catholic chaplain at Oxford, Cardinal Hinsley had asked him to accept the presidency of St Edmund's College, Old Hall. The post offered unusual opportunity for influencing the life of Catholicism in England. There were other possible advantages to be seen in the proposed appointment. Cultural as well as spiritual interests would receive a new impulse within the college itself, while to the outside world Ronald's name would acquire new prestige. Among scholars, and in the intellectual world generally, Ronald enjoyed the standing he deserved. It was to the ordinary radio-side public, non-Catholic and Catholic alike, that he was falsely presented. People still thought of him as a brilliant but frivolous sixth-former who could produce a Greek epigram at the drop of a hat but to whom the serious affairs of life were unknown. The post would almost certainly—though to Ronald this would not have appeared an advantage—lead to a bishopric.

Ronald consulted a number of people as to whether or not it would be wise for him to accept. I was at that time supplying for a few weeks at Little Malvern in Worcestershire, and he came over from Oxford to talk to me about the Cardinal's offer. I knew that he was considering the work of translating the Vulgate, an undertaking which to me ranked of the highest importance, and that he was giving up Oxford anyway. If he chose St Edmund's it would mean putting aside, in all probability for good, the translation of the Bible. If he chose the Bible it would not mean, because he had planned to do so already, giving up his work among the undergraduates at Oxford. He told me that he intended to ask other people's advice, but that he wanted to know what I thought. We walked for two hours on the hills above the town, and in the end I urged him to refuse the appointment. I asked him not to base his decision on my opinion. He said he would not, and that in order to get the same unprejudiced opinion from the others whom he meant to consult, as he had got from me, he would not let them know that I had given it. Then he insisted on dropping the subject, so we walked about saying nothing until I saw him off at the station. On the platform he asked me to come to speak to his undergraduates before he left Oxford. I had given Sunday conferences before at the Old Palace, dreading them on each occasion. As this was to be the last, I said I would. When the time came and I preached in the chapel I now knew so well, Ronald told me he had turned down the Cardinal's proposal. He told me also that of those to whom he had talked, only two—namely Father D'Arcy and Dom Justin McCann—thought as I did. I hope Father D'Arcy and Dom Justin were as unrepentant afterwards as I was.

So now, with the war going on and the chaplaincy a thing of the past, Ronald was doing his translation of the Bible at Aldenham Park in Shropshire, the home of the Acton family. Instead of seeing less of him as a result of his move from Oxford, I in fact saw more of him than had been possible before the war. Lord Acton, who owned Aldenham, had been at school with me, and I had been in touch with Lady Acton since Ronald had received her into the Church in 1938. She had been to Downside once or twice to see me and we had become friends. So when a community of Assumption nuns came with their school to occupy a part of the house, I was often invited to Aldenham to give retreats and days of recollection. In this way I was able to visit Ronald, the Actons, Princess Rospigliosi (Lord Acton's sister who was spending the war at Aldenham), and at the same time provide the nuns with a retreat-giver who was ready to come whenever his superiors allowed it. One stone was killing enough birds to satisfy even Ronald. When the War was over, and Lord Acton had returned from fighting in Italy, I went on visiting Aldenham until the house was sold and the family moved to Southern Rhodesia. More will be said about these later meetings with Ronald and his friends in the next chapter.

Writing is not like carving: it does not wait upon opportunity. To carve stone you must have not only a place for it but at least an hour at a stretch to give to it. You must also be able to have a bath whenever you want one. If you sleep badly you cannot use a mallet and chisel at two o'clock in the morning but you can write in bed. I have said above how convenient the habit became of writing at odd times: it was now becoming a necessity. The first instance of this was when the head boy of the house over which I presided asked me to let him have a play which he could put into rehearsal at the end of the same week. There was to be a competition of house plays, and the other houses had chosen one-act plays by Barrie, Galsworthy, Coward.

'So you expect me to compete with Barrie, Galsworthy, and Coward?'

'I suppose so. The trouble is the other houses have already started. We left it rather late.'

'So what you really want is to have this play for tomorrow?'

'That would be nice.'

I had written sketches and lyrics before, but this was the first set piece. It did not win the competition but at least it was ready for rehearsal next day, and in addition it showed me what satisfaction there could be in work done at high speed. Such plays as I have written since, whether of one act or three, have in each case taken less than a week to write. If I have spent a long time over some of the books (*The Holy Rule* took me a year despite the fact that I had been making notes on the subject since the time of my profession) it is usually because I have got ill or have been called away to a place where there was no library. (As now, for example, when I am confined by circumstance to writing what is in my head.) Some of the smaller books I have written in eight or ten days. I am perfectly aware that there is no merit in writing fast, and that on the contrary there is considerable merit in writing with deliberation and painstaking accuracy, but it is not a question here of merit. It is a question of method, and I am saying that my method is to rush. 'You don't really like writing books,' Ronald told me once, 'but getting books written.'

Apart from house and school plays the need for rapid composition arose when Mr Christopher Hollis, whom I then knew only slightly, asked me on behalf of Burns and Oates to write an Old Testament History for the young. 'Something to jolly up that tedious hour of scripture class.' I could make it as long as I liked but was to bear in mind that Moses described the whole of creation in seven hundred and sixty-six words. After a few months of leisurely typing I submitted some two or three hundred pages of typescript which eventually found its way to the printers. When the printing works was destroyed in the bombing of Plymouth my typescript went with it, and since in the interests of religious poverty I had thought it a waste of paper to make a carbon copy I had to begin again. Moreover in relief at having got the work off my chest I had torn up the notes I had used. The publication date had been advertised, so the rush was on. I felt like Jeremiah when his written prophecies had been burned to ashes in King Joakim's brazier, like Carlyle when he found that a housemaid had used his manuscript to light a fire, like Lawrence of Arabia when he remembered he had left the only copy of *Seven Pillars* on a railway station. *From Creation to Christmas* came out on time, and since then I have used carbon paper.*

Not long ago I was sent a cutting from an art magazine which described me as 'most likely a very impatient man'. I read this with surprise. How could anyone think me an impatient man? The writer of the article, who was not known to me personally, had of course got me entirely wrong. I read on and learned how I had completed an order for a four-foot statue 'in six days flat'. I now have to admit my impatience.

During the war years I tended to be in and out of hospital. One such visit was in 1942 when I was sent to St. Mary's, Pad-

* In a later edition the title was changed by the publishers to *Old Testament Stories*, which is what the book emphatically is not. The whole point was to show that the history of the Jews is one story: continuous and complete. Taken piecemeal it may have plenty to teach, but the full significance is missed. Under the new title the work became a textbook for schools. I hope it still jollies up the tedious hour of scripture class.

dington, where I spent an agreeable time and experienced some interesting air-raids. The priest who was acting chaplain asked me to speak to the Catholic nurses before I left, which I did in a small chapel where Mass was said for the staff and which brought me new friends. On the last evening of my stay at St Mary's I was given a party by those not on duty. The party was cut short by the siren's familiar plaint, and my hosts and hostesses returned in the twinkling of an eye to professional status. It reminded me of a ballet in which the performers dance off from one side of the stage as court ladies, and without seeming to have drawn breath dance on again from the opposite wings as shepherdesses.

At Paddington next day the corner seat facing me in the train was occupied by Mr Ernest Thesiger. He was shorter than I would have expected him to be, but actors look taller on the stage. Noticing that I had not brought sandwiches, Mr Thesiger offered me one of his. 'Only spam, alas,' he said. On the strength of this frail introduction I observed that the last time I had seen him eating sandwiches was when he was playing the gillie in Barrie's *Mary Rose*. He was delighted, and for the rest of the journey told me stories about Barrie, Shaw, Mrs Patrick Campbell, Charles Hawtrey, and Gerald Du Maurier. He told me that Shaw had once in an expansive moment offered to write a play about any character from history or fiction whom he, Thesiger, might care to play. After much thought Thesiger had written to Shaw suggesting that the play should be about Don Quixote, a part for which he judged himself well cast. A postcard came back from Shaw: 'It's been done already. G.B.S.' He told me also that if he were given the choice of spending an afternoon with any man of his generation whom he had known he would name Max Beerbohm. 'He has such charm, humanity, and social grace. With gentle magic he draws out of you all the beautiful things which you know you do not possess.'

The memory of this conversation in the train lingered in my mind when I got back to Downside, lending wings to my choir-stall so that I would find myself in Arcady when I should have been at Vespers.

Less amusing, but not without their interest, were two stretches of hospital life spent nearer to Downside, at Corston between Bath and Bristol. During the earlier I was visited by two of my closest friends who were on embarkation leave: Peter Cuffe and Maurice Turnbull. Both were to be killed not long afterwards in France. The second Corston interlude was, by comparison with the other which I associate chiefly with goodbyes, gay. George Bellord came with me to the hospital and saw me in. I was given a room with a commanding view, and together we surveyed the Edwardian character of the house which, before becoming a hospital, had passed through hands not connected with medicine or the knife. On the occasion of my first visit I had been so quickly dispatched to and from the sickroom as not to have taken in the features of the place. With George as a companion, if only for an hour or two before he went back to London, I was able to savour the richness of the establishment. The house had belonged to an extremely rich German merchant before the First World War, then had become a private school. When the school went bankrupt it was bought by the Royal West Country Cycling Club. Only when the R.W.C.C.C. had wheeled away to a countryside more challenging to their skill did a community of Irish nuns take over and turn it into a hospital. Successive occupants had each left their mark. The German merchant had ennobled the grounds with the busts of Roman emperors; the school had decorated the walls with views of the Bernese Oberland, paddy fields in China, the lower reaches of the Amazon; the Royal West Country Cycling Club had embellished the already grandiose rooms with stained glass depicting aspects of its life on the road. Thus you had the classics out of doors and the march of education and progress within.

George and I were given tea in my room, and through the window we could see the late August sun reddening the marble heads of Augustus, Caracalla, Caesar, and Trajan in the garden. The scenes of geographical interest, rendered in apparently ineffaceable tempera, glowed with all the invitation of the travel agents' poster. Light shone through stained glass which showed a gallant young man in knickerbockers helping a girl in a straw boater to mount her bicycle. George left after tea to catch his train, and next morning I had an operation.

In 1944, during Lent, I paid my third, and, up to the time of writing, last visit to Corston as a patient. For this recurrence I was placed in a large ward which was full of boys, mostly from

Downside, with whom there seemed to be nothing the matter. Also in the hospital at the time, and suffering from a bone injury, was Raleigh Addington, a younger brother of the Gurth Addington mentioned in connection with a theatre organ, and since we shared tastes which were not those of our fellow patients we braved together the ordeals of communal life in the ward. Raleigh was able to walk about, so I urged him to inspect the marble busts, the murals, the leaded lights. He told me that lest the uninitiated should mistake their period, the dates of the emperors were inscribed below their names. He told me also, after further exploration outside the ward, that lest the unobservant should mistake the direction, a scroll was worked into the design of the coloured window which bore in Gothic lettering the words 'Forwards'. 'But, after all, what else?' said Raleigh, concluding his description, 'they couldn't put "Sideways".'

The Irish sisters who ran the little hospital seemed to live in a state of constant bewilderment, marvelling wide-eyed at the ways of the English, at the appetite of Downside boys, at the strangeness of the house to which they had tried unsuccessfully to give the appearance of a hospital and a convent, and at the indifference to religion which they found among the natives. Raleigh stopped on longer than I did, but we have met again since. So at least that wartime association was not dissolved with the bubbles of a hospital sink. Relationships formed in hospital and in war are liable to be on a level with those formed on sea voyages.

Almost at once on my return to Downside I became involved in arranging for an art exhibition to be shown by the Palette Club, a painting group which I had got together a year or two before. I promised Mrs Woodruff, another of Lord Acton's sisters and married to Douglas Woodruff the editor and writer, that the proceeds of this exhibition would go to a work which she was doing for mid-European refugees. To make the project pay, we planned to have seventy or eighty pictures on show and all of them priced above their worth. At a meeting of the Palette Club I tried to be my most persuasive. One member, Timothy Matthews, who was a disciple of mine in the world of art, devoted the whole of his free time to helping me in painting the pictures, sending out notices, drawing up the catalogue, prodding the other members to activity. Two days before the exhibition was due to open he and I were still painting pictures the titles of which had been decided upon beforehand and sent to the printers. We worked in oils, water-colours, poster paints, and stayed up painting until the last moment of the July light. Of the seventy exhibits finally put on show, eighteen were submitted by the other members of the club, and then only after great pressure had been brought to bear, the remaining fifty-two being supplied by Timothy Matthews and myself. Almost all the items were sold, and we got a letter of thanks from the mid-Europeans.

It is a curious fact that three boys of more outstanding talent than any others whom I have come across in a long association with art at Downside have each given up painting. Patrick O'Higgins, whom I had nothing more to teach by the time he was twelve and whom I still see when I am in his country, works for a cosmetics firm in New York. Timothy Matthews conducts interviews with wit and an economy of words on the B.B.C., but at so awkward an hour that few of his friends can manage to listen to him. Robert Stuart is writing and re-writing novels in Greece. There may be a moral to be drawn from this, but if there is it eludes me.

Towards the end of the war, I was beginning to feel old. So was Ronald, but this was because he was working too hard and was tired of the food. His was a physical exhaustion, and his friends knew he would get over it. My exhaustion was psychological and spiritual, and was leading to a sense of defeat. I told myself that I needed more time for prayer and reading, more chance of leading the strict monastic life. But I began to wonder whether this were really true, and whether if these things were given to me I would want them any more. Had I not got out of practice, lost the knack? Would I be able to settle down in an exclusively monastic routine, in a solitude such as I had enjoyed at Parkminster, in an ascetic routine such as I had always imagined to be my proper element? I remembered how Xenophon had dreamed all his life of governing a city somewhere along the Black Sea, and how when the best of them was offered him he turned it down. What if Mr Bolt's flowering cherry became available? Would I be able to uproot myself and take possession?

This inner dissatisfaction had its effect upon my dealings with the boys, and I became less accessible. While I hope I was conscientious in seeing to their spiritual and moral welfare, I was to blame in neglecting other sides of the boys' lives. Handing out punishment became increasingly distasteful to me, and discipline suffered. New commitments irked me. I avoided having to meet parents, and when I did meet them I mistook them for other parents. I lost letters, forgot appointments, put off as long as possible the duty of meeting the prefects and discussing house affairs. It is said of Cyrus that he knew personally every man in his army, and of Themistocles that he could remember the name of every family in Athens. It was as much as I could do to remember the names of the boys in my house, and when I came to write reports at the end of the term my comments were not masterpieces of penetration.

It was suggested that I needed a holiday. Since for years I had been away only to give retreats or to go on pilgrimage to Lourdes I acted on it, and invited a party of seven boys to join me for a week in Sussex. My mother at that time had a cottage which she rented from Worth and which she was not using, so it was decided that we should go there and manage by ourselves without servants. Timothy Matthews lived near by, and came over each day on a bicycle. It was without exception the most hilarious week I have ever spent. We swam in the lake at Crabett Park and had picnics in the grounds. Lady Wentworth, to whom not everyone was welcome, liked the Matthews family enough to grant them anything they asked. That I had been at school with her son, Anthony Lytton, was no recommendation: the name of Downside worked no spell here. Fortunately I still possess a day-to-day account of this unusual week, though even without such a bulletin to remind me I am not likely to forget much of it.

On coming back to normal existence I realised that no one week, however enjoyable, could do more than relieve me for the moment. For the first time in my life I could see nothing ahead of me to which I could look forward. Hitherto I had been helped over the defeats by having a goal of some sort to lure me on—a visible goal to which I might reasonably soon attain. But now, with the future stretching endlessly in front of me, there seemed to be nothing concrete to stimulate the virtue of hope. Hope was precisely the difficulty: I had it, but there was nothing to hook it to. In his strange haunting book, *Dona Rosita*, the Spanish writer Frederica Garcia Lorca makes one of his characters say this: 'Everything is finished, yet I go to bed and get up again with the most terrible of all feelings: the feeling of having hope. Hope pursues me, encircles me, bites me.'

Then the best thing possible happened. I caught pneumonia, was taken by ambulance to St Mary's Hospital in Bristol, was given the last sacraments, and was told that the chances against my living were strong. Having waited for this for years, I lay back happily against the pillows. It was a relief to know that at last things were promising well.

Deposition

Stoneshed

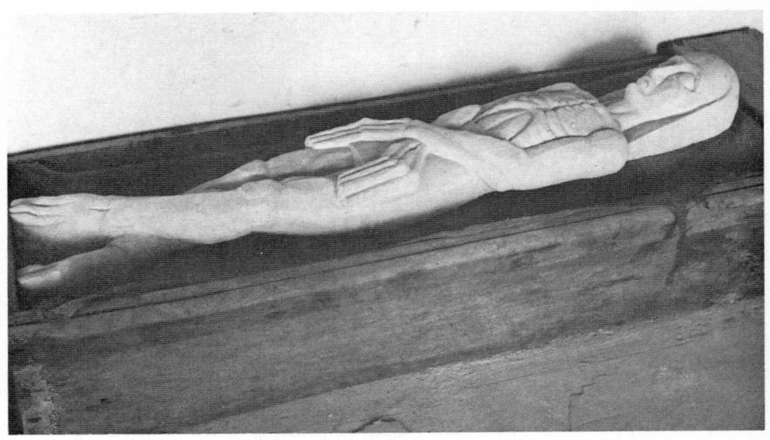

Christ Dead

CHAPTER TEN

The Change

The promise was misleading. I have learned now to hold suspect not only the prophecies of the experts, whether in science or politics or sociology, but also the wistful assurances of my own heart. There was a time when I would say, with no great show of originality, that 'I knew it in my bones'. It seems that my bones can lie. I shall not be caught again. That I did not die was attributed by the nuns to the effects of Extreme Unction, and by the doctor to the psychological relief which came with a knowledge of my condition. All I know is that having let go of life and of everything else, I allowed myself to be carried. So in a sense the nuns and the doctor were both right. The fact that as the days went on I found myself carried farther away from death was a disappointment, but since I could not reverse the direction I accepted it. Admittedly I felt that if on the doctor's showing I had got better because I had thought I was getting worse, I was the victim of a trick. But even if this is the way in which God's purpose has sometimes to be served—through the selfish purposes of men—acceptance is still the appropriate response. I could not now spoil it all by a display of resentment.

It is one of our commonest delusions to imagine that people can be interested in our illnesses, so I must be careful not to go on about this one. For the sake of unity, however, it may be noted that pneumonia 1945, when I was forty, produced the same kind of changes inside me as pneumonia 1915, when I was ten. In each case what I think of as a conversion was not something which I was bringing about but was something which was brought about for me. All I did was to stay still and let myself be turned. On this second occasion I understood of course more clearly that the essence of a conversion is not the turning from but the turning to. So long as I was willing to be released from whatever it was that had held me back until now, I knew that the grace would be there to enable me to take hold of whatever it was that God was offering me. I was willing enough. What I had clung to in the past, my chimeras, had not been so very satisfactory. I had nothing to lose.

They gave me a room to myself on the second floor where I remained from January 10 until March 19. From the bed I could see nothing but the sky and the upper branches of a single tree. In the nine weeks the variations of sky became matter of great interest, and in a fall of snow the tree would take on a new importance. Had I been inclined to loneliness, which I was not, the visitors who came despite the difficulties of wartime transport would have dispelled it. The hospital was run by the same order of nuns as that which managed the smaller establishment at Corston, so I felt I was among friends. Though not allowed to write or say office I was able after the first two weeks or so to organise my day according to a system. Without order in the day I tend to go to bits.

My mother came to see me, looking far more ill than I did, and I had visits also from other members of the family: Yolande of course. Members of the community came over by bus from Downside. George Bellord came twice, stopping the night each time in a Bristol hotel and reading to me from Ronald's translation of the Gospels which had just come out. Lady Acton, bearing messages and food from Aldenham, also came twice. Her hazardous journeys across country in weather which would have deterred Hannibal were made only slightly less uncomfortable by Ronald's wizardry with Bradshaw.

I was brought back to Downside on the feast of St. Joseph to occupy a ground-floor room in the Old House (the school infirmary) from which I was able to follow, through wide windows looking south and east, the changing scene. On the day of my arrival I watched Dom Brendan Lavery, seated high on a motor mower, moving swiftly but irregularly over the grass on the lawn to my right. Next day there was snow, but Dom Brendan disdained it. At times he would all but disappear behind the veil of falling flakes, and the rattle of the machine would come muffled across the lawn, but still he mowed on. Only when a snow-plough would have been needed to clear the course in front of him did Dom Brendan shut off the engine and leave me to meditate upon the virtue of perseverance.

Until the end of July I stayed on in the Old House, enjoying the leisure and comfort with only occasional twinges of guilt. It was a time of gaiety. My brother, who like myself is a member of the Downside community and was taking my place as house-master, came in frequently. Nevile Watts, whom I had known since I was a boy, read Gosse and Conrad to me in the afternoons. Boys drifted in and out at all hours of the day. Jack Carroll, whom I had not seen since the day when he saw me off from Paddington in 1924, sent me one of his characteristic telegrams and walked into the room a few hours later. He had been lunching at the Ritz the day before, and had overheard a conversation between two young officers of the Brigade of Guards in which one of them had mentioned my name, saying that I was ill and was not expected to recover. 'I hate funerals,' he explained, 'so I thought I would get here before they started to toll the bell.' Jack left the same day, and I have not seen him since.

The only interruption to the halcyon weeks of early summer was a fortnight's stay in a hospital on the Somerset coast where I had to have a lung collapsed. Apart from the inconvenience of the operation, the episode was not one to have missed. They warned me before wheeling me down to the theatre (so strangely named) that since my condition ruled out a general anaesthetic I would be able to hear, though not feel, what was going on. I viewed the prospect without exuberance. Sure enough, injection notwithstanding, I heard every word. My head was put under the kind of hood which used to be stretched over bath chairs in wet weather. I could accordingly not see. Through a pleasantly drunken haze I heard: 'Not that one, nurse . . . hold the dish a little closer . . . now the cotton wool.' Then there were some *ping* sounds as the instruments were dropped into a bowl.

The hospital at Weston-super-Mare was exclusively for lung cases, and was supposed to be exclusively for military personnel. It was only by the kindness of the surgeon who was treating me that I got in at all. Since I arrived in pyjamas it was assumed by the other patients that I was one of themselves; as the only civilian in the ward, and a monk at that, I did not always feel entirely at ease. But before long my status got out, and my end of the ward, to which the Catholics seemed to drift, was called the Sunday School. There was a particularly agreeable and popular Pole who used to come and sit on my bed and talk about religion. His name was Vladimir: they called him Vlud. He had tried his vocation as a Jesuit but that had not solved his problem. With a bullet in his chest which had necessitated one operation after another, Vlud was nevertheless able to help in the ward, flirt with the nurses, and entertain me. He died some weeks after I left hospital. I have written about him in a book of essays.

A thing which interested me while I was in the military hospital was the attention paid, both by staff and patients, to class. Not merely to rank, which would be understandable enough in such a setting, but to class. The only ones who did not bother about it were the G.I. soldiers, white and coloured. To the English and French it was a matter of the greatest importance to belong to the right regiments, and I remember how a major of the Sixtieth could call for his shaving water at eight in the morning without exciting the least resentment. The rest of us had washed and breakfasted hours ago. The idea of an egalitarian society had not fully caught on.

Back from this coastal retreat, without having so much as seen the sea, I was kept in bed for another month. I asked if I might say Mass on July 11, the feast of St Benedict, and this, subject to conditions, was granted. The Mass was served by a new friend, Peter Kearon, who said that if he had known it was going to take so long he would have brought a camp stool and some books. Six months had elapsed since I had last said Mass, and my movements creaked. July 11, 1945, marks for me the point of return. I was learning an old life in a new way and on new terms. As I had never quite seen before, I could now see, in the searching glare of a self-knowledge which could not be denied, the inconsistencies of my story. It was brought home to me how I had repeatedly mistaken the unreal for the real, the letter for the spirit. I saw my life as a sequence of blundering false starts, face-saving strategies, swings from worldliness at one extreme to a contrived spirituality at the other. I could have echoed Pound's soliloquy:

Thou art a beaten dog beneath the hail,
A swollen magpie in a fitful sun,
Half black half white
Nor knowst 'ou wing from tail
Pull down thy vanity
How mean thy hates
Fostered in falsity,
Pull down thy vanity
Rather to destroy, niggard in charity,
Pull down thy vanity,
*I say pull down.**

It was clear to me that I used religion to bolster up my confidence. This is not really what religion is for. I had used the Mass for the comfort it provided, for the sense of belonging which I could find nowhere else. I had need to rediscover religion and the Mass. Perhaps this was why for six months I had been debarred from monastic routine and deprived of the Mass. I was to understand religious expression not as something behind which to shelter, on which to rest, in which to find compensation, but as a means of giving worship. With the Mass I must go to God not for my devotion or peace of mind but for his glory. If peace should come along, so much the better. It would then be not so much my peace as his.

'The world would mock,' wrote Aristotle, close to Christian thought, 'if told to cast its cares on Jupiter, for men hold it the function of Jupiter to hurl thunderbolts from the heavens and not to draw men to him in their sorrows.' The difficulty as I saw it now lay in not using God simply as a receiver of human sorrows. I was not afraid of the thunderbolts, because I did not think he was that kind of God. I was afraid much more of the darkness which follows superstition, and it looked as though I had used the fifteen years of my priesthood superstitiously.

A point which has puzzled me, and to which in the nature of the case there can be no satisfactory answer, is how the mind can see the issues and then not follow up its vision. Presumably the difference between the saints and ourselves is that in them the *metanoea* means doing whereas in us it means only experiencing.

* From Canto LXXXI by Ezra Pound.

If there were changes going on inside me, there were changes going on too in the outside world. The war ended, the General Election took place, Churchill was thrown to the wolves. From my bed in the Old House I watched the bonfire which lit up the night of victory celebrations, and from a wheeled chair I listened to the polling results as one after another they fell out of a portable wireless on the lawn.

On the day that the school broke up for the summer holidays I was taken away for an examination which would decide whether or not I would be able to resume housemastering again in September. The examination providing satisfactory, I was told to go away for three weeks before starting to prepare for the coming term. The time in the Old House was over and I did not regret a moment of it. I had written a novel while in bed, and all I had lost was a lung. A permit for extra petrol was asked for and obtained—I was not allowed to travel by train—and Lady Acton came for me on August 6. The drive through smiling country-sides and festive villages, where flags still fluttered in the sun, was memorable. We tried to find the fish-and-chip shop where we had dined five years before on an equally memorable drive through frozen country, but it had disappeared. For the next three weeks I enjoyed at Aldenham a peace which, a year ago, I would not have believed could come my way again.

Each morning Ronald and I served each other's Masses in the Acton chapel which had a beauty all its own. From breakfast to luncheon we worked. The girls of the school were of course away, so we were not disturbed. Lady Acton saw to her pigs, her accounts, her wrangles with the local authority about chemical manure. Ronald and I wrote. We gave ourselves an hour after luncheon for hanging about, and then worked again until tea. After tea we prayed. In the evenings, after dinner, we talked. It was the kind of day one plans but can seldom secure.

While in hospital I had read Hollis's *Death of a Gentleman*, which had come out shortly before, and one night at dinner I said how much I would like to be able to write like Chris.

'You never will,' said Ronald, 'he's a pro.'

'A pro?' Daphne Acton asked.

'He knows how it's done. Belloc is a pro, and so is Evelyn.

Arnold Lunn is very much of a pro, and I like to think that I am too. It's just that Hubert isn't.'

'Is Maurice Baring a pro?' I asked. We were praying for Maurice Baring every day in the chapel so he was much in our thoughts.

'I wouldn't say he was a pro quite,' said Ronald. Then, with his mouth dropping at the sides as it did when he pronounced the thoughtful negative, 'No . . . but you must remember that he has two great advantages over you. He has read everything, and he happens to be a genius.'

'Tell us how Hubert can become a pro, Ronnie,' said Daphne, 'like you.' Daphne always knew when she was on to a good thing, and used to push him along by gently teasing.

'For heaven's sake don't let him try. I can always tell where Hubert has taken a deep breath and tried to write properly, and it's disastrous every time.' Turning to me: 'No, your best bet, Hubert, is to write without trying to.'

He told us that Maurice Baring, my fellow amateur, wrote as though writing a letter and did the minimum in the way of correction. He said that while he, Ronald, had to spend hours making his sentences seem flowing and spontaneous, Baring had no difficulty here at all. The things which held Baring up were whether to use reported or direct speech, whether to say 'one' or 'you', and when to end a chapter and begin a new one. These were not points which exercised Ronald in the least. He told us further that Baring had once asked him to read the manuscript of a novel which he was writing, and which came out eventually under the title *The Coat without Seam*. Ronald understood from Baring that the book was about half way through. He read it and liked it, but the comment he made was to the effect that if the holy coat went on reappearing much more—the theme of the story was that at intervals in Christian history, in times of great crisis, it manifested itself for a time and then got lost again—the repetition would become monotonous and the book would become too long. 'All right,' said Baring, taking the manuscript from Ronald's hands, 'let's stop the reappearances here. There can be one more chapter to wind it up, and the book's finished.'

'That's what I mean about Maurice not being a pro,' Ronald

said, 'because if I had been writing the book I would have been in a sweat months before starting the first page; I would have planned exactly how many reappearances I was going to have; I would have measured the length of each account so that they balanced one another.'

'And also,' said Daphne, 'you wouldn't have listened to anyone who said it was going to be too long.' She turned to me and said: 'Anyway this lets you out, Hubert, because now you don't have to bother any more about how it's done but just go straight on.'

I told them about how Eric Gill had told me, before advising me to drop it altogether, not to allow my carving to be cramped by a formula—either his or anyone else's.

'Well, that's what I mean,' said Ronald, adding with characteristic diffidence, 'though of course I know nothing about sculpture.'

On August 15, a special day for the nuns of the Assumption who were in the other part of the house, Ronald decided to write a short book about the moral and ethical issues raised by the recent destruction of Hiroshima and Nagasaki. He began it the same afternoon, and for the rest of my visit he used to read each evening to Daphne and myself what he had written during the day. It was probably the only rushed writing he ever did. He felt that if it should come out at all, *God and the Atom* should come out soon, while people were having to form their minds about atomic warfare, and though he wrote at speed on a subject which lay outside the field of his normal work, the book is in its way a classic. Each evening he would ask for comments, and though we doubted if he would alter a line whatever we said we did our best to put forward intelligent criticisms. Once or twice Princess Rospigliosi, who had moved out of the house and had taken a cottage in the village, joined us for these readings. Though her presence made it more amusing for the two listeners, and though she found no fault with what was read, the alteration of the original number made Ronald feel uneasy. He had planned for a symposium of three. That the book when it was published bore my name on the page of dedication was, as may be guessed, a gratifying reminder of the Aldenham readings.

The bomb was of course the current topic of discussion in the papers and on the wireless. I asked Ronald if he ever listened to the Brains Trust, a panel which seemed to me to have interesting ideas about the bomb as about everything else. He answered: 'Huxley is Joad, and Joad is Huxley. That's all ye know, and all ye need to know.'

Either on the occasion of this or an earlier visit some proofs arrived for me to correct. It was a book of prayers for girls, and Ronald was pleased to learn that two of his own flock at Aldenham had asked me to write it. 'I hope you will put in a prayer which you seem to have left out of the book you did for boys,' he said. When I asked what prayer, he said: 'A prayer of thanksgiving when someone who has written to say he's coming to see you sends you a telegram at the last minute calling it off.'

On August 28, my holiday over, Daphne Acton drove me back to Downside. The sun shone so we had our picnic on the grass. I did not know it but this was to be the last of these drives for I went only once more to stay at Aldenham and on that occasion travelled by train. The end of the war brought about almost as many changes as its outbreak had done. The nuns stopped on, with now nearly sixty girls and four on the lay staff, until Easter of the following year. Lord Acton, back from the army, found post-war farming an uphill and frustrating labour. He sold the property to Daphne's father, Lord Rayleigh, and took his family to Southern Rhodesia where they are now living. The chapel was closed, and Ronald moved to Mells where Mrs Raymond Asquith had invited him to stay for as long as he liked. He stayed for nearly ten years, until the day of his death, August 24, 1957.

So back I went to the new term full of new resolutions. But one cannot, at least I cannot, live on resolutions alone. The year which followed was the kind of indeterminate year which is known in retrospect to have been unsatisfactory but which cannot be put in any one unsatisfactory pigeon-hole. I kept a diary, but I cannot find anything worth using from it. The house which I was supposed to be running more or less ran itself. The teaching, writing, retreat-giving went on, but that is about all that can be said about them. The boys did not irritate me or get under my feet, but they made me realise I was an ageing schoolmaster. I was not giving them much. Beyond telling them not to say 'after you' and 'don't mind me', not to write 'last' when they meant 'past', and not to carry a comb in their pockets, I showed them little of the way in which to face life. Whenever one of their relatives died I helped them to compose their letters of condolence; when they left their tortoises and goldfish with me for the holidays I fed the brutes; when one of them in a moment of jubilation kissed a maid in the refectory I smoothed things over in official quarters. But I did not have to be a Benedictine monk to do these things: they were the common run of the housemaster in any public school.

Throughout the school year I felt disconnected, like the loose flex of a lamp, and wanted to get back into a settled monastic routine. So when in the summer holidays of 1946 the newly appointed Head Master, Dom Wilfrid Passmore, telephoned me one evening while I was giving a retreat at Grayshott, and told me he would like me to hand over my duties to someone else, I was neither surprised nor disappointed. I knew I had not been a good housemaster, and I knew that others knew it too. Though it meant adding another to the list of failures I was not in the least sorry for myself—any more than I had been sorry for myself after the earlier ones—because if left to myself I would have brought my term of office to an end long ago. Looking back along the way at the signposts of defeat, I could trace without cynicism a course which was like the uncertain silver trail left behind on the bark of a tree by a snail which has failed to make the ascent; and I wondered what was coming next.

During the four or five months which followed I occupied myself with sculpture, writing, digging every afternoon in the kitchen garden. They were restless months, however, for I was still not plugged in. When there is nothing on the agenda to happen, the tendency is to fear that something might. In January 1947 Dom Romuald Alexander, chaplain at St Mary's Abbey, Talacre, in North Wales fell ill and I was sent to take his place for a few weeks. I stayed for nearly three years.

CHAPTER ELEVEN

The Second Dawn

I arrived at Talacre on January 20 in a blizzard. 'In January,' one of the nuns told me, 'it is nearly always like this.' Next month another nun said that the sleet which we were getting every day was a feature of the Welsh February. March, I was told when the time came, was known to be the coldest and wettest month in the year. When July poured down upon us I was assured that 'it is hardly ever as bad as this'. Experience of four subsequent summers at Talacre (where I am writing these lines in May during a hailstorm) leads me to believe that heat in this part of Wales is like jam for tea in *Alice*.

Hitherto my contacts with convents had been restricted to retreats: now, when it became clear that Dom Romuald would not return, I must adapt myself more radically. But the nuns proved so accommodating, and the timetable was so much in line with my own inclination, that there was very little adapting to be done. The community at Talacre is enclosed, has no school, supports itself almost entirely by the work of its hands, and devotes itself to the contemplative life. The liturgy is carried out with care, religious poverty is interpreted strictly, silence is emphasised and faithfully kept. Not everybody likes this sort of thing, but I do. Living only on the fringe of such a Benedictine community, as I was in the capacity of chaplain, afforded me ample opportunity of developing certain aspects of St Benedict's Rule which for practical reasons I had found difficult to develop before. While it is true that for the chaplain to a Benedictine convent there can be neither participation in the Divine Office in choir nor any semblance of the common life, it is just as true that nothing need prevent him from ordering his life according to the day-to-day observances in the monastery. This challenge I found to be stimulating, so made it my business to attend the

Divine Office from the extern chapel and to rule my occupations throughout the day by the convent bells. The holy Rule provided my reading at the midday meal, the martyrology at supper. Since I was able to get to bed by nine there was no difficulty about getting up at four, and since there were no demands to be met from outside I was able to study and write in the mornings, walk and dig in the afternoons.

I had been warned at Downside before coming that the chaplain's lodgings were so cold that approaching them along the concrete path you felt an icy blast coming at you through the letter-flap of the front door. Forebodings proved justified, but I had endured worse among the Carthusians and refused to look upon the prevailing temperature in the priest's quarters as anything more than a temporary bedevilment sent to try the soul. Once I had got the house and myself into a state of steady furnace heat, which is the only kind of atmosphere I can live in and which I am glad to say I maintained from January 1947 until June 1949, I could afford to look round and envisage the possibilities which my new life offered.

Priests who have come on supply are prone to complain that there is nobody to talk to at Talacre and nothing to see. Admittedly if you want conversation you have to go out for it. If you want something more to look at than the chapel and the outdoor shrine of our Lady of Lourdes you have to leave the grounds and climb a hill. From the hill you can get a view of fields, a railway line, caravans, huts, sand dunes, and finally the sea. It is my good fortune that I can manage on little conversation and no views. When conversation comes my way I gladly take part in it, but if during my nine years in Egypt I did not ask to see the pyramids, I can go quite as long in Wales without asking to see Snowdon. If today, while stationed at Talacre for the third time, I am taken for a drive I am not indifferent to the scenery. But I do not ask to go again. This digression is introduced in order to sustain the contention that most places are bearable to me, even when there are no people about and no objects of interest to look at, provided I do not very much want to be somewhere else. During this first period of residence at Talacre I did not very much want to be somewhere else.

A detail connected with the Talacre scene which I noticed on the first morning of my stay, and one moreover which I did not have to climb a hill to see, was a thick metal plate screwed to the bars of the gate at the entrance to the drive. In raised letters the notice proclaimed 'Private', a reminder to which few would take exception. It was distinctive only because at some time in the past the gate had been reversed, so that the notice now faced inwards and along the drive towards the convent. So placed, the notice carried a more forceful implication than it had carried before, suggesting that those inside the convent bounds must be careful not to trespass or intrude upon the privacy of the rest of Wales and of the outside world generally. To any who feel as I do about the preservation of the unexpected it may be of interest to add that the notice is in the same position today, seventeen years later.

Solitary study after the bustle of work in the school might have turned out badly: I might have been bored stiff. I was accordingly glad to find how much the writings of the mystics, the commentaries on the Rule, the history of monasticism still appealed. The difficulty was getting hold of them. Since there were no books in the house except the Catholic Directory and some poetical works of Father Faber, and since the public library in Prestatyn did not promise to deliver within a month, I had to borrow from Downside. It took time but was worth it. I trudged along with the Fathers, romped through the counter-Reformation with Mabillion and de Rancé, took wing with the Flemish mystics.

Besides books I sent for chisels and mallet, files and a saw. But after defacing some rocks in the neighbourhood I gave up carving: not only was the local stone too hard but however apparently deserted the site, people would spring out of the ground and watch. So in a triangle of garden not much bigger than that which goes with the Carthusian cell I toiled and was content. I still think there is no substitute in a monk's life for manual labour of some kind, and each time I come back to it after a period of other work, illness, or laziness, I am more convinced of this. Well, I told myself, at last I had found the formula. In point of fact I had not.

Designs for living are not tabled, as motions are tabled before a committee, but are found to have emerged. Rarely does someone come upon the blueprint which is to determine the nature of his life. Still more rarely would such a blueprint be one which he has himself prepared. More often a person finds that by an instinctive and not very clear process of the mind, by a system of selection from a pool of experiences, by what seem to be fortuitous influences from without, a principle has gradually evolved which narrows itself down to a few key tenets. Or even just to a single idea. It is like the pin-pointing of sunlight through the lens of a magnifying-glass: you could not do it without the glass, but neither could you do it without the sun. Or a better simile would be the kind of trick photography which presents on the screen a design of great complexity and then so simplifies it as to leave in the end only a single dot in the centre of the space. Everything else is seen to fall back into the distance and fade away; nothing but the essential remains to stand clear in the foreground. Unless the pattern to which this final presentation belongs had been shown in the first instance, the essence which is now seen on its own would not be understood. The pattern's function is to reveal the essence, and once the essential significance is appreciated there is no longer any need for the design as it appeared originally.

This is always happening in religious life, and I suppose in other ways of life as well. The elaborate design reduces itself to a simple concept, to a point of focus. This is not necessarily because the original composition is found to be unworkable or unattractive, but because it is found to be unnecessary. What is often forgotten is that without the multiple structure to begin with there would be no appreciation of the final simplicity. There would be nothing to construct.

So when I imagined at Talacre that I had discovered for myself the scheme of religious living best suited to my particular spirit, I was really doing no more than what I had been doing all along: I was scratching yet another surface. I was re-arranging the composition upon which I had been engaged since my clothing retreat in 1924. So by the time I left Talacre in 1949 it was clear to me that my pious practices, my mapped-out day, my rigid frame, my elaborately simple life, my readings and examinations and so on were not as important as I had thought. All I had done was to push forms and symbols about on the board. But out of the experience was emerging what I like to think was a more unified and simplified outlook. The vehicles of what had been formulated and symbolised were receding. Like the design on the television screen, the original pattern had to be kept in reserve, ready to be brought to the front in support of the significant feature which is always in danger of getting overlooked, but it had to be kept subordinate. It must not be allowed to swallow up the significant feature. The significant feature of religion is love, and when this is drawn to the front by God—and it cannot be drawn without him—everything else can take second place. If there can be a formula, this is it. When the formula has emerged, evoked by the grace of God, you find you have known it all along.

A truth which is known all along is not necessarily understood, not necessarily applied logically. Appreciation of reality does not always guarantee continuance at the level of reality. I had invented no new formula; I had merely discovered new meaning to one which had been staring me in the face. How it was to be applied I had no idea: I knew only that the applications I had made before were the wrong ones. Truth had been coming to me in glimpses all my life, but I had never co-ordinated the glimpses. I had been so busy card-indexing the aspects of truth which I had glimpsed that I had not related them to living. The filing-cabinet was there, but I was constantly losing the key. My mistaken approaches had been pointed out to me as mistaken by Father Bede, Father John Talbot, Abbot Trafford, and Ronald Knox. They were sympathetic, sorry to see me going about my vocation the wrong way, but what they said made no difference. Not until the light of reality is brought to bear upon the single scorching point of the soul, brought there through the lens which sees everything and spares nothing, can some people fully understand what is going on.

So described, the process may convey the idea of a sudden illumination. There must be many to whom truth dawns in such a way. No sudden transport took hold of me. What lessons I learned came imperceptibly over the years when I was at Talacre. And even then I forgot them. It is one of the strange things—to go back to the television simile—about watching the design simplify itself until it compasses the essential in a dot that the vision so easily fades. The shrinking outlines become blurred, the presentation wobbles, the central and all-important object becomes so small that it cannot be seen, the square of light narrows on the darkened screen. Then there is a blank, and life goes on very much as it did before.

In 1948, when I was well into the second year of my time at Talacre, news reached me of my mother's sudden death. She had had a heart attack, and the whole thing was over in twenty minutes. That she was spared a long illness was a relief to me, but I felt the loss all the more because there had been no time for explanations. It was my father's death over again: I had missed my chance of showing gratitude. Both my parents had given me everything that was theirs to give, and I could point to nothing that I had given in return. I had excused myself while they were living by pretending that had they shown their affection differently I would have responded more. But this was a too easy way out, and I doubt if I really believed it. When they were both dead there was less room for self-deception. My mother's Requiem and funeral were carried out in the greatest simplicity by my brother and myself. He and I had often heard her say how much she disliked 'all this middle-class preoccupation with the extras of death' so we were glad that we could keep the *pompes funèbres* down to the minimum.

Berthe died in the same year. But this time the *pompes funèbres* abounded. My holy old aunt was buried at the mother house of the order which had sheltered her for the last years of her life, the procession to the nuns' cemetery consisting of several religious communities, the children of the orphanage, and a ragged line of laity of different denominations and classes. 'Goodness,' said Yolande, 'I'm sure there won't be such a lot of funny people at mine.'

In case I am giving the impression that the Talacre interlude was divided between wrestling with the spirit and mourning the losses in my family I must add that there were diversions. For instance George Bellord came for a few days, taking me for walks deep in the heart of Flintshire. On one of these walks we came upon a cottage, grey and depressed, which bore in a front window a placard reading: 'Madame Zarima. Fortunes told from October to March. Five shillings per séance; or course by request.' George's visit was shortly after Easter so we had missed Madame Zarima by a fortnight. George, who said he had never met a Welsh witch, promised to come back in October. The cottage was miles from anywhere. What sort of custom do Welsh witches hope to attract during the winter months?

'And where do you suppose Madame Zarima is during the summer?' I asked George.

'Epsom,' said George.

Another visitor to Talacre was my brother, who said in answer to Beryl Fitzherbert when she asked him what he had been praying about for so long in the chapel: 'that I may never be sent here.' Yolande spent a week in some rooms near by which were let by some people who wanted to teach her esperanto. 'Imagine, darling,' said Yolande, 'esperanto . . . me.'

Ronald came twice to my Welsh retreat: once for the day from Chester where he was preaching, and the second time for longer. He said it was because the trains to Talacre called for the kind of mental exercise he enjoyed. He showed no longing for the sea, for the hills, for the road, or even to have his fortune told, so we sat all day by a roaring fire and went through his manuscript of *Enthusiasm* which by then was nearly finished. *Enthusiasm* was to Ronald what *The Holy Rule* was to me: a work for which notes were for ever stacking up and one which could be added to in intervals.

Besides my own friends there would sometimes be priests who were guests of the convent. One such was a Jesuit from Ireland, a bluff but kindly man, to whom the contemplative life made no appeal. 'Now what you should do with so much time on your hands,' he said, 'is write a book.'

New friends were not wanting. I got to know a family of five children whom I used to see playing ball in the lane. Their father was a postman, a Mr Coffey. In the village the children were known as the Koffee Kids. The family was not Catholic, but this made no difference. The Coffeys had migrated to Wales from London during the war, and, despite the Welsh names given to the two children born since the migration, had retained the flavour of the south. The two elder girls, witnessing to the influence of the time, were called Shirley and Marlene, aged thirteen and eleven respectively; then came John, ordinary enough, aged nine; another little girl, Glynis, aged seven; lastly Towyn, a boy, nearly six. It was in honour of Towyn's sixth birthday that I took the Koffee Kids to an early but comprehensive tea in Prestatyn, and then to a film in which Mr Niven was playing Bonnie Prince Charlie. The tea went on for so long that we were late, and, with little help from the young woman who held a torch and took our tickets, had to grope our way past unsmiling knees. 'Ruddy battery run out, Miss?' asked Shirley, in whom the idiom of London was still strong. Our first misfortune was when Glynis, tiring of Mr Niven, who was miscast anyway, crawled under the seats and for a time was lost to us. This put us in the wrong as regards the lady with the torch (must I use the word 'usherette'?). We were put farther in the wrong at the stage in the film where Charles Edward was nearing his homeland in a little boat. There, bobbing up and down on the waters of Eriskay, were brave men with red hair on their arms. Towyn had eaten more than was good for him at his birthday tea, and the sight of heaving seas did the rest. As the boat grated on the pebbly beach and a dapper Pretender splashed briskly ashore, Towyn put his head on my knee and was sick over my legs. I took the little boy to the back of the cinema, but as he was more interested in Mr Niven's than his own plight, we had to do what we could on the spot with handkerchiefs. The girl with the torch leaned against the wall and was no help. The mishap had not increased our standing. So when during one of the battle scenes I came back a second time, now with Marlene and Glynis, and asked if she would be so good as to show my friends to the ladies' lavatory I received disagreeable looks. It was a long film, but the children wanted to stay on for the cartoon, the trailer of next week's big attraction, the advertisements for furniture and plastic suitcases, even for the opening scenes which we had missed of the highland epic. I felt at the end of it that, compared with the afternoon's exertions, Prestonpans and Culloden were child's-play. On the way home in the bus, Shirley leaned over to me and said very sweetly: 'Our Towyn ain't half a God-help-us doing what he done to your poor pants.' It was an appraisal in which I concurred.

Another household to which I had free entry was that of an elderly couple, a Mr and Mrs Brooke-Stevens. They were Catholic, poor, childless, rather eccentric. They lived in two rooms on the ground floor of a farm high up on the hill behind the Abbey. They asked me, after I had been calling on them for a year, to call them by their Christian names, Willie and Agnes. In the cold winter of 1948 Willie had to spend longer days in bed, and once when Agnes was out of the room he told me he thought he would not live until the summer. 'I want you to be here when I go,' he said, 'and you must see that Agnes is provided for out of the estate. She has not had much of a life, you know.' I looked at the papers which told of the 'estate', and judged that twenty pounds would cover it. It had not been much of a life for him either.

In early March I got back from a retreat which I was giving to the Cistercian community at Nunraw in Scotland to find Willie dying. After the funeral I did my best to attend to his second wish. With her pension, with the 'realisation of the estate', and with something scraped together by Willie's relatives, Agnes was soon established at St Joseph's Home, Wrexham, where I visited her at intervals until she too died.

In June of 1949 the first of my Talacre chaplaincies came to an end, and I was transferred to the chaplaincy of the Oratory School, Reading, where I remained for four school terms. Father (later Monsignor) Tomlinson was then Head Master. He had been given the uphill task of raising the dwindling numbers and declining academic level to what they had been in the days of the Oratory's prime. He managed it, deserving more thanks than he received. I know that I for one did not appreciate the work he was doing, and this is as good a place as any to say so. I know too that he proved a better friend to me than I to him, a fact which again I acknowledge here.

Being chaplain at the Oratory meant being a schoolmaster again, with all the old dreads of taking class. It induced a state of bemused vacuity in which I continued for the fifteen months that I was there. I missed the quiet of Talacre, the Divine Office, the daily sung Mass. I missed our Towyn and his brother and sisters. But against this I made many friends among the boys at the Oratory, and quite a number too in the schools, both of boys and girls, to which I was giving retreats. Young people are always a joy to me provided I have no authority over them. In addition there were some local children who came to be prepared for the sacraments. Among these, two little girls who came from opposite ends of the village, and whose respective parents were not on speaking terms, stood out for their intelligence and looks. They each bore the name of Kathleen, and one was dark (Black Kathleen), the other fair (White Kathleen). When I left they both cried. I still hear regularly from Black Kathleen.

The Oratory masters at that time were easier to draw than any I have come across on the six school staffs with which at one time or another I have served. But apart from acting as subjects for the caricaturist, the masters were an agreeable lot and with several of them I kept up correspondences long after I had returned to Downside. To Mr Headlam* particularly—'Bones' as he was known to generations of Oratory boys—I owed much in the way of relief from the more professional side of my job. Distinguished, tall, shy, wise, a lover of music, possessed of a wit which was all the more telling because he rarely smiled, Bones embodied all that most of us would want to be (or want to be thought) at the age of seventy. Years before, when I was still at school, and when Downside and the Oratory attended the same O.T.C. camps in the summer, I had admired old Bones from a distance. Though commanding the Oratory contingent, he was old even then. Among us he was not known as Bones, but, because of his long thin body and long thin neck, as the Pull-through. His air of aloof indifference to everything and everyone made a great impression, and now again, nearly thirty years later, I found myself admiring the same detachment. With a feeling for clothes as well as for words, Bones more than anyone else I know suggested style. At the Oratory when well into his seventies he would be seen loping with dignity through the wood in all weathers towards the chapel, a sheaf of organ music under his arm, and always perfectly dressed. I have only two regrets regarding my association with Bones: first that I did not keep his letters,

* Gerald Erskine Headlam. Born October 21, 1877. Died June 15, 1954. A convert to Catholicism, he served successively at Edgbaston, Caversham, and Woodcote on the staff of the Oratory School, of which for a time he was Head Master. A good account, impressionist and anecdotal, of his Oratory career can be found in the *Oratory School Magazine*; No. 3; 1955.

each one a model of concise literary elegance and very funny; second that I did not draw him more often.

A break in the sequence of school terms and holidays occurred when Dom Gregory Murray and I travelled in mid-winter at the request of the Abbot President to Ampleforth in order to discuss a minor matter connected with the Congregation. There was snow a foot deep on the moor when we arrived, and it snowed steadily throughout our short visit. This was before the new guest quarters had been equipped with central heating. Only on one other occasion in my life have I slept the night through wearing a hat. We were shown the greatest hospitality, and I remember with what edification we noted the number of voluntary servers who came up from the school for the early series of Masses. We would have liked to prolong this enjoyable stay, particularly since we were both in high holiday spirits, but there were other things waiting for us. When later I told my brother about the hat, I found him deeply shocked to learn that a member of his family—of *his* family, if you please—should have so lost caste.

One of the things which awaited me on my return to the daily round, but quite unconnected with the trip just mentioned, was pneumonia. It was a timely intervention, for I was feeling at the Oratory the absence of the Divine Office and silence. It was the third time in my life that pneumonia had rescued me. Knowing how easy it is for a monk to become submerged in mundane affairs, I was glad to get back to the monastery. Though I did not on this occasion receive the last rites, I heard once again the now familiar warning against doing more work than would be assigned to a child in kindergarten, against getting up early, against catching chills.

While convalescing at Downside I was able during Holy Week to see something of Evelyn Waugh—who I think was still Mr Waugh to me at that period—and to hear about a recent visit of his to the United States. He suggested that I might like to try out my retreats in America for a change. The same evening I put the idea to the Abbot (now Dom Christopher Butler in succession to Abbot Trafford of the war years) and was somewhat surprised to find that it met with his warm approval. Shortly after this I received a letter from a Mr Hugh Garvey, Secretary of the

Campion Society, Springfield, Illinois, telling me he had received from Mr Waugh an assurance of my willingness to give a retreat to a group of Benedictine oblates and others in Springfield or some neighbouring city. He added that Mr Waugh had himself addressed a Springfield audience the year before and had apparently survived. In conclusion he said that if I accepted the offer he would be glad to meet me in New York at any date convenient to myself, that I could proceed thence to the Midwest by either rail, car, or plane, and that all expenses would be paid whichever I chose. There followed between Mr Garvey and myself an unusual correspondence, the writer at each end trying to form some sort of picture of the other. I was puzzled by this Mr Garvey. He seemed to be speaking the argot of the executive, of the tycoon even, yet with a gentle mockery. Fluency, efficiency, courtesy—they were all there—but I had the feeling that someone was being teased. Since it could not conceivably be Mr Waugh who was being teased—I dismissed that idea instantly—it must be myself.

'What's this chap Garvey like?' I put it to Evelyn the next time we met.

'American,' was the answer, 'he can't help it.'

Ronald was by this time only a few miles from Downside, living at Mells with the Asquiths, and when I went over to see him I told him of the American project. He was not encouraging.

'You'll hate it,' he said, 'they have meals out of heated cardboard boxes, and put cellophane covers on their hats when it rains. Why go? Evelyn put the thing to me, but I wouldn't look at it. He's probably asked D'Arcy as well. You must be last on his list.'

Father D'Arcy had not, it turned out, been asked. I explained to Ronald why I thought it might be a good idea. I was forty-five; I had performed the few tricks I knew and was getting stale. The retreats I was giving were becoming repetitive, the statues I was carving were the same statues over again but with different titles. My twenty-third book was about to come out, but it had nothing new to say. Perhaps three weeks in a new environment, I said, would fill me with fresh ideas.

'I suppose so,' said Ronald, drooping, 'but America's not my idea of fun. Besides I *loathe* fresh ideas . . . other people's, anyway.'

To complete my convalescence, though I was now back to my normal routine the warnings notwithstanding, George Bellord took me in a car, together with two of his children, to France and Spain. I had not been to France since before the War—when I had been, in 1938 and again with George, to Lourdes—and had persuaded myself that I did not care for the French. It was Vichy. But ten days in France, under the scorching sun, cured me of that. After a dutiful but rapturous look at the châteaux of the Loire, we stopped with some friends of George's in whose private chapel I was able to say Mass. We spent a night at one of the loveliest of all medieval shrines, Rocamadour in the Dordogne. To kneel where St Bernard, St Dominic, kings of England and France, pilgrims from all over Europe have knelt—specifically on a stone floor in front of a small weathered Madonna—is not something to be forgotten. From Rocamadour to Lourdes and the Pyrenees. Lourdes with its memories of pre-war pilgrimages was almost too painful: so many of those who had come with us before were dead. If Lourdes can hurt, and in one way or another it hurts every time, it cannot disappoint. There were the crowds, the processions, the rumble of recited rosaries at the baths, the roared responses during the litanies, and, more impressive still, the silence at the grotto. There was the authentic smell, evocative throughout France but found in its quintessence at Lourdes, which is an amalgam of coffee, new bread, fried onions, benzine, French tobacco, drains, incense, wax, sweat, inexpensive soap.

From Lourdes, we went by way of Roncevalles, to Spain. Against all calculation we found Spain less exciting than France, so came back by another way. The Bellords wanted to linger in France so I left them for England: my leave of absence was running out. Ten days later I took off again, bound for America. I had a feeling in the plane that this Midwest venture—two weeks in the Springfield area and one in the East on the way back—would be significant. My feeling proved correct.

The mysterious Mr Garvey, who could not help being an American, met me at Idlewild. In spite of the ten years that separated us in age, he being thirty-five and looking younger, we got on instantly. He took me to his brother-in-law's flat in New York where we spent the night, and next morning served my Mass. We picked up Robert Fitzgerald, the poet and translator of the Greek classics, who was to make the retreat, and started on the three-day journey by car which was to take us—Springfield being exactly central—half across America. We stopped one night at an hotel, one night at the home of Hugh Garvey's parents, and late on the third night we arrived at Springfield.

Here I must be careful to avoid overstating the effect which America had upon me. M. Maritain has written a book called *Impressions of America* for which he has been criticised. He has lost his head, the critics complained, as well as his heart; the book is a love story; M. Maritain has seen only one side; M. Maritain is such a simple kindhearted man that he would probably, if he went there, write the same kind of book about Russia. The critics can say what they like, but so far as I am concerned it is of all M. Maritain's books—of all, that is, which I can understand—the one which I would most like to have written myself.

The effect produced by this first short tour may be explained by an analogy drawn from the photographer's darkroom. Before I had been in the country a week, meeting first Hugh Garvey's family (his parents and younger sister at Sharon, Pennsylvania, his wife and children at home in Illinois) and then the retreatants who in turn introduced me to their families, I felt as a roll of film might feel which has been used for its proper purpose but has been lying, undeveloped, in the back of the camera. Once put in the tank of developer and acted upon by the right chemicals, the film is on its way to fulfilment. Whether over-exposed or under-exposed, whether showing the object tipped crooked or out of focus, the strip of celluloid does not have to worry. As a setting, the darkroom gives scarcely more light to see what is going on than did the setting of the camera's interior, but the immediate setting is the dish in which it floats rather than the darkroom which produces no direct effect. The negative will in the course of things become a positive. The final print, in spite of the flaws, will represent the purpose of the operation. The ontogenesis or 'becoming what it essentially is' will have taken place. America was for me the ontogenesis.

Though it amounted to a liberation, an awakening, this was again no supernatural illumination. The way in which a negative becomes a positive is not phenomenal. The combination which opens a safe is not a thing of magic but simply a matter of getting the weights rightly placed. The new awareness which came to me was a matter of placing. Hitherto I had known no place, I had been psychologically a nomad. I might even now be camping in tents, but at least I knew I was in the right desert.

Why anyone should feel perfectly at home in a foreign country after a few days and not at all in his own after many years I shall not attempt to explain here. I think that the sense of belonging which can come when objectively one does not belong does in fact admit of explanation. But another book would be needed to give it. All that need be said in this one is that America woke me up. I made no deliberate attempt to like the country. If anything I had been prepared rather to dislike it. Americans did not understand half of what I said but this did not matter. What mattered was that they came out to meet me more than half way. I found that I was instinctively collaborating, compassionating, congratulating—these are words which St Paul uses when speaking of the individual's relationship with Christ and his faithful—and that this produced an affinity. In the affinities rather than in the geographical settings I found that which I had long ago ceased to expect from this life. The aloneness which had been part of me for years (I avoid the term 'loneliness' because for much of the time I had not been lonely, and also because it has a self-pitying sound) had not prepared me for the experience of becoming part of other people's existence and of their becoming part of mine. With successive visits this interchange developed over the years, so that I have come to see my particular apostolate as directed more towards America than anywhere else.

The retreat which I had been brought across the Atlantic to give took place in great heat at the Benedictine Abbey of St Bede, Peoria. Since many of the retreatants were Benedictine oblates, St Bede's was the right place for it. We attended the Divine Office and were looked after by the monks. Half way through I discarded the notes which I had so carefully prepared in England, and spoke freely on the points raised in interviews. Towards the end I was asked to give a talk on the Benedictine life and its relevance at the present day. This meeting turned into the equivalent of a press conference and lasted nearly two hours. When the retreat was over I was driven to Chicago so that some of the men who had been at St Bede's might introduce me to their families. In a private room at the Lake Shore, after a large luncheon, I was asked to give a discourse about our Lady. The request surprised but did not embarrass me. Had the same request been made at the Dorchester, I would have felt foolish talking about our Lady across the coffee cups and crumpled napkins in an atmosphere of cigar-smoke and Chanel. I doubt if the request would have been made at the Dorchester. The Chicago connections led to further preaching engagements, so that by the time I got back to New York I had covered a fairly wide range.

Since frequent mention is made of retreats, an amplification may be called for. Preached retreats are a cross between a revivalist mission and a course of lectures. If they lack the intensity and emotionalism of the mission, they lack also the academic quality of the lecture course. The retreat is designed to stir the intellect and the will rather than the warmer sentiments, but essentially it aims at eliciting the *metanoea* or giving of self. Retreats may last from three to eight days, and there may be as many as five discourses a day. Between the discourses the retreatants are supposed to observe silence, practise mental prayer, and give themselves to spiritual reading and various devotional exercises. From the point of view of the retreat-giver there is stimulus in adjusting to new audiences, new environments, new needs. I have now given nearly three hundred retreats in my thirty years at the job, and I have found no two to be alike. Some have been a great joy to me, some have occasioned fruitful correspondences and friendships, some have fallen completely flat. From the point of view of the retreatant there are corresponding hazards and compensations.

Where a pulpit orator addresses a larger congregation, and consequently tends to preach a more formal sermon, the retreat-giver may well have to equip himself with a wider range of subjects for his more intimate talks. He is speaking now to monks, now to nuns, now to school children and now to diocesan clergy. A recent development has been the retreat to engaged couples and to husbands and wives. Reviewing my own association with the work I feel pretty sure, and I say this without the least fear of false humility, that I have derived from retreatants more benefit than they have from me. And certainly a lot more fun.

The week before flying to England was spent at the Sacred Heart Convent, Greenwich, where I spoke twice each evening: once to the nuns and once to the girls. With Greenwich as the centre, my preaching activities fanned out to other Sacred Heart houses and to the Benedictine community at Bethlehem, Connecticut. It was not easy, when the time came, to leave behind so many contacts and so much affection. The verse from the psalms which for years now had been the theme of my prayer, *spiritus tuus bonus deducet me in terram rectam*, had been verified. All along I should have trusted more that it would be. My mistake each time had been to think I could hack my way through the jungle to get to the 'right land'. So long as I felt I was following a hard course I imagined the explorer's reward would be granted. Had I trusted more to 'God's good spirit' and less to toughness, I would have found what I was looking for. In future, I told myself as I boarded the plane, I would do well to leave both planning and fulfilment in God's hands. To arrive at such an elementary conclusion may not seem much. Yet failing such a conclusion there is little value to anything that is done.

What with invitations from my recent hosts and hostesses, what with prophecies on all sides and the assurances of prayers, I felt confident that without pressure from me the *spiritus bonus* would bring me back one day and perhaps for good. On the flight from New York to London the heating in the plane broke down, and although I did not on that occasion wear my hat through that long night, I had not been so cold since the visit with Dom Gregory to Ampleforth the year before.

On the impulse provided by the American experience I plunged with zest into the old occupations which had served me well in the monastery. The hopes expressed to Ronald before my departure were justified, and I started writing jollier books, carving less stereotyped statues, preaching less stuffy retreats. America had effected a catharsis which was long overdue, and I was able to work in a lighthearted spirit and without having to drive myself on the one hand or use work as an escape on the other. Having now no duties in the school I was able to spend longer in the cabbage fields and grubbing about with the roots of trees. Seeing me one day as I strode out in my big boots, my patched habit, a pick on one shoulder and a spade on another, a member of the community who has a gift for the neat phrase stood still and slowly nodded. 'Well, my dear Father Hubert, if there were more people like you in this community,' he said, 'there would be fewer people like me.' Happier relations prevailed everywhere, at home and abroad, and when in the following year the jollier books started coming out (two of them about Downside) I was told how much more normal I had become and how pleased people were. Why had I not thought of writing jolly books before? It was nice not to be thought a fanatic any more. Ronald noticed but made no comment. It would have pleased Father John Talbot had he lived to see the change in me, for he had repeatedly told me that 'this monastic thing of yours, you know, is really all bosh'. America was teaching me a new formula.

Hugh Garvey meanwhile, without prompting from me though with my blessing, wrote to the Abbot asking if I might give another retreat some time, and proposing that I make a longer stay. The Abbot agreed to this at once, so in September 1951 the second and more ambitious mission got under way. In addition to the Campion Society retreat, which remained the constant among the variegated engagements of all my American tours, I was down for visits to Benedictine, Cenacle, Sacred Heart, and Franciscan houses. When I got there I found myself agreeing to give three short retreats to the clergy of scattered dioceses, and being called upon to give unprepared discourses at unlikely places to non-denominational audiences. With each of my six visits to America between 1950 and 1963 the field was enlarged, but since I do not mean to turn this into a travel book I shall give the names of places and people only where the narrative seems to demand them.

This second tour differed from the rest in that it gave rise to a project which, even though it never came to anything, engaged the interests of others as well as of myself to an extent which warrants mention. It may be remembered that at St Bede's I had spoken and answered questions about the Benedictine ideal, and whether or not it was a practical one in the contemporary scene. The proposal now came from some who had attended this meeting that a Benedictine community be founded in America along the lines discussed the year before. It was suggested that a house of this kind would soon be able to support itself, and that a need existed in America for just such a foundation to which laymen could come for direction and retreats. As a primary condition it was insisted that no responsibilities outside the enclosure might be undertaken: the community would devote itself exclusively to the liturgy, manual labour, study, attention to guests. To me was entrusted the job of laying the scheme before the Abbot and community at Downside. In a memorandum which was to be laid before the chapter it was stated that Bishop Bennet of Lafayette was anxious to have a foundation of this kind in his diocese, that a property had been offered, that two or three young men were proposing themselves as postulants, and that financial security would be guaranteed over the first five years. To me, as may be guessed, the idea appealed greatly. It seemed to incorporate everything I had been searching for since novitiate days. I came back from America in a state of elation. Approaching the front door of the monastery I read as if for the first time the text carved in stone over the central arch: *Dominus custodiat introitum tuum et exitum tuum*. I had had my share of both coming in and going forth, and it was comforting to know that the Lord had been watching over each. Which would it be now, with the memorandum from the Campion Society in my suitcase? The great thing to remember, I told myself, was that so long as the Lord kept up his watching it did not really matter which of the two resulted: as far as I was concerned the alternatives came together to represent the one thing which really did matter.

When the plan was submitted to authority it was decided after much discussion, correspondence, sympathetic consideration, prayer outside as well as inside the community, that the undertaking was not one for which we at Downside were trained. In principle the work proposed recommended itself, in practice it posed too many problems. The project was dropped.

I had talked of trust. I had preached to myself the will of God. I had tried to school myself to a measure of detachment. But for a while the disappointment robbed me of these things. I bowed to the decision—how could I not?—but it is one thing to bow to a decision and another to preserve peace of mind. There were no personalities involved, no antagonisms to get over. It would have made it twice as difficult if there had been. Resentment was not the difficulty so much as the sense of emptiness. I was listless, unable to work at anything creative. My brethren, with true family feeling, told me I was exhausted after zigzagging across five states and preaching ninety-one times in six weeks. But I knew it was not because of this. It was because I had lost my new formula. I was back where I was before. It seemed to me that the same story was repeating itself and I was spending my life going over the same ground with the inescapable insistence of the Athanasian Creed. I would get just close enough to the realisation of a hope to feel secure, then would come a setback invading and even apparently destroying trust and the foundations of peace.

In this state of unreasonable dejection, trying to rally a sense of proportion and well aware that there were others in the world who were having to endure infinitely worse trials, I wasted the best part of three months. Father Bede and Father John would have helped. Ronald at this time was no help. None whatever. He was himself suffering a period of gloom. When I said I supposed I would sooner or later have to cheer myself up and get back to writing, he said, 'You're lucky to have an up to cheer yourself to. I don't think I have.' He said that when people got to my age (which was forty-six) they must not expect to do anything original any more, and that if they were writers they must resign themselves to writing what they had written more amusingly already.

'Look at me,' he said, 'I haven't been funny for years, and as for originality *that's* worn pretty thin when you look at it. For politicians and actors it may be different, but for writers you can take it as a general rule that after fifty at the latest they are only light-houses: the same old light going round and round . . . and it is only because their public is so dashed kind that this is seldom discovered.' I did not at that moment possess the energy to challenge a theory which, in his own case at least, was manifestly false.

Fortunately the creative urge, never dormant for long with me, revived. Even on Ronald's strict estimate I still had another four years to go, so I took the lid off my 1931 typewriter and began another book. It was not a jolly book this time (it was called *The Choice of God*) but it took my mind off myself. A factor which helped more than anything else to restore a sense of perspective was the encouragement given by Frank Sheed. He and I had been meeting irregularly over the past few years, and I like to think we had much in common. Certainly we shared the same enthusiasms, the same religious approaches, to some extent the same literary interests, and the same ideas about America. More clearly than most of my friends, many of whom were his as well, he understood what I was aiming at. He knew the religious climate in America, he knew Bishop Bennet, he knew me. So not only in the field of books but more significantly in the field of spirituality and monasticism, Frank gave me a confidence which I doubt if I would have received from anyone else.

Helpful also at this time of flagging effort was the stimulus given by the books which kept pouring from Thomas Merton. We were in correspondence but had never met. (I went once to Gethsemani in Kentucky in the hopes of clarifying a point of spirituality—he had in a general way invited me—but permission was not granted to speak.) *Seeds of Contemplation* was exactly what I needed just now, having on me the effect which his later books, *Sign of Jonas*, *Waters of Siloe, No Man is an Island*, invariably produced. When he sent me some of his unpublished notes and conferences, Father Merton did me a service for which I cannot be too grateful. These files of mimeographed sheets, which he called *Monastic Orientations*, not only gave me assurance but were useful to me also in my work on *The Holy Rule* for which I was still making notes. Every time I went into hospital between 1953 and 1957, *Monastic Orientations* went with me. All four files of them.

So if Frank Sheed put me on my feet, Thomas Merton kept me there. From a very different quarter came another support. I was introduced by Dom Christopher Leyne to a group of young artists, mildly eccentric in character, whom he was teaching in the school at Downside. The reason for the introduction was the need in which these gifted young people were placed to find a sponsor and censor in the production of an entertainment which they had in mind. The duty of carrying the project through its highly tricky stages, official and unofficial, should properly have been Dom Christopher's. He was in charge of the art department, and had himself founded the Angelico Society to which these boys belonged. But one glance at the proposed script must have told him of what lay ahead. 'You know about plays,' he said to me in the middle of a conversation about something else, 'I wish you would just preside occasionally at these people's rehearsals. You won't have to produce, but just give a few hints. It's all quite informal, and will take up little of your time. You will like the performers because they are plumb crazy to a man. Here are the keys of the art attic where everything takes place.' There was no warning, no hint of caution. I was accordingly imposed upon the Angelico Society. It was years since I had worked in the school, and I did not relish being drawn, an elderly and unwitting Cincinnatus, from my seclusion into the world of light entertainment. Thus into my lap fell dynamite.

It was soon clear that the society's name vested its activities with a nature which it did not strictly possess. I felt as the horse might have felt at Coventry when conducted from the stable to meet Lady Godiva. The choice had not been mine, but once accepted it had to be pursued with vigour. Between us we staged two revues, *The Hole in the Floor* and *The Hole in the Roof*. The painting of scenery, programme covers, posters was left to me. The lyrics also were my concern, and since most of the numbers were in rhyme there was plenty to do beyond 'looking in occasionally at rehearsals'. Despite quarrels, resignations, cancellations, differences of interpretation and temperament, interruptions caused by exams, games, epidemics, the Angelico continued to exist as a unit. It continued also to buoy up its sponsor's psyche. I was back with Maisie Gay, Teddy Gerrard, Gertie Millar, whom I had known in the twenties.

Some years later another such group was to form, not this time to require my services in the theatrical field but simply to share the shelter of the stoneshed where I worked, and it would be ungenerous if I were not to say how much this new circle meant to me. Citation of names is invidious. It is also tedious to those who have never heard of them.

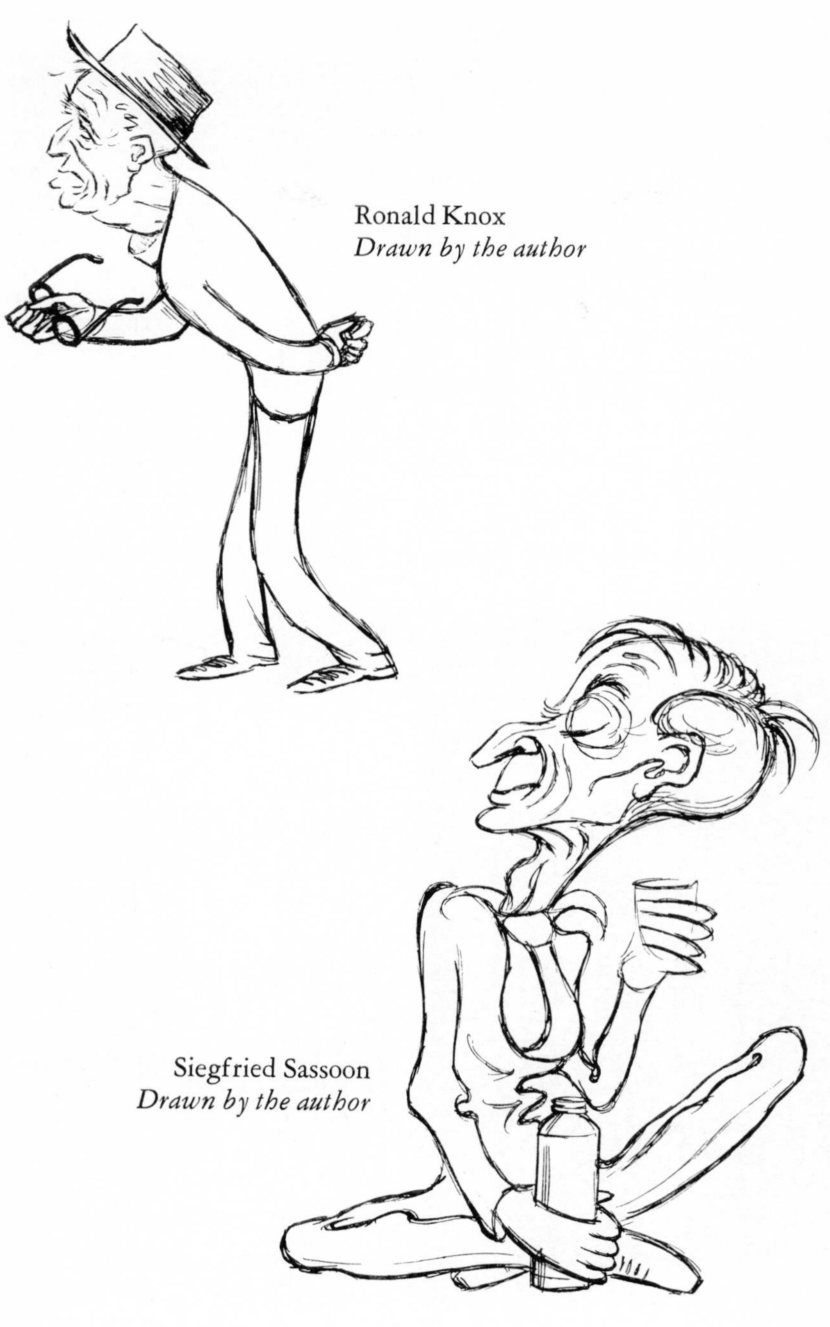

Ronald Knox
Drawn by the author

Siegfried Sassoon
Drawn by the author

St. Christopher

Head of a soldier

In bringing the narrative up to date I must go back to 1952 when I was appointed chaplain at All Hallows Preparatory School, Cranmore. The school being only a few miles away, Downside had supplied it with chaplains since it had moved into the neighbourhood shortly after the War. Though the chaplain was able to reside in the monastery, coming over by car twice a week and spending only Saturday night at Cranmore, I did not relish the appointment. I felt myself to be too old to be of much use with boys of preparatory school age, eight to thirteen, and also that the work would take me away too much from the monastic life. In the five-day week which was left to me at Downside I did not see how I would be able to get through either the orders which were coming in for statues or the series of books which I had undertaken, by contract, to write. Against all expectation I came to like the work and the boys and the whole spirit of the place. Mr and Mrs Dix, who had founded the school, could not have been kinder, and though it is a long time now since the chaplaincy has passed to other hands I go back to see the Dix's whenever I can.

Teaching catechism, hearing confessions, saying Mass, preaching to small boys once a week and watching their cricket matches. The familiar cycle. For me there seemed to be no escape from recurrently renewed contact with schools. I wondered what would happen when the number of Catholic schools requiring my services as chaplain finally ran out. 'Where will all the cowboys go,' as the song has it, 'when there ain't no cows no more?'

The appointment imposed restrictions upon my activities in the United States. It meant that I would be free to go only during the summer holidays, and August in America is not the favourite time for making retreats. That year, as it happened, I could not go anyway, because before the summer term ended I was in hospital. It was the first time I had been a patient in the Lansdowne Hospital, Bath, and I was glad of the change from Corston and St Mary's, Bristol. Indeed I enjoyed everything about it. With its embossed brass flower-pots, its turkey carpets, its wheezing lifts, it was more like an old-fashioned hotel than a hospital. It reminded me, especially when from a wheeled stretcher I saw bottles of champagne outside the door of a private room, of the Cavendish. The glass door-knobs did not fall off, there were no brass bedsteads, and there were not half a dozen douches to choose from in the bathroom, but from the feel of it I might have been in Jermyn Street. It is the feel that counts.

Back from the Lansdowne I was swept into scene painting for *The Gondoliers*. All Hallows was taking more of my time. Orders were coming for stone stations of the cross, a panel of the last supper, a figure of our Lady and another of St Joseph. I felt like a juggler, tossing a number of things into the air and knowing that sooner or later something would drop. I was seeing the audience—boys, retreatants, my fellow monks, God—as a blur. It was difficult to focus. Which mattered more, the audience or the performance? Where did my real duty lie?

I remember particularly the Saturday and Sunday afternoons which I used to spend in the All Hallows chapel trying to get the balance right, trying to go deeper into what really mattered. The chapel at All Hallows is immediately above the kitchen, and through the floor would come the smell of cooking, the clatter of plates, the voice of the German maid singing *Aufwiedersehen*, *Drei Rote Rosen, Ich hat ein Kamerad,* which, for their associations, tore at the heart.

Lacking a clearer light there was nothing for it but to live this divided life, partly among senior and partly among junior boys, partly as a monk and partly as a missioner, and to trust that somehow or other it was what God wanted and would come right in the end. It did not feel very satisfactory, but I knew that to take the initiative and ask for a change of place and work would leave me feeling less satisfactory than ever.

CHAPTER TWELVE

The Second Noon

With a mission to preach in the American sector of Germany, 1953 began well. It meant that at each of the appointed stopping-places down the Rhine, I was to say Mass, hear confessions, and preach three times. The tour was to end up at Munich, and I was to fly back. On the outward journey I would be provided with a military plane as far as Frankfurt, and would then proceed by train or car. The itinerary was worked out in great detail. For weeks before the date of starting, January 2, I was getting letters from the U.S. Army containing passes which would be valid when service transport might not be available, hotel reservations, lists of addresses to be consulted in the event of failure to establish contact. It was this last which should have told me that I was in for the unexpected.

Since the venture was sponsored by the military, I left from a military airport in Middlesex. Driving me there in his car, George Bellord switched on the radio and we learned from the weather report that rough weather could be expected over the Channel. 'But you will be flying with generals from the Pentagon,' said George, 'in a plane which laughs at blizzards.' He gave me his overcoat to take with me. I told him how the last time I had travelled to Munich I had done the journey in trains with wooden seats, and how I would like to be repeating that sort of attitude towards travel. Pompously I pointed out that 'travel' and 'travail' had the same origins. Once a schoolmaster, always a schoolmaster.

When we arrived at the airport a light snow was falling, and on the pavement where it had not had time to settle the wind was blowing it into small white rolling strings. There were not many people about. A few military policemen were stamping, and blowing on their hands, and a girl wearing a cap such as I had seen only in photographs of the Pandit Nehru told George that he could not accompany me beyond the barrier marked 'military personnel only'.

'Not many chiefs of staff taking off today,' I said to George.

'They're all drinking Grandad Specials in the V.I.P. lounge,' said George. He told me, as always, that he would meet me with the car when I got back.

The plane was not pressurised or heated, but at least it started punctually. The passengers sat along the sides facing one another, reminding me of a Dublin tram, and on seats of shining grey metal. The blizzard began shortly after take-off. Bumping and waving uncertainly over the Channel the flight made some of the plane's occupants feel unwell, and communal buckets were slid across the floor from man to man. I was not myself sick, being too solidly frozen inside for such a movement to be medically possible. Nor, because of the uneven passage, was I able to type as I had intended to do and as I normally do in planes. Instead I fixed my mind upon the shortness of the distance between Middlesex and north-west Germany. My duplicated schedule told me I was to reach Frankfurt at 14.20 hours. At 16.20 hours we landed at Brussels Airport, where I sent a telegram to the man who was to meet me, a Major Saslec, saying I was delayed by the weather. Before boarding again we had to shelter under the wings against the body of the plane until the door, which was frozen on its hinges, could be forced open. Later in the day we came down in various parts of Europe, disembarking each time to press against the driving snow in our walks to and from the terminal buildings. We arrived at Frankfurt just before midnight, the journey having taken nearly twelve hours. Understandably the army car which was to meet me had given up, and while recalling the luxury of my previous entry into Germany I found myself addressed by an unshaven crumpled man in clothes much worn and frayed. His walk was English, and his accent was what is called, arbitrarily, Oxford. I took him to be a spy. In no time he had secured an American army car, and together we drove through the snow-covered country into Frankfurt. I could only think that spies have to be efficient or they would lose their job.

That night was full of entertainment, because not only was my companion extremely amusing but when we arrived at the house where I was to lodge we found in the landlady, who wore a henna wig and played the French horn, a subject rich in humorous possibility. Only when seeing me off on the southbound train from Frankfurt, the first of the obligations fulfilled, did the crumpled man tell me he had been at school with me. Having failed to recognise him, I failed also to remember his name: all I could recall was a small boy, a fag, whose intelligence was of a kind that drew suspicion from the masters. There was no time, while we were saying goodbye, to learn more about him. As a good spy he would in any case have told me little.

Mannheim, Heidelberg, Stuttgart, then south-east to Munich. At Munich I preached four times in what had been General Patton's headquarters, a severe barrack in the outskirts of the town. The young soldier who was detailed to show me over this building told me to notice especially the two elevators (lifts) which side by side, went slowly up and down, down and up, throughout the day and night all through the year. They did not pause at a floor, so when the lift you wanted drew level you had to nip in, and when it reached your destination nip out. My guide told me that when he had gone on leave he had frequently paused during the day, and on waking during the night, and had thought of those lifts going ceaselessly up and down, down and up. 'Kind of scares you,' he said.

When the Munich duties were over, and as there was still half a day left, my military hosts asked if there was anywhere they could drive me, any place in Munich I would care to see? I said I would enjoy a look at the University and the Ottilienkolleg where I had studied for a short while twenty years before. So they drove me to both places. I did not go in. Through the railings of what was called the English Gardens, presumably because in the days of the great Ludwig it must have reminded someone of Hyde Park, I gazed at the scenes and recalled the mood of that earlier but abortive expedition, Newman leaning on the gate at Littlemoor.

Back in England I was met at the airport by the faithful George with his Bentley. He took back his overcoat, which I had worn with almost the incessance of General Patton's elevators, and returned me to Downside only just in time for the opening of the Lent term at All Hallows. Perhaps because it had been such an exhilarating experience, the mission in Germany gave to the mission at All Hallows a new urgency. I saw it as the appropriate apostolate between what seemed to be the more fruitful apostolates which I was trying to further among grown-ups. There was plenty of work to be done at All Hallows, and plenty of enjoyment to be derived from it. One of the things which I enjoyed most was saying Mass each year at the scout camp, particularly when this took place near Wells. Saying Mass in a barn, with cows nosing through the bars of their stalls on either side of me, with the boys kneeling in the straw behind me, with the rain rattling on the roof over my head, is something not easily forgotten. I enjoyed also the informal Sunday evening sermons, at which one of the boys was instructed to wave a handkerchief if I went on longer than seven minutes, and the much that was made of First Communions.

There is a book to be written by someone who can steer a course between pedantry and condescension: a book about preparatory school life which tells of its timeless jargon, its gangs, its hobbies, its pets, its taste in locker-decoration and garden arrangement. Can anyone be more conservative than the English preparatory schoolboy? Certainly the diary which I was keeping in 1954 during the All Hallows terms might equally have been written at Ladycross or Worth years before. Entries record cries of 'I'm in next . . . nobody asked you . . . dirty cheat . . . hop it, can't you? . . . Oh, aren't we *con*-descending.' At All Hallows the chapel overlooks the courtyard where the boys play, roller-skate, fight, and shout. The worshipper in the chapel will accordingly find his devotions interrupted not only by the sound of *Drei Rote Rosen* coming up through the floorboards but by the authentic *argot* just alluded to coming through the window. In parenthesis it might be added that the courtyard serves also as a car-park for the use of parents visiting their children. So the worshipper in the chapel will sometimes hear comments from more adult speakers. On a Sunday morning while making my thanksgiving after Mass, a window open at my side, I heard one mother who was sitting in her car saying to another: 'The chapel isn't bad, and my son tells me the chaplain isn't bad either.' It was a gratifying thing to hear, but the same voice went on after a moment's pause, 'Oh no, I remember now: it's the brother who is supposed to be nice. There are two Fathers van Zeller, you know.'

In religious literature much is written about zeal for souls. The term has an unfortunate do-goody ring but there seems to be no substitute. In order that what follows may be better understood, I would like to say something first about, for want of a better label, my own zeal for souls. In the two pastoral works on which I had been engaged, one at Temple Cloud and one at Whitehaven, my failure in each case could be attributed to the inability to reconcile the parish with the monastic life. The difficulty would not have come up, or at any rate would not have amounted to so much, had I been fired with a genuine zeal for souls. Until I started going to America the only thing which roused my zeal for souls was giving retreats; particularly retreats to contemplative communities. Then and later the only times I was happy were eight-day periods spent in Trappist or other enclosed houses, expressing a combined love of observance and zeal for souls.

Now, with the American work, zeal for souls came into its own. With it, in many instances, came the opportunity of exercising it either in or from contemplative communities. 'The soul,' writes Père Teilhard de Chardin in his *Milieu Divin*, 'is wedded to a *creative* effort. The will to succeed, a certain passionate delight in the work to be done, form an integral part of our creaturely fidelity. It follows that the very sincerity with which we desire and pursue success for God's sake reveals itself as a new factor —also without limits—in our being knit together with God who animates us. Originally we had fellowship with God in the simple common exercise of wills; but now we unite ourselves with him in the shared love of the end for which we are working. And the crowning marvel is that, with the possession of this end, we have the utter joy of discovering his presence once again.'*

When preaching in America I began to experience this 'will to succeed' and 'passionate delight in the work to be done' which in the above quotation are taken to be an integral part of our fidelity

* *Le Milieu Divin*, p. 35, in a section which he calls *Communion through Action* (English edition. Collins, London, 1960.)

to the service of God. Launched now on an enterprise which I felt at last I could perform, environed by circles of people whom I felt I could help, the whole scene was changed and instead of guilt, fear, listlessness there was confidence. My retreats were not something tacked on as an extra, as a sideline to the service of God: they *were* for me the service of God. Such a service of God, according to Teilhard de Chardin, inheres in the creative activity of God. 'I become not only its instrument,' he says of God's creative power, 'but its living extension.' When acting under the animating influence of grace, the soul coincides with the divine will and shares in the divine operation. In all this there is natural animation too, but this is allowed for in the postulate. It is the supernatural animation which does the work.

So were I to deny the actuation I would be denying the work of grace. If grace meant what I thought it did, it must permeate energies, activities, aspirations and human faculties to such an extent that works done under its impulse were not only in a general sense 'the work of God' but in a more strict sense works done *by* God. There may well have been some self-deception here, for there is a margin of self-deception in everything one does, but certainly it was in these terms that I saw the work which was waiting for me to continue in America. Since I had never seen it so in England, either on the parishes or in the schools, I concluded that for me the service of God was becoming localised in the west. That the service was more in demand on the other side of the Atlantic, and was felt to be more rewarded, made a difference. Essentially I believed it to be a question neither of need nor of success, but of vocation. So as soon as this was clear, namely that vocation and not simply predilection was involved, the vindication of the American apostolate was made. It is in virtue of this conviction that I have returned to America whenever my superiors have thought fit.

In this matter of following the call of grace, or what is believed to be the call of grace, it is a commonplace to observe that sacrifices have to be made. The price to be paid is nearly always that of allowing the external order to yield to the interior. With me it was a question of letting the monastic frame take a different outline. Under pressure of retreat-giving the frame was looking a little bent. Having cast myself for the role of the monk tethered to his choir-stall I was turning out to be more of a friar-preacher. Having seen in manual labour and enclosure my natural habitat, I had to admit that there was not much of either in the American programme. Ten years later the American programme included both manual labour and enclosure, as will be accounted for in another chapter, but at the 1953-1957 stage it was not always easy to secure the measure of silence which I needed for prayer and reading. Given the choice between living the full monastic life and being the itinerant preacher I would always choose the full monastic life. I tried to choose it again last year in 1963. But here I was not given the choice. In order to lead the full monastic life I would have had to do greater violence to the existing setting than if I were to become a whole-time missioner. So I settled back to watch the monastic frame twisting itself out of shape. Against this I enjoyed the conviction, supported as it was by the sanction of authority which was not solicited, that I was following and not pushing the wishes of divine providence.

It was now just over two years since my previous visit to the States, and in the meantime I had witnessed the collapse of my hopes regarding the contemplative foundation. Those who had worked for it bore me no ill will. They were confident that their hopes and mine would one day be realised. When I pointed out that I would soon be too old to launch out on a monastic foundation, one of them reminded me that the Holy Spirit was getting no older.

With the 1953 tour a new circuit was opened to me. After the Campion Society retreat I spent three days at St Walburga's Convent, Boulder, Colorado, and if confirmation were needed for what I have written above I found it here among the Benedictine nuns at the foot of the Rockies. The pieces of the puzzle were fitting neatly into place. I remember standing outside the chapel at dawn, watching the mountains as they changed colour, and how there came upon me the sense of being held in the hand of God. I suppose such moments come occasionally upon us all, however indifferent. *Levavi oculos meos ad montes: unde veniet auxilium mihi . . . auxilium meum a Domino.* The impression left me with something which has never quite evaporated. I came away from my too short stay at St Walburga's feeling that if human happiness were still in store for me it would declare itself here.

I had the sense to put this in writing, for ten years later the hope, without benefit of hindsight, was verified.

On the same circuit were retreats at Chicago, St Louis, Tulsa. When I left from New York, after a final round of Sacred Heart convents on the east coast, I had preached just over a hundred times. Being seen off from anywhere, but particularly from New York at the end of these tours, is to me an emotional ordeal almost past bearing. On this occasion my suitcase was weighed down by gifts presented by the children of the MacGuire family whom I had come to know on an earlier visit. Aware of my interest in sculpture they handed me on the morning of my departure large grey damp lumps. These objects were not easy to explain at the customs. Whatever they were meant to represent, for they defied identification, to me they represented—after the overweight charge had been met, after I had dragged them across London, after the shirts in which they had lain were sent to the wash, after they had finally dried out and now stood uncertainly on my desk—something very valuable.

In air travel I am fortunate. On the return flight that year a propeller fell off. I wish I could say that I had seen it spinning down silently into the Atlantic but I must have been typing and did not notice. The pilot, a man with a practised aisle-side manner, walked slowly the length of the plane assuring everyone that there was 'absolutely no need for panic' and that we would have to go back to New York and board another plane. Mention of the word 'panic' and the emphasis laid on 'absolutely' were unfortunate, causing some of the passengers to feel alarm. I remained calm because I did not think that a four-engined plane was likely to fall into the water on losing one miserable propeller and partly because I would not have minded in the least, so far as my own life was concerned, if it had, though I was anxious for the safety of the others. When we got back to Idlewild we were told how other planes had suffered similar misfortunes and were now, as we were, grounded. It had something to do, they explained, with electricity in the air. I was glad it was not the lumps in my suitcase.

For the next two years I was unable for one reason or another to resume the American rounds. 1954 was a race, chisel and hammer in hand, against the stopwatch. A figure of St Benedict, nearly lifesize, went to St Benedict's School at Beccles; a crucifixion in deep relief became an altar-piece in the Abbey at Downside; a madonna and child was ordered and bought by the Earl of Craven, who had worked with me years before and who had carved nothing but penguins; a seven-foot statue of St Francis, commissioned by Francis Dix, was hauled away on a truck which carried a crane and given a commanding site at All Hallows. It was gratifying to get these orders, and I took pleasure in surprising my customers with quick delivery. It was like the books: I do not know if I enjoyed the carving so much as having delivered the carvings.

A monk who has taught in several schools will find himself frequently invited to perform weddings. Baptisms too I had long since come to regard as an occupational hazard. I shrank from turning into the kind of monk who stands beneath crystal chandeliers. But there were some weddings and baptisms which I could not turn down without failing in charity. On several occasions Ronald was asked to preach while I was asked to perform the ceremony. In this way I came to hear a number of his wedding sermons which later came out in book form. At the McEwen–Laver wedding, which took place in the McEwen's chapel at Marchmont and for which Ronald and I were exercising our respective functions, Douglas Woodruff, who delights in weddings more than in any other thing, told me he thought Ronald's style was deteriorating. He instanced the sermon we had just heard, and which I of course had thought faultless, producing by way of proof a skilful parody. He instanced further a book of Ronald's, *Off the Record*, which had been published by Sheed and Ward a short while before and which I had thought masterly. 'I'm glad Ronnie didn't offer the book to us,' said Douglas, 'because we would have had to turn it down.' Then he added with a wicked chuckle, 'but of course Frank snapped it up.'

A few weeks later I called at Frank Sheed's London office on my way to give a retreat at Grayshott, and while I was debating in my mind whether or not to repeat the comments Douglas had made I was handed across the table a bundle of my own typescript. 'You know, Hubert, this simply isn't good enough for us,' said Frank without apology. Then he added, 'send it to Douglas:

he takes anything.' Frank's chuckle was every bit as wicked as Douglas's.

It was at this meeting that I outlined to Frank a scheme which had suggested itself and which I thought might be worth attempting. Would Sheed and Ward be interested in producing a series of 'Approaches'? I proposed that a list of titles be drawn up, and that writers whose names were already connected with the subjects envisaged might be asked to contribute; the books were to be the same length and would appear at regular intervals. 'You do like a *set* of everything, don't you?' said Frank. 'Come and have lunch and we'll talk about it.' He took me to the Café Royal, and on the back of a menu I wrote in block capitals 'Approach to', and then 'Education, Philosophy, Theology, Liturgy, Nuclear Warfare' and one or two other subjects which I now forget. Against each we put a name in brackets. Frank entered into it with gusto, promising himself to write an *Approach to Cricket*. I do not know what happened to our plans, and whether or not he wrote to the people whom we had chosen, but in the end I was the only one to approach. I wrote five of them, not one of which was on the original list, and was rewarded by seeing myself referred to in the *Trumpet* as Sheed and Ward's favourite approacher.

At another of these meetings in London, Frank suggested printing some lighthearted drawings I had made for private circulation among the Downside community at Christmas. Some time before, when he was spending a few days in Bath with his wife, Maisie, I had shown him a portfolio of these yuletide frolics and now he wanted to bring them out as a book. I demurred, saying that if they were to be printed at all it would have to be as a posthumous work. 'But that will be no fun for me,' Frank objected, 'because by that time I shall be just as posthumous as you.' I said I did not think the Abbot would agree. It would be easy enough, my host insisted, to find out: he would write at once. By return of post Abbot Butler agreed, so under the pen-and-brush name of Brother Choleric four slim volumes of claustral cracks have since appeared. Frank was quite right about my liking to have things in sets.

It might be added that though conceived without malice and executed with hilarity, these books of drawings have been to me a not unqualified pleasure. By many they have been taken amiss. A number of retreat bookings have, on discovery of authorship, been sharply cancelled. In the un-fan mail which the first of these publications elicited, I was charged with blasphemy, an attempt to undermine the authority of the teaching orders, lowering the dignity of superiors, turning away vocations, and being in the pay of the Communists. Some letters were anonymous and abusive, others were signed by every sister in the community and cold. It so disturbed me to think that there might be souls who were harmed by what I had thought to be harmlessness itself that I consulted both with Frank and with my superiors as to the advisability of going on with the series. Reassurance came without hesitation from both quarters. 'If people are such boobies,' Frank observed, 'they deserve to be boobied.'

One reason why I did not go to America in the summer of 1955 was that I was in hospital having operations on my feet. This was again at the Lansdowne which had provided innocent amusement on an earlier occasion. With both legs in plaster up to the knee, I returned to Downside after a restful three weeks during which I wrote *The Gospel Priesthood.* After another three weeks the plaster was cut away to reveal the necessity of another operation. 'Eh, you've done yourself a proper mischief,' said the orderly 'what kept you from hollering before it got like this?' I explained that had I hollered I would have been told that I could hardly expect to be very comfortable with enough plaster over me to make me look like one of my own carvings. So taking Father Merton's *Monastic Orientations* I went to bed again and had another operation. Feet are farther away than lungs, and I cannot say that I minded these operations very much.

In America my relationships were by now so well established that to miss out a year or two was not matter for anxiety. I had every reason to believe that the moment I got back I would go on from where I left off. At Downside my circle of interested spectators and fellow workers in the stoneshed gave me reason to be content. The boys were not unheeding to what I was trying to do for them, and for their part they gave me much in return.

While giving a retreat to a Bernardine community I began a

work which I had been wanting to do for some time: a careful book on the spiritual life which would be dedicated to Ronald. *The Inner Search* was published by Frank the following year, and only just in time for Ronald to read it before careful books were beyond his strength. It was probably already beyond him. 'The dedication,' he wrote in a letter of thanks, 'is the best part.'

In the spring of 1956 a member of the staff from the Middlesex Hospital wrote to me asking if I would give a lecture. Catholics and non-Catholics, men and women, patients and friends: there might be twenty, there might be two hundred. The subject chosen for the lecture was the religious life in general and the Benedictine life in particular. But it is not because of the subject, or because of the attendance when the meeting took place some weeks later, that I record the circumstance here. The reason why this particular engagement stands out is that I was to be lodged for the night at 109 Lancaster Gate. In the early part of this book I have referred to my grandmother's house as the cradle. More than any other house, more even than 45 Lower Belgrave Street or Carrigduv where I spent my school holidays, more even than the ugly house in Alexandria from which I looked out upon my fort at the end of the bay, 109 Lancaster Gate has a claim on me. It had, since my grandmother's death, changed hands several times. When the Duchess of Westminster bought it from us, it was, according to 1913 standards, modernised. A lift was put in. During the First World War it became a hospital for wounded officers. Since the hospital was a private one, and the Duchess of Westminster was running it, the patients were somewhat hand-picked. The house was empty for a long time when the Westminsters gave it up, and then, after a short lease, it became the Marlborough Court Hotel. I went to see it in its early hotel period, but got no farther than the downstairs rooms. I would be able now, on the occasion of the proposed visit, to explore it at greater length. These Brideshead are a mistake. They produce emotional exhaustion.

The room which I was given was one of three into which the morning-room of my grandmother's day had been divided. The delicate moulding on the ceiling ran straight into the dividing wall, and the two new walls did not quite match the old ones. The dining-room, now with its complement of small tables where before there had been one long one which had been made even longer when big dinners were given, was bright and shining and airy and infinitely depressing. There was electric light where there had been gas, there were radiators instead of open fires, telephones instead of speaking tubes, electric bells instead of thick silk-tasselled ropes which connected with a wire high up against the ceiling which in turn connected with a line of pendant bells in the servants' quarters; there were basins with running water where before there had been sets of flowered china. There was a reception office, bristling with metal-labelled keys and pigeon-holes and typewriters and cash-registers and an air of clinical efficiency, where before there had been an umbrella-stand, a long oak chest containing music-scores and prayer-books, and Berthe's goloshes. There were lifts and bathrooms galore. The old smell, a mixture of dried rose-petals, log fires, leather, velvet curtains, violets, had quite gone. When its smell goes, the feel of a place goes with it. At Marlborough Court Hotel there was no smell at all.

That night I did not sleep but lay awake remembering. At one point I got up and started typing my diary, but sounds from the room next door told me that there were others sleeping on the same floor. More wakeful were the shades of uncles and aunts, of servants whom I had loved, of my grandmother herself. I thought of her as she lavished her devotion upon Bret Harte dying in one of the rooms upstairs yet had denied affection to her own children. I thought of her as setting off on tiring journeys to Farnborough to spend the day with her friend the Empress Eugenie, yet she had never crossed the Bayswater Road to speak to the old lady who sat all day opposite the morning-room windows selling balloons and paper windmills. I thought of Berthe: busy, fiercely independent, loving the poor but angry with the rich. Yolande: sad, sensitive, responsive to beauty in art but unaware of it in nature, fearful of extravagance, resigned to the puzzle of human existence. Beatrice: beautiful, kind, but to me unknown. Rita: volatile, spendthrift, affectionate, as ready to cry as laugh. Then there were the uncles: the two who were reputedly wastrels, and the two who were elegant anachronisms. I reflected how the Edwardian profligate of the upper classes was lucky if he could keep a foothold on this island, and how, in contrast to several of my male relatives who ended up in one or other of the colonies, Maurice alone rode the storm to remain beyond reproach, urbane, decorous, the soul of respectability.

The company of aunts and uncles, grandmother and domestics kept me occupied for so long that I wrote off the night, packed my bag, and let myself out in the early dawn before the hoovers began their morning hum. The streets at that hour were empty, and as I followed the route which we used to take on Sundays to Farm Street I found association on every pavement. I remembered the man who locked the side entrance to the Park, but could not remember why he needed to and I remembered the men who hosed the streets. I also remembered conversations with Georgie as we walked together to Benediction at Tyburn Convent, and with Ellwood as he took me to sail my boat in the Round Pond. I wished I had remembered these snatches of talk while I was writing *Family Case Book*, but it was something that they should be coming back to me now. Georgie telling me of her life at the orphanage, of her prayer that she would one day settle with a family who would make up for the lack of a home in her own life, or being down to her last shilling when she was recommended to us. Ellwood telling me endless London lore, gravely pursuing the subject as though he believed what he said was true. 'You see the Marble Arch, General? Well, just under where it stands today there used to be a prehistoric village, and I'll tell you something which not many people know. There are animals living deep down under our feet in caves and dark tunnels, waiting for the day when they will be able to come up above ground and breathe the open air like you and me. Of course they *could* come up this minute, General, through the Serpentine. You know that's how the Serpentine got its name? . . . because of the prehistoric serpents which lived in it. Well, those serpents could come up through there any day.' 'Then why don't they, Ellwood?' 'Ah, they know better, General, than get themselves stuck in a dusty museum along with a lot of prehistoric skeletons. That would be no fun at all, General, not for them it wouldn't.' 'Hey, steady on, Ellwood,' I would always say when fancy exceeded belief, 'how do you know all this?' 'I used to do a lot of digging in these parts, General, deep down. Now I can tell you something about Hyde Park Corner which you wouldn't find in a book . . . .'

It was still so early when I reached the church at Farm Street that the doors were locked. I sat on the steps, and went on sorting out scenes from the past. Even here there were ghosts: Rodney coming to Mass after our rides in Rotten Row, the girl who rode ahead of us and became a Sacred Heart nun, Father Bampton and his threats about a flowing white silk made-up tie for serving Mass. When the doors were opened and I was shown to an altar, the names of those who had occupied my thoughts figured prominently in my intention. The pilgrimage would have been incomplete without a final station: 45 Lower Belgrave Street. The ground floor was now a shop, and since this killed my memories stone dead for that part of the house, I did no more than peer down the area steps and recall one or two in the broken line of Berthe's preposterous servants.

The threefold revisiting had a curiously subduing effect. If I felt a little as St. Benedict might feel if he walked today through the cloisters of Monte Cassino, I felt also the need to hurry on and not look back. Once again in my experience I did not know to which world I belonged. Each seemed equally the stuff of fantasy, like Ellwood's stories, and more than anything else I wanted reality.

Accordingly I have not been back in the intervening years to these three places. They tell me that Lancaster Gate has lost tone and has rather gone downhill. It happens in big cities. The lorgnette moves out and the cosh moves in. There is no stopping it. The march of progress.

In the autumn of the same year I set off for America. The Suez affair was going on at the time, and on the way to London Airport in the sparkling sunshine George switched the radio on and off so frequently that Eden's fighting broadcast remains in my memory more as a surprise than as an argument. In the plane everyone was talking about it, speculating upon the consequences, and wondering whether or not to come straight back next day. I could afford to be detached. I would not have altogether scorned the excuse to stop on in America indefinitely. Someone was taking my place at All Hallows and I was given eight weeks leave of absence.

The tour included engagements, or as they are called in America 'assignments', at a number of places to which I had not been before. In the plane from Denver to Los Angeles, typewriter on my knee, I began a book of which I had roughed out a plan while at St Walburga's, Colorado. The air hostess, much made up and dazzling, asked me what I was writing that it should command such urgency. I said I was pushing along the opening chapter of a book, and was I making too much noise? 'Why, no,' she said, 'that's what this little caboose is for, right back here in the plane, so business executives can knock hell out of their typewriters. Go right ahead.' I thanked her, and rattled on. 'But what's it about, for heaven's sake, this book?' It was about prayer I told her. 'Boy, am I just crazy about prayer.'

This improbable response was shown to be not so improbable after all. She told me that in a few months' time she would be trying her vocation among the Ursulines, and had already ordered the clothes which she was to need as a nun. When she moved away to attend to the other passengers, and as I was working down the page in the typewriter, a man who had overheard our conversation came and sat next to me. He told me he was a regular passenger on this flight, and that the girl who had been talking to me had provided out of her savings for the training of a priest. 'Guess you just can't tell, can you?' he said.

At Sacramento, California, I gave two retreats and spoke to various groups in the town. While there I was driven by a Mr and Mrs Frank McNerney to the newly founded Cistercian monastery of New Clairvaux, Vina, where I preached to the monks at six in the morning. Seldom have I received such a warm response as from the brethren of New Clairvaux; I came away with reluctance, feeling I had drawn near to the spirit of old Clairvaux. Then back with the McNerneys, who correspond faithfully but whom I have not seen since, to Sacramento.

On reaching Downside at the end of the eight weeks I learned that Ronald had been asking to know the date of my return. This was unusual so I guessed that something was wrong. Within a few days of my arrival I had a letter from him asking me over to Mells and characteristically excusing himself for not taking the trouble to come over to Downside. This was in the beginning of December.

'I'm not telling people,' he said after he had asked about America and told me of the movements of people we knew, 'but I'm feeling pretty mouldy.' Certainly he looked far from well. 'The doctor isn't awfully pleased . . . I'll get myself looked at after Christmas.'

I guessed that this summons outside our regular times for meeting was because he wanted to be pushed into seeing a doctor in London. It showed me how mouldy he must be feeling. I talked to Mrs Asquith when he was out of the room, and she did not seem very happy about him. She had the greatest confidence in the local doctor, and so had Ronald. The next thing I heard was that the local doctor had recommended London on his own.

An operation was performed in London on January 20, 1957, which revealed cancer of the liver. The findings of this operation were not disclosed to Ronald, who went back to Mells early in February expecting to convalesce in the warmth of Mells Manor and take up work again before the summer. I went over twice, and he looked worse than he had looked before Christmas. In March the Waughs took him off to the Devon coast where they hoped to get the sun, but the weather was against them and Ronald came back exhausted. I imagine Evelyn was exhausted as well.

'I've always been stinkingly irritable,' Ronald said to me when he was settled again, 'but never until now with the people I'm most fond of. It's an effort to be nice.'

By now it was April, and before the middle of May it was clear to Katherine Asquith and to me that Ronald was very ill. His speech was slow and slurred, his ankles were swollen, his colour was yellow. He had no appetite, and apart from soups could drink only fruit juice. He was told at last that he had cancer, that he would not get well, that it would do no good to have another operation. In the hope that a second opinion might reverse this judgment he arranged, with the local doctor's glad approval, for an appointment to be made with Sir Horace Evans, the Queen's physician.

While staying at Combe Florey with the Waughs and at

Rackenford with the Eldons, Ronald had been at work preparing a lecture which he was to deliver at Oxford on June 11. This was the Romanes Lecture, and not everyone is invited to give the Romanes Lecture. The first was delivered by Gladstone in 1892, and since then among those nominated for the honour have been Curzon, Balfour, Theodore Roosevelt, Asquith, Winston Churchill. Anyone seeing Ronald on May 22, as I did, would have said that the chances of his being able to travel from Mells to Oxford, give his lecture, and get back without collapsing somewhere along the course were low. 'He'll manage it,' Katherine said, 'you'll see.'

Knowing the amount of work he had put into the preparation, and how anxious he was to fulfil the obligation, I asked him if he would like me to go with him and do any little jobs which might arise. I argued that he might rest more if he knew someone was looking after the tickets and seeing about taxis. 'Rather poor sport for you, Hubert, wouldn't it be?'

So I got permission from the Abbot, and it was arranged that I would see him to his lecture, take him on next day to London for Sir Horace's verdict, and then bring him back to Mells on the day following. Lord Hylton lent his chauffeur-driven car for the journey to Oxford (after two accidents while learning to drive I was told to stop) and we started on the morning of June 11. Not since our joint retreat at Caldey more than twenty years before had I been given a chance of spending so long with him at a stretch. We hardly spoke at all on the way, Ronald needing all the voice and strength he could muster for the strain which was to be put upon him later in the day. We stopped once for the sandwiches and chicken soup which Katherine had packed for us, and Ronald's patience during this picnic luncheon was impressive. Things which might have exasperated him—the cork from the thermos coming away with the slight splash and plop which apparently cannot be avoided, crumbs falling on the floor of the car, the greaseproof paper and rubber bands—he put up with, making no comment: he was a model of control.

At Oxford we were received by Mr J. C. Masterman, the Vice-Chancellor, who had invited us to spend the night in his house at Worcester College of which he was Provost.* He had long been

* He retired in 1961 from this position, receiving a knighthood.

a friend of Ronald; I had not met him before. He told me, when Ronald was lying down, that he had arranged for a doctor to be standing by in the Sheldonian, and for a reader to take over, if Ronald should collapse while speaking. This was to be kept to ourselves. When the time came there was no sign of faltering. Ronald spoke for more than an hour, and even seemed to gain strength as he went along. The response of the audience carried him. For those of us in the packed Sheldonian who knew that he was dying, that this was his last public appearance, that he would not see Oxford again which of all places in the world held for him the most associations, it was an hour of the deepest feeling.

After the lecture, the text of which has been published together with some essays and has also been issued separately, he was taken off by friends who had been present. Of the rest of the Oxford visit I have written, in answer to a request from Evelyn Waugh who was working on the Life, 'He was less tired than was to be expected, sitting up till eleven while friends from various colleges—dons, mostly from Trinity—talked with him while he sipped fruit juice. J. C. Masterman could not have been a better host, and I think Ronnie was as happy as I have ever seen him. But it must have been a strain because when I called him in the morning he looked desperately ill.'

In case he should need anything during the night I had been given a room next to his with a connecting door between. Since the sound of shunting and puffing from the near-by railway line kept me awake most of the night, I was able to assure our host at breakfast that Ronald had not stirred. When I asked Ronald if the noise from the trains had troubled him at all during the night, he said '*I* never mind trains . . . train noises are music to my ear.' Bradshaw close in spirit.

On the morning of June 12 we went together to London where his first stop was at the Dowager Lady Lovat's flat for luncheon. Here I left him and went off to lunch with George at his club. Ronald's appointment with Sir Horace was for some time in the afternoon and was to take place at 10 Downing Street, where Ronald was to spend the night as the guest of his friends Mr Harold Macmillan and Lady Dorothy. I came to pick him up at Lady Lovat's, and as our taxi turned at the corner of Downing Street I suggested that he had better stay where he was, sitting with his feet up, while I rang at the door. On the steps of Number Ten were two policemen. 'Do I have to explain who we are, and that the Macmillans are expecting us?' I asked him. 'I think it will be enough,' said Ronald, speaking with difficulty, 'if we don't *look* like people who throw bottles at the Prime Minister's windows.' There was no difficulty: I left him with his host and hostess and came away.

Next morning I was at Paddington half an hour before the time of the train's departure, and the tickets were in my pocket. Never before had I allowed so wide a margin or shown such efficiency in travelling: it was a tribute I paid to my fellow traveller. As the car drew up, I could see through the window what Sir Horace's verdict must have been. Mr Macmillan got out first, holding the rug, and then helped Ronald out of the car and in to the station. After I had assured the Prime Minister that we lacked for nothing—he had himself arranged that we should have a private compartment—and that I would report to him on Ronald's progress, we shook hands and Mr Macmillan walked back to his car. Ronald, who had heard this exchange between the Prime Minister and myself, told me as we walked at snail-pace along the platform not to bother about reporting to Downing Street on his progress because from what Sir Horace had said there was not going to be any.

In the train he told me he had no wish to die. 'One clings,' he said, 'and I can't think why. You would have thought anyone would prefer heaven to fruit juice.'

Back at Mells he refused to lie down or have a tray sent to his room, so we all lunched together and Ronald went over the events of the three days that he had been away. Though speaking slowly he enjoyed telling Katherine and Lady Helen about whom he had met, many of them their friends as well as his. He did not say a word about the Romanes Lecture; this was where I filled in. He was touched to learn that twice while he had been away Lady Dorothy had telephoned from Downing Street to ask if he could eat this or drink that, saying she would get a scolding from her husband if anything went wrong, 'I like to think,' said Ronald, 'that the nation's business is held up while I am debating whether to take tea or coffee, and then deciding to take neither.'

I saw him once again in June, and twice in July. For the July visits he was in bed, and on the first of these I suggested that he might like me to anoint him before I left for America at the end of the month. Both of us knew he would not be alive by the time I got back in October. 'Wouldn't the parish priest feel a bit left out?' he objected, 'we don't want him to think we are being sniffy about it.' So in the end he was anointed when I was away, and by, quite properly, the parish priest. Was there nothing I could do, then? I knew he had been translating *The Story of a Soul*, a favourite book of his, so suggested that perhaps he might like me to read some of it to him.

'Not unless you can endure to read it from my version. I'm bound to say I would rather have St Theresa in the Knox than in the original.'

'All right, I'll be back in a week's time,' I said in parting, 'and if there's anything I can do, you must tell me.'

'You could pray for me I suppose.'

Well or ill, serious or amusing, Ronald never said anything that was not in character. The slightly dated idiom was part of him. More often than not his observations on subjects connected with religion and spirituality came as a surprise, yet when you examined what he had said you wondered why you had not expected it. It was the same about his humour: you were caught off guard each time. The choice and economy of words, the exactly correct form, the accompanying facial expression: these things had a lot to do with the individual character of his wit. Many good conversationalists can manipulate the talk to their advantage, can fold their ideas neatly into pat phrases, but there are few who use none of the tricks and are simply themselves. Many of Ronald's most typical remarks were those thrown away, thrown over his shoulder for anyone to pick up. I, an instinctive Boswell, was assiduous with my spiked stick and basket. I remember once at Aldenham when he was working at his translation with a quantity of books open in front of him, and when I happened to be standing at the window looking down the drive. The drive at Aldenham is exactly one mile long and straight all the way from the steps of the house to the park gates. A prospective caller can therefore be seen as a dot in the distance. In silence I watched such a dot coming closer up the drive and becoming a male figure in black.

'It's a priest,' I said, hardly thinking that Ronald was listening, 'I wonder where he comes from?'

'Cork,' he barked instantly from behind his barricade of books.

The last time I saw him was when I went on July 19 to say goodbye before going to America. He did not want to be read to; he wanted to talk. There was not very much to be said, and for this I was glad because it was an effort for him to speak. We went to confession to one another, as we always did, and I think this helped matters for both of us. I told him that the nuns of Hengrave whom he had known at Aldenham were having prayers said for him every day, and gave him messages from Downside. We spoke for a while about Siegfried Sassoon who, fairly recently, had come into the lives of both of us. We agreed that we should have got to know Siegfried years ago, and that he would have been the right person for the Caldey retreat before the War. 'He's more a First War man than anyone I know,' said Ronald, 'you must draw him.' I did.

'So, Hubert, you are going to America next week.'

'For two months.' I got up to go. It was no good prolonging it. 'But there is something I would like you to do for me,' I said, 'which neither Father Bede nor John Talbot nor Abbot Ramsay has done for me. When you get to heaven, Ronald, I want you to see about this death wish of mine.'

'Oh . . . so you are still on about that.' He knew it was a request which he was meant to treat seriously. He considered it for nearly a minute before making his comment. 'I'm making no promises,' he said at last, 'except that I will pray for you *wherever* I am. I never have liked this game of yours, as you know, because it seems to me fishy, but I suppose that's your affair.' I knelt for his blessing and left.

On August 24, while in Springfield, Illinois, I learned of Ronald's death. Hugh Garvey telephoned from his office to tell me. I was waiting for it. I took my mourning and my memories to the chapel of the Dominicans at Siena Hall.

The suggestion has come to me since his death that I should write a book about Ronald as a man of prayer. From several quarters, religious and lay, the need has been expressed. Evidently it is felt that what the Life has so admirably done in presenting the scholar, the priest, the apologist, the master of style and craft, might be supplemented by a biography which aimed specifically at giving a picture of the subject's spiritual life. If such a task is to be performed, and it would certainly make a contribution to the story of holiness in the contemporary setting, it will not be performed by me. To account for the interior life of a man whose confessions you have heard off and on for a quarter of a century would be a breach of taste.

CHAPTER THIRTEEN

The Second Evening

In an attempt to bypass the gloom occasioned by Ronald's death, more invading to thought in England than in America, I resorted to the distractions of overwork. By Christmas *The Holy Rule* was finished and in the hands of the printers, by New Year's Day I was well into *Approach to Monasticism*. Every afternoon found me sloshing through Somersetshire mud, loosening up for planting a strip of ground which a label on a stick proclaimed as Hungry Gap—a name calculated to please my Midwestern fancy. By the end of March the big stone panel of the *Last Supper*, in deep relief and weighing two tons, was almost finished. In the middle of April, after giving the Holy Week retreat to Downside's old boys, I collapsed.

But this was no hospital affair. On April 23, the feast of St George, I went to Buckfast Abbey to rest, and by the kindness of everyone concerned, the respective abbots of Buckfast and Downside especially, I was allowed to stay there for six months. It was a period of gradual rehabilitation, spiritual and monastic, and one of greater tranquillity than I had known for some time. The freedom from interruptions as were inevitable in my own monastery, the comparative simplicity of the life, the rhythm set by the Divine Office, set hours of study, silence, manual work: these factors combined to restore me so completely that I came back to Downside in October (1959) feeling ready for anything. I would have been ready for America, but after so long away in another monastery a further absenting would have been unsuitable.

Though I gave only one retreat during that time (it was to a community of Poor Clares in Scotland) I can look back to the Buckfast interlude with the liveliest satisfaction. I made a number of friends, both in the community and outside it, and if for this alone it was not time wasted. Among those from outside were five who were under the age of seven, and with these I have kept in close touch since. The Anderson family were doing for me what the Rochford and Garvey families had done for me at an earlier period of stress, and what the Leonard family were yet to do: they were giving me something natural as well as supernatural to live for.

Also while at Buckfast I had written two and a half books and had received the largest order for work in stone that I had yet received. The architect who commissioned the undertaking—fourteen stations of the cross in panels of two feet by two feet to be delivered in America by July of next year—communicated his wishes always by telephone and never by letter. Since his office was in Quincy, Illinois, I did not like to take him up on his injunction 'call me back'. Moreover, since on each occasion he chose to telephone before leaving his office in the evening, the difference between American and European time being of no interest to him, our negotiations would be conducted round about midnight. I have met Mr Benya several times to discuss the possibility of further orders, but I have still not had a letter from him.

As though to launch me on this major venture in stone, and certainly to facilitate its execution, the bursar at Downside, Dom Vincent Cavanagh, moved me from the stoneshed where I had worked intermittently for close on thirty years to a solid and well-lit workshop which had been cleared of onions to make way for me. In this building, which by the law of association was called a shed, I worked for the next three years. The move was a timely one: the roof of the old shed let in the rain, and an impatient movement would send a foot through rotting floorboards. In the new shed there might be a smell of onions but there was also a gas fire. As soon as the stone had dried out I went to work on the stations. I had taken great care over the drawings, and though these were not returned after I had submitted them, I had the designs firmly fixed in my head. With me it is the designing that takes the time. The carving in this instance took four and a half months, interrupted only by an attack of flu. The flu was not so severe as to bring all activity to a halt, so I used the time to decorate the whitewashed walls with lifesized figures of monks engaged in one or other of the mason's functions. These very simple murals, carried out in red tempera, are probably still there. A good flu germ knows when it is beaten, and as soon as it gave up I got back to carving.

At the risk of saying something which already is known to all, I record here my belief that an interest pursued with absorption is the most effective of prophylactics. The creative aptitude, if acted upon with enough zest, not only prevents ordinary light illnesses but also shakes them off if they happen to come upon him while the subject is not looking. It is unfortunate that this principle does not cover ills which call for surgery. At the end of May, 1960, when fortunately the last of the stations had been completed, I sustained an injury which for the time being meant the end of work, creative or other. The accident destroyed the hearing of one ear for good, and prevented me from walking straight. It might have happened at a worse time—had I been half way through a job instead of having just finished one—but even so it was inconvenient. When I found myself in bed without knowing how I had got there the first thing I thought of was the Campion Society retreat which was to open on August 11 at Notre Dame, Indiana. Notices for this and other retreats had already been printed, reservations had been made, and tickets for the flight were on my table.

Three weeks before I was due to fly I was still falling off chairs and supporting myself on two sticks. Food tasted of plastic artichoke cooked in linseed oil and I could not distinguish between tea and coffee. (I still, four years later, cannot always tell the difference, but at least they do not taste of carbolic. Nor can I be sure of walking straight, and this can lead to embarrassing misunderstandings. Most of the other faculties, except the hearing in one ear, seem to have returned to me.) Medical opinion was divided, but in the end I was allowed to go to America on the condition that I rested every afternoon and did not do too much. That America is not the best place for such a regimen I did not feel it my duty to reveal.

George took me to the airport on August 8 with my two sticks and my bottle of steadying pills which were supposed to do something for my balance. 'I know of a better bottle than that,' said George, and ordered champagne. He noticed that this was the first time he had seen me off without my typewriter. I explained that I could neither type, draw, carve, nor write more than would go on a postcard. 'Well, let me know if you find you have taken on too much,' he said, 'and I'll come over and fetch you.' I said I would send him a postcard. In the meantime I had nearly three days in which to rest before the opening of the Campion Society retreat.

Mention has already been made of my good fortune as an air-wayfarer, and how I am seldom subjected to a dull flight. The claim was not disproved on this occasion. When the plane was well over the Atlantic a radio message told of the possible presence among us of an unexploded bomb. In imparting this information the pilot reminded us how frequently this was reported and how rarely a bomb was discovered. 'Just some crackpot,' he said, 'who has a compulsion.' Nevertheless we would have to go back as far as Shannon, he said, for a search of plane, luggage, and passengers. 'It would be too bad if this crazy guy was right after all.'

Seated next to me in the plane was a German who had spent the first hour of the flight telling me the story of his life. On hearing the pilot's announcement, which I translated for him into bad German, he took off his boots. 'Warum?' I asked, pointing to his stockinged feet. It was because, he told me, a swimmer would find it twice as hard to keep afloat if water got into his boots. I looked out of the round window at my side, and saw the last of the evening light reflected on the calm surface of the Atlantic far below.

By the time we reached Shannon it was dark, and we were told we would be there for at least two hours. The search was nothing if not thorough, and when they had finished with me I shaved and recited Matins for the next day: if an undiscovered bomb should accompany us it would not find me unprepared. Whether in the sea or before the judgment seat I must be like the warriors of Thermopylae, groomed within and without.

When the two hours were up it was announced by loud-speaker that passengers who felt uneasy as to the success of the search might proceed later by a different plane. A number decided to act on this proposal so my German and I had the plane almost to ourselves. In the course of the night the German told me, though not before removing his boots in case the bomb was still there after all, the rest of his story. He was on his way from Hamburg to Cincinnati to visit his divorced wife, who was ill. Was I shocked by this? Did I consider the procedure *unangenehm*? Not at all, I considered it very proper: a happy reconciliation. 'Ah, but I have not told you all,' he said, crying softly and showing me a photograph of his divorced wife, 'I have married since. She too has married since, who knows how many times?' Until dawn broke he showed me photographs of wives and husbands while I marvelled at a concept of matrimony which could produce, at Cincinnati as well as at Hamburg, so variegated a pattern of domestic life.

There was no explosion, and three days later I was being cared for with hospitable solicitude by Father Foran, the Holy Cross priest who looks after the retreat house at Notre Dame. Since discovering the Fatima Retreat House and Father Foran, the Campion Society has gone nowhere else for its retreats; I have now given three there, and a more excellent setting could not be imagined.

Another Holy Cross priest, Father Lauck, who heads the art faculty at Notre Dame, deserves my gratitude. He took me, between retreat conferences, to see the great master, Ivan Mestrovic, who was working in a studio provided by the University on the campus. From the time that I first started speaking and writing about sculpture thirty years ago, I have hailed Mestrovic as the greatest exponent of Christian sculpture of the age. Perhaps of any age in Christian history. To be meeting him now in person was for me a momentous occasion. A lesson was going on when I arrived, so I was able to watch him at his work, surrounded by students and apprentices. When the class was over he drew me into the private part of the establishment and we talked in a mixture of French, German and garbled American. He was a gentle, diffident man, not at all what I would have expected. He spoke sadly of the decline of Italian sculpture, attributing it to the decline of religious spirit among Italian artists generally. Several times I got up to go, wobbling on my two sticks, but he pressed me back into the chair. When we said goodbye he asked me to come again, which I did the following year.

From Indiana I moved south, fulfilling one or two short preaching engagements on the way. I felt ill and my balance was getting no better. Every time I went up in a plane, and often when I was not up in a plane, it was as though little bubbles were bursting in my head; this would be accompanied by a kick which knocked me sideways. Once, before landing at Memphis, Tennessee, I felt I would have to abandon the assignments, send the postcard to George, and go back to England. The bursting bubbles on that occasion had become bursting bombs, and the kick had become an explosion. I reminded myself that a drop in altitude made things worse for the time being, and that there was an injection waiting for me at my destination. But I did not like the idea of having to be hopped up by the needle in order to preach, and had I not feared to offend Dr James Furrie, a particular friend of mine in Springfield, who regarded it a point of honour that I return to England at the end of the trip as a standing witness to America's medical superiority, I would have dispensed with injections altogether. I am glad I did not turn back at Memphis for I would have missed an eventful and rewarding retreat farther south to the Carmelites at Jackson, Mississippi, of which I have written in *You Don't Have to Read It*.

From the deep south my duties took me northwards again to Pittsburgh, and thence to the Benedictine monastery of Mount Saviour, Elmira, where I gave another eight-day retreat. The monastery here is so remote, even more remote than Madame Zarima's cottage of mystery and clairvoyance in North Wales, that without a doctor within call to give me the prescribed injections I wafted uncertainly through the grounds (and I suppose also through my obligations) and have no clear recollection of the day-to-day events. I know only this, that its spirit impressed me as much as that of any Benedictine community I have come across. My feeling is that if St Benedict were to find himself at Mount Saviour, he would not have to bother about making allowances for the march of civilisation, not have to listen to talk about the law of adaptation: he would be able to walk in, sit down, and know that here was something which he had set out to establish.

After Mount Saviour came the Sacred Heart convents in the east to which by now, after so many visits, I felt myself to be affiliated as honorary chaplain. Unable to write, and therefore without the backing of the diary, I see this 1960 tour only in outline and through a waving astigmatic haze. Though I would be hard put to it to give an account of my movements at Greenwich, Manhattanville, Duchesne, and Noroton, I remember that that last two days were spent, as on previous tours, with the MacGuire family and what we did during them. The children had lost their interest in modelling, so this time I had no fears about carrying damp clay back to Europe, but culture still ranked high among them. So when the question was put to me 'What would you like to do on the last miserable day?' I answered, as I had answered the same question each year, that I would like to see the Cloisters. The Cloisters is an offshoot from the New York Metropolitan Art Museum, and is situated on high ground overlooking the river; it is approached by turning off one of the main four-lane highways running just outside New York. As a kind of holy foundation from the urban and secular motherhouse, this museum is redolent with aesthetic and monastic ethos. Father Merton refers to it in his autobiography. Every year new exhibits are added, reproductions of which are reproduced in religious as well as in art magazines. Sculptors, painters, students, churchmen and architects visit it in droves. I seemed to be the only person in America who had never been there. I had come to think of the Cloisters as Kafka's castle. For one reason or another the five MacGuire children and their mother had always borne me off, however carefully planned the Cloisters expedition, to see something else. This year proved no exception, so once again a mocking laugh came rolling down those noble slopes as we went purring past the signpost in the MacGuire stationwagon which is as long as a bus. Not until last year, in the hilarious company of Frannie Kemmerer (to whom half of the present work is dedicated) and Dr Bob O'Clair (a member of the faculty at Manhattanville), did I finally reach the Cloisters.

The astigmatic haze was my companion throughout the next few months, so that I can only say of them what the Abbé Sieyès replied when questioned as to what he had done during the Revolution, 'I survived'.

On my return to England I found that *The Benedictine Idea* had been out for some weeks and was getting bad reviews. After *The Holy Rule*, which did not get particularly good reviews either, it was the book which I had most wanted to write and which I am most glad to have written. This and the commentary—the first commentary, so far as I know, to be written in English—expressed my monastic creed. To both books the German and Italian reviewers, notably those who were Cistercians, were favourable; the English and Irish were not. Had the books been well received on all sides, I would have doubted whether I had made my meaning clear.

It is a curious fact that the more you want to write a book, the more obstacles you come across in the writing. Either you cannot get hold of the necessary books of reference, or you run into trouble with the theologians, or someone writes a better book which comes out while yours is at the printers. In its various stages *The Benedictine Idea* several times nearly met extinction. The first occasion was when I left all the notes I had made on a bench in the grounds at Downside, remembering them only when woken by a storm during the night. I went out with a torch and collected them. The second time was when I forgot to pick up the three concluding chapters, the summing up of the whole argument, from a chair at London Airport. This section of the book had occupied me during a retreat to some nuns near Edinburgh, and on being met at the plane by George I was more interested in telling him about the Edinburgh Festival than in gathering up the typescript. Several hours later, when we came back for it, the heap of sheets was where I had left it.

Since, following the accident to my ear, I had been relieved of my duties as week-end chaplain at All Hallows, I was now more free to develop interests within the enclosure. The trouble was that, being too unsteady on my feet to dig and too uncertain in my vision to write, the scope was narrowed. When I tried to carve I either fell on my face or hit inaccurately; when I tried to concentrate on people's problems I would hear a bomb ticking in my head which after a few minutes would blow up and I would have to close the interview. The punishment for having done too much in America was that I was now forced to do too little at home.

Having lived at comparatively high pressure for some time, I did not like to think of myself as condemned to idleness, as on the shelf. It seemed clear at that time I had made my last journey to America, given my last retreat. I refused to believe, however, that I had carved my last block of stone, so I had some pieces moved into a position which would allow me to attack them sitting down. It was humiliating, as well as from the practical point of view difficult, to swing a mallet from a seated position, but it was better than not swinging one at all. Working for twenty minutes at a time and then lying on the floor, I eventually finished three figures, two of which were sold. Having proved to myself that it could be done sitting down and with blocks of stone two feet tall, I wanted to prove it could be done leaning against a wall in an upright position and using blocks of stone four feet tall and larger. This arrangement took much longer, but as an exercise of do-it-yourself therapy it gradually accustomed me to balancing on my two feet and even to walking without sticks.

Fired by the hope of returning to normal all along the line, I tried some tentative writing. This did not go so well, half an hour at the typewriter being more than enough. But if I could hit stone why could I not hit the keys of a machine which had come to be almost an extra limb to me? So I typed on, and in the week after Easter was taken to hospital where I spent the next five weeks.

This time, with little the matter with me beyond the need for rest and a cessation of curative experiments, I was back at St Mary's Hospital in Bristol where I had not been since 1945 when the war was in its final phase. Having been a patient in several hospitals since 1945, including one in America for a few days, I felt I was beginning on a second round. A detail which encouraged this feeling was the sight of the same treetop against the sky which had held my attention on the previous visit. I was now one floor higher in the hospital, and the tree had grown in the fifteen years. For a variety of reasons I did not greatly enjoy this second experience of St Mary's. The nursing was as good as ever, and I met with nothing but kindness. The drawback lay in the recognition of hopes frustrated and relationships severed. Opportunities and people were slipping away. I was tired, and the world was growing old and tired as well. 'The corn grows now where Troy once stood.'

This Bristol mood was not a mere haphazard melancholy. Looking back I can see it in its appointed place and as having a spiritually educative work to do. The immediate causes were physical; the purpose was spiritual. The dejection which asserted itself at St Mary's and developed throughout the months which followed was the appropriate prelude to the peace which came later on. This in mind, a brief analysis of the preliminary process will make the resulting satisfaction more intelligible.

There was a difference in the present sense of defeat and that which has been described earlier. Where before I had had to face my failure to live up to a clearly defined ideal, now I was beginning to doubt the ideal itself. Where before my self-confidence was blown sky high, now the threat was to confidence in any direction. When a man doubts the validity of an aim which has dragged him through the badlands throughout his religious life, he is left not only without a light to follow but with the sense that he ought never to have started following it.

I had lost touch with myself before, not knowing where I stood, but this time I was losing touch with what I believed to be the essence of monasticism. Always in the past there had been, along with my personal inadequacies and acting as compensation for them, a certain structure of conventional certitudes. These certitudes had lit up the darkness of ordinary external life, and had provided the stimulus as well as the principle of my action. But now all this was gone. I could no longer generate the electricity. There was no source of energy to tap.

To ring the changes in metaphor it was like trying to accelerate and finding yourself in a dummy car, like trying to grow and realizing that nature has withdrawn the principle of growth. Hitherto I had believed myself capable of starting up the engine, but now there was nothing to connect; hitherto I had imagined I could add a cubit to my stature, but now I was being reduced to nothing.

As a child in Alexandria I believed that I and nobody else was responsible when a house fell down. Now as a man in my middle fifties I believed that the house had fallen down again, and that it was all my fault. How could I not feel guilty, having built in the wrong tradition? I had used the wrong materials, faced the wrong way, surrendered to the wrong pressures. There seemed to be no chance of building it up again. Without a fulcrum, even a lever cannot lift the world. Without a plan and a purpose, not even a born architect will produce a house.

The spiritual books would say that a man's very inability is the point of leverage, and that he ought to be able to hoist himself up from there. 'When I am weak, then I am strong . . . virtue is made perfect in infirmity.' At the time, however, the books and the texts are of little help. It is as though an airman who is given a precise course to follow so that he may pass through the sound barrier finds himself *in* the sound barrier and unable to read the instructions. Navigation, so far as he is concerned, breaks down. All he can do is to wait at the controls for something outside himself to take over. This is exactly what I did, and when the forced landing was finally made, it seemed the most natural landing in the world.

Before going on to recount the manner in which this conclusion was brought about for me, bringing confirmation along with relief, I quote relevant passages from the author already cited, Teilhard de Chardin. 'At every moment we see diminishment, both in us and around us, which does not seem to be compensated by advantages at any perceptible level . . . man does not move upward in any direction that we can perceive. He disappears or remains grievously diminished. How can these diminishments, which are altogether without compensation, wherein we see death at its most deathly, become for us a good?'* The writer goes on to show that God operates in the domain of the diminishments themselves, and that the specific factors in our lives which have occasioned our greatest failures, and made us suffer the greatest loss, combine to become the immediate and effective factor in the ultimate release. The barrier is at once the break-through.

'The essential marvel of the divine *milieu*' says the same writer describing the happy outcome of all this, 'is the ease with which it assembles and harmonises within itself qualities which appear to us contradictory.'† Though these words do not excuse the inconsistencies which we allow into our lives, they explain the irreconcilables which we sometimes so disturbingly see there.

The law of growth in the spirit is invariable: the upward thrust

* *Op. cit.*, p. 67. † *Ibid.*, p. 100.

occasioned by combustion. The obvious analogy is that of launching a rocket into space. The soul mounts to God by utilising elements which of their nature are destructive but which, utilised by the action of grace, are the means of elevation. How else? 'I, if I be lifted up, will draw all things to myself.' The magnetic influence is there, constant. All it wants is the explosion of selfish interests to provide the motor force.

So it is in the spiritual order that what looks like the betrayal of an ideal is in fact the ideal's translation into new terms and to a new level. It is, in technical language, a 'procession'. The old forms are reversed. Hitherto it was a matter of establishing superficial equilibrium by the removal of disturbance; now it is a matter of essential equilibrium resulting *from* disturbance. What sort of life it is that emerges out of all this combustion is not the individual's concern. This is where trust comes in. It would spoil the whole thing if we could design our own Phoenix, and enjoy it as a pet.

After five weeks in bed I came back, at the beginning of May, to Downside. Carving, whether it was a physical effort or not, must now be the outlet. It will surprise nobody who has followed the drift of the foregoing section when I say that the first piece of sculpture I attempted on my return was a figure of the dead Christ. Stone, more than clay, bronze, paint, or any other material, seems to me the medium best suited to such a subject. The dignity of death, which is so much more dignified than that of life, is matched by the classic tranquillity of stone. Wood is less static than stone, carrying on a life of its own. Stone is petrified life, and as such was the perfect material for what I wanted to convey. To those who are not artists this may seem an over-elaboration, but the artist knows that if he is to produce something new and worth while he must first dig inside himself and then go right on beyond himself. If this is true about any subject he proposes to himself, it must be particularly true when he attempts to carve the figure of Christ. More especially the dead Christ. It would be bad art if the artist stopped short at himself and did not aspire to something above himself. It would also be bad Christianity if he represented Christ only as a reflection of himself. As far as

Christianity goes it would be better to have a sculpture which tells only what it knows from books than one which talks only about itself.

So while working on *Christ Dead* I needed to have more to go upon than my death wish, more even than the experience of destruction which had clouded my time in hospital. I had need of a closer understanding of Christ, alive and dead. How far I was successful in suggesting the combined ideas of majesty, acceptance, death and waiting, I would be the last person to judge. I know that artistically the work was far from good, just as historically and on their literary merits *The Holy Rule* and *The Benedictine Idea* were far from good, but in the same way that I am glad to have written the books I am more glad to have carved *Christ Dead* than anything else I have done in stone.

Throughout these months of interior strain I was unable to give retreats. If I did not know where I was, it would be no good trying to tell other people where they were. The greatest relaxation came in the form of visitors to the stoneshed. Whether talking, eating, working, reading, quarrelling, or getting in my way, the boys who daily drifted in were the best distraction I could have asked for. Ranging from fourteen to eighteen, they gave me more to think about than some of the earlier circles that had delighted me. Preoccupied as I was at this time, I cannot think that I made a very entertaining host, but it is one of the endearing qualities of young men that they persevere. Not only young men but also young women. The eight girls of the Quinn family, several of whom I had baptized, used to come often to see me. Paul Quinn had been at school with me, and had settled at Shepton Mallet. It did not take much of a crisis in the household to bring his children over to Downside. Since the ages of the Quinn girls ranged from six to nineteen at the period of which I write, our meetings in the stoneshed were sometimes noisy. So from 1959 until recently when I was transferred to Wales there was always a faithful following, male and female, which brightened my days when the stoneshed was not closed by my commitments elsewhere.

Over the years I can see that the stoneshed cemented as many relationships as the retreats. Yet neither sculpture nor religion was necessarily the reason for this. Among my visitors from

America were Maurice Lavanoux, the critic and editor of *Liturgical Arts*; Monsignor Driscoll, who did not come to do business but who bought the two-ton *Last Supper*; Ned O'Gorman the poet; the entire Garvey family of ten who came in a van. From nearer home, Peter Watts would look in, but all too rarely, to talk about stone and his projected lecture tours in America. Princess Francesco Borghese, whom I had known as a girl at school and who had taken up modelling in clay, came with whirlwind effect and dazzled even the most phlegmatic among the residents into life. Some of those who came as customers returned as friends, and this was very reassuring indeed.

A weekly visitor during the summers of 1961 and 1962 was Siegfried Sassoon. He would arrive with a thermos and a bag of biscuits, and have his tea in the stoneshed while I went on working. Sometimes he would bring a guest who was staying with him, Edmund Blunden or Ian Davey, but mostly he would come alone. Though I suspect that sculpture bores him, I know that people do not, and when there was nobody else present we would talk endlessly about the friends whom we had in common and about Ronald. Joining us when they were free from classes were some boys who attended the stoneshed regularly and who much admired Siegfried's work. For me their arrival was a signal to put down my chisels. We would sit outside on the grass and talk until it was time for me to go in to Vespers. Usually Siegfried too would come to Vespers, but the boys—David Gallagher, Brian Cotton, John von Knorring, Nicholas van den Branden de Reeth—would have to go down to the school and resume the liabilities of youth. I look back upon these evenings as among the happiest of those years. Every now and then, on the occasion of a holiday or when for some reason they could get off, the boys and I used to motor over to see Siegfried at Heytesbury. Here we would play bowls, discuss books and authors in the library, have an enormous tea, and arrive back later than we meant to.

In June 1961 a letter came from Monsignor Driscoll asking me to come to his parish at Jacksonville, Illinois, and carve two six-foot figures which he wanted to put up at the entrance to the Catholic cemetery. I could choose the stone, decide how the work was to be mounted, take as long as I liked over it, and stay as his guest throughout the undertaking. He added that the assignment might leave room for another Campion Society retreat. Monsignor Mike Driscoll had given the staunchest support to the scheme for the foundation of the contemplative community of primitive Benedictine observance, was himself a Benedictine oblate, and had Hugh Garvey for a brother-in-law.

Though wanting very much to accept the invitation, I did not at once put the proposal to the Abbot. I still could not count upon being able to do sustained work: on bad days I had to go back to sitting on a box and gripping the block of stone between my knees. This was an important and costly commission, and I did not want to risk saddling Mike Driscoll with a lot of half-finished sculpture and a corpse. So I wrote back saying I would go into practice, working six hours a day, and let him know in a few weeks if it seemed possible. On judging that it was possible I referred the request to authority, received permission, booked a flight, and started making a great number of alternative designs. In submitting the designs I suggested that as I did not feel equal to much preaching, and because I could not be sure how long the cemetery carvings would take, the Campion Society retreat at Notre Dame would be enough in the way of apostolic commitment. The designs were approved by return of post, and Mike wrote in his covering letter 'that's fine about doing only the Notre Dame retreat, but will you really keep to that?' I did not, because in the end I finished the carvings sooner than I thought I would, and preached ninety-seven times.

In the meantime I got ready by reading up the subject of American-quarried stone. The findings showed me that the chisels which I had used for years on Bath stone would make little impression on Indiana limestone, which appeared to be the softest available, so I obtained leave to spend a day in London buying new equipment. In London I chose the strongest instruments on the market, and also bought several little handbooks which I studied in the train on the way back.

This plan to go into the technique of sculpture was prompted by a sense of duty. I felt I owed as much to the pastor of Jacksonville. Here was the largest order I had yet been given, so I had better find out how carving was done. How did the pros go about it? Like my mother who has been described as making short cuts wherever possible, scorning method and carrying things off on her flair for style, I too had gone on in my own way and trusted to luck. 'You see, no hands,' had been the line I had taken, and now it was time I investigated seriously the mechanics of sculpture. My father would have approved.

With mounting discomfort I learned from these books that I had been doing it wrongly for thirty years. But I still had a month before America in which to put myself on a professional basis. It was no good. The books, with their diagrams and warnings, with their photographs showing how the chisel should be gripped and at what angle it should meet the stone, confused me. So I put the books away, and instead gave myself slightly longer each day at the actual material.

The Campion Society retreat was by now, after so many times round, such an informal and intimate affair that the three or four discourses a day hardly ranked as preaching. It gave me no sense of strain. Once again, and by the kindness of Father Lauck who arranged it, I was able to call on Mestrovic. This time the master introduced me to his students as 'my friend and fellow sculptor' which made me swell with pride. Hugh Garvey tells me I have never quite got over it. Mestrovic seemed to have aged a good deal. He told me that though he was allowed by his doctor to model, he was forbidden to carve. Yet because his method of modelling, he explained, consisted largely of throwing lumps of clay at a mass of built-up material, he set little store by the wisdom of the advice. To show me what he meant he hurled a thick pat of clay with great force at a figure on which he was working. And there it stuck, in exactly the right place. 'Striking with the hammer is far less tiring,' he said, adding with a Yugoslavian look, 'so I do both.'

On this occasion I was in his studio for longer, and he evidently wanted to talk. He told me he had seen my book on sculpture, published since our previous meeting, and had liked it. He did not say he had *read* it but that he had *seen* it, and from this I gathered that though his English was limited he chose his words with care. And with regard to truth. At the mention of my book,

Father Lauck showed him a photograph of my *Deposition*. Mestrovic studied it and said it was good. 'It is not so much good van Zeller,' I said, with what I hoped was a deprecating smile and not a smug one, 'as bad Mestrovic.' He thought about this statement for a moment, translating it into his own language, and then roared with gratified laughter. Holding the print in his hand he left Father Lauck and myself where we were sitting, and we could hear him repeating the joke in the next room to his students. 'That has made him very happy,' said Father Lauck, 'and of course you *have* taken quite a bit from the Professor.'

Before we left him, Mestrovic drew me aside and asked me to pray particularly for his son who had died shortly before. 'It has affected me. I feel I am . . .' and he snapped his fingers to imply finality. This had been an even more satisfactory meeting than the one before, and I felt I was saying goodbye to someone whom I was coming to know and like, not merely to someone whose work I admired and whose name I held in honour.

Less than four months later, on January 16, 1962, Mestrovic died. His body was flown to Yugoslavia, where it was to have lain in state for two days in St Mark's Cathedral, Zagreb, and for another two days at the church of the Holy Cross in Split. He was to be buried with full solemnity on January 28 in the family crypt at Otavice. Though these arrangements had been agreed to by the Yugoslav authorities they were not carried out. The coffin was hustled in and out of Zagreb without ceremony, taken straight to Drnis where orders were given that Mass should be said at once before the mourners had assembled, and thence to the family mausoleum. Here, at Otavice, where some three thousand loyal Catholics were gathered for the last of the ceremonies, the Bishop of Split began his sermon of eulogy. He did not get far. Paying tribute to the dead sculptor as 'a Catholic and a Croat', the Bishop was interrupted by a gang of Communists who heckled and threatened so persistently that the Bishop, in order to prevent bloodshed, had the coffin carried into the crypt without further ceremony. Those who had tried to silence the agitators were afterwards arrested. 'I am nearly eighty,' he had told me a few months before, 'so maybe it is time for me to go.' It is only a pity that one of the greatest

Christian artists that the world has ever seen should have to go quite like that.

I have told how much impressed I was by the Benedictine convent of St Walburga, Colorado, the first time I went there. The second visit in October 1961, which lasted a week, impressed me even more. It was to this, and to all that developed from this, that the trials of a year ago were leading me. A long enough time has elapsed since then for reason to pass judgment on what might have been something emotional. I know in 1964 that what I felt in 1961 needs no qualification: nothing calls for apology or retraction. The dawn which is glanced at between snatches of sleep may turn out to have been a false dawn: there is no doubting the dawn which goes on providing more light.

Having learned while giving the Campion Society retreat that Mike Driscoll was to be away from Jacksonville until the end of the month I arranged to go first to St Walburga's before starting on the stone. Accordingly I arrived at Denver Airport in the middle of October where I was met by three members of the community and a Mrs Leonard whom the Reverend Mother had asked to act as hostess to me for the afternoon. The Leonard family consists of nine children and their mother. John Leonard, the father, had died earlier in the year, in April, after a long illness endured with the greatest resignation. I had heard about the Leonards, and about the father's death, from one of the nuns. But I was quite unprepared for the impact. In the ordinary way it takes me a little time to get used to a big young noisy household, and it takes the household a little time to get used to me. There was none of this with the Leonards. The exchange was immediate and, as it has turned out, lasting. Since I was engaged to speak in and around Denver during the week of my stay at St Walburga, not twenty miles from Denver, I was able to see more of the family than I had a right to expect. Whenever I came down from a platform, there they seemed to be. The reason why I drag them into the story here is not only because they might as well know that I think them worth putting into a book—they have been mentioned in print before now and do not seem to like it—but more because, if I left them out, the story of my waking up would be incomplete. The picture as presented by St Walburga's needs the companion picture as presented by the household at Denver. I hope this can be said without causing embarrassment in either camp.

In close association, then, with the twofold ideal—one aspect of it reflected in the supernatural family life of the convent where I was staying, one aspect of it aspired to in the natural family which I was coming to know—I found myself closer than ever before to what evidently had eluded me throughout my life. It was like looking into the back of a camera while the photographer is getting his subject into focus. It showed me that I had never really seen the whole thing—God's world which included the entire range of people, created good, religious service, human affection, suffering, happiness—properly in focus, in true perspective. Always it had been more or less blurred. Or I had seen one aspect of it at a time, and often to the exclusion of the others. Where before there had been a divided loyalty—God claiming his rights and human beings claiming theirs—now there seemed to be no conflict. Life appeared to be simpler than I had understood it to be. When light is brought to bear upon simplicity the consequence is peace. Life can now become, in the full sense, alive. By the end of my week at St Walburga's convent I had passed from strain to calm, from blindness to sight. When I said goodbye to the nuns at the gates of the enclosure, and next day to the Leonards at the airport, I knew that the verse from the psalms which had seemed so significant to me at my first visit had now been verified. Even if I should never come back again to the Colorado Rockies I had 'received my help from the mountains, the mountains to which I had raised my eyes in hope'. As the plane moved towards the strip to take off, I could see two of the Leonards waving at me from the terminal and in the distance the broken line of the range gleaming white against the October sky.

Monsignor Mike was still not at home in Jacksonville, and there had been a hitch or two about ordering the stone, so I filled in the time with some sermons and lectures which I had been asked to give but which were dependent upon the Jacksonville dates. I spoke in Boston, in and about Kansas City, Chicago, Pittsburgh, and baptised a baby in Rhode Island. By now the blocks of stone and my ecclesiastical patron were waiting for me so I arrived on the eve of All Saints to begin the work for which I had come. All Saints went out, because it was a holiday of obligation, but at least I was able to get things ready and make drawings on the stone. The workshop—or as I preferred to call it, the stoneshed—was Monsignor Mike's garage fitted out with moveable arc-lamps and a heater.

On the first day I broke three chisels. This was not because I failed to carry out the instructions in chapter two of the handbook *How to Hold and Where to Hit*, but because the stone was harder than the London tool-makers had envisaged. At the end of a wasted morning I decided to try with a pressure hammer and an instrument called a skillsaw, both worked by electricity. Having held out for years against what I looked upon as clockwork toys, saying grandly that I would carve with my fingernails and teeth before I stooped to battery-operated instruments, I humbled myself and learned the new techniques. I found that certain effects could be produced with powered tools which could not be produced by hand, so now I no longer spurn these things. Also the speed and the roar were exciting.

Never have I enjoyed fulfilling an order more. It was not only that the recent transformation at St Walburga's had worked wonders with my psyche, but that on a more material and social level the Jacksonville setting was ideal. I was able to average seven hours a day on the stone and fit in weekly conferences to two religious communities in the town. The Garveys came over often from Springfield, twenty miles away, and a number of the townspeople made a habit of looking in. The carving—or perhaps it should be called drilling—went well and I was jubilant. So was Mike, who would bring in parties of people to watch me work. He was a Lorenzo di Medici, shouting through the din and dust, displaying magnificence. 'I have my sculptors imported from Europe,' he would roar—to the mystification of his friends.

Mike more than anyone else knew what monastically, artistically, socially and spiritually I was trying to do in America, so it was a delight to be under his roof for these four or five weeks. Together we celebrated Thanksgiving at the Garveys, returning the same night so that I could begin work early next morning. With Mass every day next door to the stoneshed, and freedom to arrange my hours of prayer, work, and reading as I liked, I did not mind how long it took me to get the figures done.

One of the joys connected with this time was the way in which boys and girls of all ages came in to see me on their way to and from school. In the mornings there was not much time, but in the afternoons they stopped on for as long as an hour or more. A thing which particularly struck me about my new friends was that they contrived in no time to reproduce exactly the pattern of stoneshed life as it had been at Downside. They formed distinct and mutually exclusive groups, they violently resented the presence of the single casual spectator, they settled down to a recognised routine in a selected part of the room. Once their rights were established they produced food and began disagreeing with one another. The moment another group came in, or a stray called, there would be complete silence and the duties of host would be left to me. Even the comments made about my work, and the jokes about me, were the same that I had been hearing from several generations of Downside boys. The only difference lay in accent and dress; for the rest I might have been on the other side of the Atlantic at almost any time between 1930 and 1960.

Before I came away early in December, the stoneshed restored to its status as a garage and cleared of associations with the rapidity that a blackboard is cleared of its chalked lines, I had the satisfaction of seeing the two carvings placed in position. Mounted on brick and standing nine feet high at the entrance of the cemetery they excited remark not always favourable. The press notices were extravagant, pointing to a revival of interest in sculpture throughout the length and breadth of Jacksonville, but I was not fooled. Had I not enquired of the citizenry about the sculptured monument in the central square, and met with blank faces? If here neither the date, the name of the sculptor, the material used, nor even the occasion commemorated had survived, what chance had I?

From the same square during the last days of my time in this friendly town, Mike and I watched Father Christmas coming down from the skies in a helicopter. It was a sparkling day, sunshine and frost, with everyone looking pink and seasonal. The yells as Father Christmas touched down, heard only through my one good ear, were as exhilarating as the colours of the people's clothes. From where we stood, discreetly on the fringe of the crowd as became serious ecclesiastics, we could see little of the grounded Father Christmas but only the slow whirling of the blades as the propeller over his head came to a stop.

Since there was still a margin of time before I was expected in England for Christmas, I agreed to do a series of four broadcasts which even now left me a gap for my usual invasion of the Sacred Heart empire of convents and colleges in the east. But I am no broadcaster, and the atmosphere of the broadcasting studio, though hospitable, I found oppressive. I found the same when delivering a Christmas sermon the following year from Denver. Speaking in a glass box in front of a soundless man touching switches and holding a cup of coffee which cannot be heard to rattle, is to me like talking to hot pipes that have been turned off or trying to pray before an empty tabernacle with the doors open. Some have a gift for it. I have not.

At Manhattanville the last few days were spent in something of a rush. On one day I spoke seven times, driven by car from one community to another. According to the rules it should have been distracting, but in fact was not. I was anchored in reality and nothing else mattered. A line of Pound's kept coming back to me: 'What thou lovest well remains; the rest is dross.' I knew now what I loved; everything else was shedding itself as I went along.

Just before the return journey to England a letter reached me from the Abbot. In it he told me he had had a request from a Cistercian superior asking that I should be allowed to give five eight-day retreats, one after the other, to the Cistercian communities strung across America. The date for this was to be early in 1963. The Abbot said he had consented to this proposal. It was my Christmas present.

CHAPTER FOURTEEN

The Cycle Repeated

On this the last lap of my odyssey I attempt no moralising and draw no conclusions. There has been enough of that already. So to continue the record of events I can say that from the return to the monastery immediately before Christmas, 1961, until the next visit to the States in the autumn of 1962, calmness reigned inside and out. During the Christmas holidays I tried going back to digging but it was no good. I might be able on a day of dizziness to hack stone sitting down, but for manual labour one has to be standing up. Reluctantly I decided that work among the cabbages and potatoes would be no longer possible for me, and that I had better get on with the two industries which were left to me: writing and shaping stone.

But I was not able to act as typist and mason for long, because Dom Julian Stonor, chaplain at Talacre, got ill and had to be replaced. Myself expendable because not on the teaching staff at Downside, and also because Talacre would not mean new ground, the obvious subject for the replacement lay to hand and I was sent. When giving me my instructions Abbot Butler assured me that this did not cancel the retreat bookings which he had agreed to for the following spring. He added that since he had received further requests—one of them from the Prioress at St Walburga asking that I should be allowed to spend some months at the convent carving eight stone panels for the outside walls of their building—I might have to come away from Talacre in the summer. He would let me know.

It was fitting that I should arrive at Talacre on January 21, the date of my arrival fifteen years earlier. 'You will like it,' everyone said, 'you know the ropes.' The ropes were all right, but the hands which pulled on them were stiffer. Everything was the same, yet nothing was the same. The notice on the gate saying

'Private' to the nuns was still there. The Koffee Kids were not. From someone in the village I learned that the Coffey family had migrated once again; this time to Australia or New Zealand, nobody knew which. Nobody ever does know which. Our Towyn must be twenty-one now, and goodness only knew what had happened to Shirley and Marlene by this time.

The difference lay not so much in outward things but in me. I was able to see by this return to Talacre, certainly more clearly than I would have been able to see otherwise, that life was no longer the rudderless quest which I had felt it to be fifteen years ago. I had come full cycle, and was getting back now to the unquestioning acceptance which I had enjoyed as a quite small child—before I had started enquiring into everything, and doubting. At the age of six it does not do to analyse. Nothing so easily forms a habit as experiment in introspection. It does not surprise me that today, more than ever before, the age of infancy is idolised: it is idolised because it is envied. We in this self-conscious age get occasional glimpses of what it was like to feel affection without guilt, to feel hope without fear that our hope would be blocked, to feel enthusiasm without being committed to a policy, to feel sad without wondering if we were giving in to self-pity, to feel piety without worrying about sentimentality. There is much to be said for the state of childhood, and though I would not have my life over again for anything in the world I would not object to living permanently in the nursery, and never advancing beyond the age of, say, five. Things being what they are I have no need, since it is a spiritual nursery that I inhabit now, to turn wistfully to the toys and joys of long ago.

But I said I would not moralise or form conclusions.

During the eight months I spent at Talacre in 1963, months of a lost spring and summer, I wrote books and amused myself in solitude as best I could: the same horarium from four in the morning till nine at night. It would be of little interest to the reader if I recorded how I went for a walk, took a bath, and ate a fried egg for supper. So I can go on to what for me, and I hope for those who are following me, is something more worth while.

On October 1, Father Abbot being as good as his word about

sending me well in advance of the Cistercian commitments, I arrived in New York. For once it was raining fit to drown, but this daunted neither me nor my backers, and a week later, having spoken twenty-eight times, I found myself dazed but happy in Chicago. Here I was engaged to address a club called the Medievalists. I had supposed, when accepting the invitation, that this was a society, parochial in character, similar to the Knights of St Columba or, at a secular level, the Elks. The name had conjured in my mind a picture of devout scriveners and clerks, merry men of Sherwood Forest, vaguely religious Morris dancers. I had prepared the material for this talk with care but not, as it turned out, with correct destination. During the formidable dinner which was to act as an overture to my discourse, I became increasingly aware of having made a mistake. Seated on the right of the society's president, I learned from a retired judge who sat on the other side of me that the Medievalists, for the most part lawyers and professors, had over the years listened to talks from Hilaire Belloc, Cardinal Mundelein, M. Maritain, Georges Bernanos, Chesterton, Father D'Arcy, Frank Sheed, and I think Bishop Sheen. Tonight they were going to listen to me. 'In case I miss you afterwards,' said the secretary of the society, coming over to me from another table while the microphone was being got ready for the president who was to introduce me, 'I must ask you to accept a small honorarium to cover your expenses.' The cheque was for a hundred and seventy dollars. There had been no expenses to cover because Michael Carroll, with whom I was staying the night, had driven me to the meeting in his car.

'How long do you want this talk to last?' I asked, wondering what would be considered a moneysworth.

'Please yourself, Father, the night is young.'

Eleven talks later I was enjoying the now familiar surroundings of the Fatima Retreat House at Notre Dame and addressing the Campion Society. It was while we were here that the Cuba situation reached its crisis, and none among those present for the retreat is likely to forget the feel of those fateful days. Some of the retreatants cut short their stay to go home to their families, their newspapers, their radios, their air-raid shelters. The majority stopped on to pray and orientate themselves spiritually towards the imminence of nuclear war. These, when not kneeling in the chapel to my enormous edification, sat in their cars and understandably listened to the hourly bulletins. Any Englishman who needed to be converted to a sympathetic view of America would have found during these few days an irresistible persuasion. This was October, 1962. The tragedy of November, 1963, and all that followed it, would come to confirm such a conversion.

While at the Notre Dame retreat I learned that Monsignor Mike wanted me to come at once to Jacksonville and carve him a dog. The magnifico was on the march again. He had built a Dominican convent opposite the church, and had apparently just discovered that there was no *Domini canis* to signify the order to which the community belonged. The nuns had not yet moved in, but would I please hurry because he hoped to have everything ready for the ceremonial opening? He did not give a date for this. So from the Cuba crisis I went in great haste to Springfield, where Hugh Garvey was making enquiries about stone, hiring equipment, obtaining from the public library illustrated books about dogs, and receiving telephone calls from his clerical brother-in-law at Jacksonville. Animals might belong to a different planet so far as I am concerned, and I cannot even make a caricature of a dog in pencil, let alone make a serious model of a dog in stone. It had been difficult enough showing Bobby Craven how to carve funny penguins; it was going to be much more difficult to produce a convincing dog for Monsignor Mike. But the experiment was well worth it, because for two days I worked with the men at the bench in a Springfield stoneyard. In England I had worked with masons, but so far not in America. The proprietor of the stoneyard, who owned a quarry and who operated as a contractor, was a man of considerable charm and distinction named Mr Baum. The man next to me at the bench was of a cheerful disposition, agreeing with me that someone whose name was Baum should deal in timber and not stone. Either that or his name should be Stein. We thought this a very funny joke. Never have I met a more genial mason.

The dog was delivered, and had to wait months before the space on the outer wall of the convent was ready to receive him. But bringing this not very creditable piece of carving to Jacksonville gave me the opportunity of seeing the two-ton *Last Supper* in position in the community refectory, and making final alterations. I was also able to put my head round the door of the garage. I missed the friendly litter of stone chips, used and blackened bulbs from the arc lamps, chisels, saws, files, curling sheets of sandpaper. My forearms throbbed from the memory of the drilling, and the palms of my hands ached in retrospect. I missed also the wrappings from the bars of chocolate, the silver paper off the chewing-gum, the sticks and cores of toffee-apples, and I missed the throng who had left them there. One never learns.

From Jacksonville to Dubuque, Iowa, where the eldest of the Leonard girls had entered at Mount Carmel, the novitiate house of the Sisters of Charity, B.V.M. Having last seen her among her family at Denver I was a little apprehensive about how I would find her as a religious. I need not have worried. Between the conferences that I was asked to give, six of them in the three days that I was there, we saw much of one another. That part of Iowa must be thick with religious houses because I seemed to go from one to another. A community which I was particularly pleased to address was that of the Cistercians originally founded from Europe. The only shadow across the memory of the Cistercian expedition was that I mistook the Abbot, who was not wearing either cross or ring, for a lay brother.

Leaving Dubuque was not easy, but it would have been a lot more difficult if I had not been heading for Denver and St Walburga's. On the flights between Dubuque and Denver I reflected upon what was now to open up. Allowing for the chain of Cistercian retreats which would occupy six weeks, I could look forward to spending in all some four months in Colorado at the convent. I knew that the nuns had accepted a few local preaching engagements for me, but since my work with them, necessarily carried out within the enclosure, would take up most of the available time, I was not likely to be out of the place for long. The prospect could not have been more agreeable: it promised exactly those things which I had most longed for in life and which I had seldom had a chance of enjoying. Certainly never for as long as four months.

Early in November, then, I was established at St Walburga's Convent in a room which looked out upon the Rockies a few miles away. Not wanting to benefit by the nuns' hospitality without having something to show for it in return, I was anxious to get down to work as soon as possible on the eight five-foot stone panels which were the main reason for my being there. The kind of stone to be used was the first problem, and for a time it looked as though Indiana limestone, which was what I had worked on at Jacksonville, would have to be transported at considerable expense from a distant quarry. After much investigation, and long negotiation with owners of widely separate quarries, we decided to order a certain greenish stone, hard but with a fine grain and a smooth surface, from Cheyenne in the neighbouring state of Wyoming. To judge from the piece on my table it looked ideal, and I started sharpening the chisels.

Delay followed delay. The man who quarried the stone fell ill, and did not want to entrust the order to a subordinate. When the illness subsided and the quarryman was back and ready to blast, the temperature dropped to below zero and no work could be done on the rock. For myself I did not mind if matters were held up indefinitely. I was giving conferences to the novices and the community—only seventeen in all, which make a cosy kind of audience to address—and writing, concurrently, two small books for the *In Other Words* series which Templegate was publishing. I had plenty to do in catching up on my reading and praying, and would have been happy enough to sit all day in the exquisitely simple chapel, but I did at the same time feel slightly uncomfortable being a guest almost on false pretences. Here the Prioress, Mother Gertrud, came to the rescue. On her own initiative she asked if it might not be possible for me to stay on, whether the stone were to come this winter or not, and assist Father Augustine, the resident chaplain, who was often ill and in need of someone to say the community Mass instead of him. I could be usefully employed giving short retreats to groups near by, continuing my weekly conferences to the community, perhaps pottering about on the farm and helping generally. If I agreed, she said, she would write to her own and my superiors and obtain the necessary permissions. I agreed with alacrity. Since the offer had come from St Walburga's I felt no guilt; I was not manœuvering. Until the stone came from Cheyenne and I would be able to earn my keep, I could content myself doing odd jobs like sweeping the snow from the paths and opening the chapel doors at four-thirty. I had not expected anything quite so good as this.

By way of following up Mother Gertrud's letter to Abbot Butler, I wrote one of my own. Rarely do I make a rough draft of a letter: I made one on this occasion. In it I said how I had now been at St Walburga's long enough to judge of its effect on me, and how I would be glad to settle 'for an indefinite period' in the terms of reverend mother's petition. I said I could be put under the proximate jurisdiction of the Abbot of the Benedictine community of Holy Cross, Canon City, which was only a few hours drive away. Before posting the letter I put it on the altar and said Mass. (I have been informed since that this was un-liturgical, if not irregular.) Mother Gertrud told me one morning that the nuns were praying for a favourable reply from England. This pleased me greatly, and I told her that the Leonards were praying in the same sense. The reply, reaching me in the middle of Advent, was indeed favourable. I was told I might stay for three years with the possibility of having the time extended to further periods of three years, and that authorisation for this arrangement was being obtained through the official channels in Rome. I was jubilant. This was the second year running that Abbot Butler had sent me a Christmas present.

So at last I had reached the fort at the end of the bay: this time there was nothing to disappoint. That myth had now been exploded, disproved by actual experience. In my letters to Yolande, who was in her nineties and writing to me once a week, I told how completely serene, confident, and happy I felt, how the disappointments of the past twenty or thirty years were well worth it if they had led up to this, how I could now laugh without feeling obliged to out of politeness, and that there was nothing more to worry about. To George I wrote that the past, with its restless changes, had dropped from me like a shirt full of ants, and that I was so content to be here, with the silence and the farm and the round of the Divine Office at which I was assisting more closely than had been possible at Talacre, that I had no desire to leave even to give retreats. My letters that Christmas must have been monotonous in theme.

Of the two books I was then working on, one was about the psalms. Every day I was finding new applications. Particularly the gradual psalms expressed my gratitude: 'If it had not been that God was with us . . . we shall not be moved for mountains are about us . . . delight now fills the heart, and peace shall be upon Israel.' Though I have spent less time in Colorado than in either Egypt, England, or Wales, I look upon it as my home. Without a home somewhere in the world, there is not much that a man can do for the homeless.

Though Christmas at St Walburga's was to me a novel experience, it combined the essential elements of every Christmas I had spent. Unique in its simplicity and spontaneity: familiar in its liturgy, monastic routine, and charity. 'Unsophisticated' might be a better word here than 'simple': the symbols of festivity more conspicuous than what would be seen in England. Most of the nuns being German, the customs brought over from the mother house were preserved with the greatest fidelity. Christmas at St Walburga meant more wreaths, Christmas trees, stars, tinted fircones, sweet biscuits, flaming red flowers bursting from crinkly silver paper, coloured candles, cribs, carols, cards, presents and *Grüssgotts* than even the Americans could match. To help things along, it snowed throughout Christmas eve and Christmas day.

The religious side of Christmas attended to, and before the anti-climacteric winds had time to blow, the Leonards came to fetch me for their family celebrations at home. They had fetched me for their Thanksgiving dinner the month before, but this was a tribute I valued even more. It was the first Christmas dinner I had shared with a family since 1923.

'You have got at least three more of these Christmases with us, don't forget,' said the youngest of the girls as the whole party drove me back to the convent. It had snowed for two days and the journey took an hour.

'I'm not forgetting,' I said.

On the morning of the Epiphany (1963) I started out on the six packed weeks of the Trappist retreats. It was something which I liked doing, but I felt now that my roots were in St Walburga's and I looked forward to coming back. The first two retreats went off all right—at least so far as I was concerned, and it is not for me to speak for the monks who were making them—and the other three might have followed as smoothly. At Portland, Oregon, I was met by the Abbot of Our Lady of Guadalupe, Lafayette, who very kindly brought with him to the airport a telegram addressed to me. It was a cable from England giving the news of Dom Julian Stonor's death, and instructing me to take his place as chaplain to the Talacre nuns as soon as I could dispose of my obligations in the States. Dom Julian had been at school with me, and was only slightly junior to me in the habit, so I felt his loss. The cable reported that his death was sudden, and I wondered whether he had received my letter before he died: a letter I had timed to reach him on February 11, the feast of our Lady of Lourdes. Today was February 12, so it seemed hardly likely.

There was now a considerable change of programme to be made, and I suspect that thinking about this and trying to adjust myself to it must have weakened what I was trying to do in these retreats. I found it hard to concentrate on the material and get it across. I could no longer look forward to three years of quiet at St Walburga's; I must cancel the order for the Cheyenne stone; I must either get out of or antedate engagements which were spaced over the next year; I must uproot myself when for the first time in my life I felt myself to be settled.

While I was still at the monastery in Oregon I received a letter from Abbot Butler which had been sent in amplification of his cable. It was the most gracious letter I have had from any superior: it went far towards reconciling me to the disappointment. A few days later, when I was with the Cistercians at Huntsville, Utah, a letter reached me from Dom Julian, written the day before his death. It was in answer to mine which had arrived on the right date. In it he said how pleased he was that at last I was settled. 'Happiness has come to you late,' he wrote, 'so hang on to it with both hands and be grateful.'

The rest of the story can be told in a few paragraphs. Since some of the preaching engagements could not be cancelled without causing inconvenience, I was given permission to extend my stay until after Easter. As soon as I had finished the last of the monastic retreats I went back to St Walburga where I was anxious to spend every moment that remained to me. Even had the stone been ready, there would have been no time to do more than one or two of the proposed eight panels, so I did not regret the cancellation. But I did regret having to come away without having satisfied the obligation, so offered to model the panels in clay which would take only half the time. I had never worked in clay, but there was no reason why I should not learn. In Passiontide, working even in Holy Week, I modelled the eight slabs of clay, showing scenes from the life of St Benedict, so that they were finished in time before I left. At least my debt to manual labour, if only in part my debt to the nuns, was fulfilled.

Having said goodbye to the community, which was a sad business, I spent my last day with the Leonards. Except for the eldest boy who was in his seminary at San Antonio, Texas, they were all at home for it. They came to my Mass at St Joseph's, which over the past two years I had come to think of as a launching pad into spaces grave and gay. The Mass was served by two Davids, uncle and nephew. David Leonard, the uncle, had to go to his work so did not see me off.

'It's just the way the hand gets dealt, I guess,' he said on parting.

'I guess,' I said.

Assembled at the airport, waiting to board a plane for South America, were twenty or so evangelists, lay missionaries, who were leaving their homes in Denver to work in a region of Peru where Christianity had not taken hold. Standing somewhat apart at the ticket gate they sang a hymn together. It was impressive, reminiscent of Lourdes. Some of them were crying while others forced a brittle cheerfulness. The relatives who were being left behind were more visibly distressed than the missionaries. The relatives and friends were thinking of poverty and jungles; the missionaries I suppose were trying to think of God. The Leonards and I sat watching this group, feeling increasingly uncomfortable as though we were looking through a keyhole. We turned away, but, in intervals of our own melancholy conversation, found ourselves turning back.

'They will probably all get tortured to death,' said Kathleen.

'Well, what's so wrong about that?' said her younger brother.

'Don't they have some sort of priest or minister to go with them?' asked Dorothy.

'He's having trouble with the parking-meter,' said Colette.

'At least, Dom, you are going to Europe,' said Mary, 'wouldn't you hate to be going with this lot?'

'I'd love it,' I said.
'Me too,' said Colette.

That was the last I saw—and supposedly the last the evangelists saw—of Colorado. A few days later I was in Wales where I have remained in the one place since. The appointment as chaplain to the thirty-eight nuns of Talacre Abbey is for terms, renewable, of three years. Now that I am well into the second year and can review the cyclic course in an objective spirit, I have no reason to be other than content. Even though I might not live in it, I have discovered my Alexandrian fort to be peopled and alive beyond all expectation. Far from being cheated I have been rewarded. Perhaps heaven will be like that: a discovery that there is now no chance of disillusion. And in any case the guilt-ridden are not good subjects for prolonged security.

Index

Aachen–Andernach journey, 155
Aboukir, 37, 38, 41
Acting guestmaster, 142, 143
Acting in school plays, 84, 89
Acton, Lady, 180, 190, 194-197
Acton, Lord, 180, 197
Addington, the Hon. Gurth, 174
Addington, the Hon. Raleigh, 185
Agate, James, 120
Agius, Dom Ambrose, 159
Alexander, Dom Romuald, 198, 199
Alexandria, 4, 8ff, 25, 30, 35, 39, 48, 52-54, 97ff, 165, 255
Ali, 15, 25, 36, 43, 98
Allenby, Field Marshal Lord, 100
All Hallows School, 221, 222, 225, 226, 253
Ampleforth Abbey, 209
Anderson family, 247
Angelico Society, 220, 221
Arbuthnot, Robert, 135
Archer, Mrs, 112, 117
Aristotle, 193
Armstrong, Hilary, 169, 170
Armstrong, William, 115
Art course in Bath, 157-159
Asquith, Lady Helen, 144, 242
Asquith, Mrs Raymond, 144, 197, 210, 239, 242

Bampton, Father, S.J., 49, 237
Baring, the Hon. Maurice, 88, 194, 195
Barlach, Ernst, 78, 157, 174
Barrie, J. M., 46, 183
Barrington, Georgina, 5, 25, 49, 236
Baum, Mr, 271
Beatrice, aunt, 61, 64, 65, 78, 235
Beerbohm, Sir Max, 183
Bellew, Lady, 105
Belloc, Hilaire, 88, 270
Bellord, George, 75, 116, 151, 162, 184, 190, 204, 205, 211, 223, 225, 241, 248, 249, 251, 253, 254
Belmont Abbey, 149
Bennet, Bishop, 217, 219
Benson, Mgr R. H., 7
Bernanos, Georges, 270
Bernhardt, Sarah, 26
Berthe, aunt, 33, 34, 46, 49, 56, 60, 66, 69, 76, 78, 107, 125, 152, 159, 161, 204, 235
Berton, Louis, 26
Beuron Abbey, 151, 156
Bishop, Edmund, 104
Blunden, Edmund, 259
Borghese, Donna Virginia, 259
Brompton Oratory, 48, 108, 162
Brooke-Stevens, Willie and Agnes, 207
Brooks, Robert, 110
Buckfast Abbey, 246, 247
Bull, Cyril, 126
Butler, Abbot Christopher, 103, 209, 232, 268, 269, 274, 276
Butler, Abbot Cuthbert, 118, 134
Butt, Archbishop, 149

Café Royal, 120, 125, 232
Caldey Abbey, 168, 169
Camberley House, 4, 34
Campbell, Mrs Patrick, 183
Campbell, Roy, 120
Carmelite Convent, Jackson, 251
Carroll, Jack, 126, 151, 191
Carroll, Michael, 270
Carter, Ernest, 35, 36, 42, 46, 49, 57, 74
Cavanagh, Dom Vincent, 247
Chapman, Abbot John, 103, 150, 151, 157, 158, 161
Chesterton, G. K., 88, 270
Chorley, the Hon. Mrs, xi
Christmas, Father, 266
Cistercian Order, 108, 109, 139, 141, 148, 161, 170, 171, 272, 276
Cloisters, the, 252
Clonmore, Lord (now Earl of Wicklow), 151
Coffey family, 205, 206, 269
Connolly, Cyril, 155

Cotton, Brian, 259
Corney, Dom Austin, 59, 66, 79, 80, 81
Corston Hospital, 183-185
Corvo, Baron, 170
Cracks in the Cloister controversy, 232, 233
Craven, Earl of, 231, 271
Cuba crisis, 271
Cuffe, Peter, 184

Dante, 126, 163
D'Arcy, Father Martin, S.J., 180, 210, 270
Davey, Ian, 259
Davey, Dom Richard, 127, 130, 138, 148
de Caussade, Père, 144
de Halwyl, Comtesse Hydeline (author's great-great grandmother), 26
de Launay, Count, 26
Delatte, Abbot, 118
de Löos-Corswarem, Princess (author's great-great aunt), 26
de Reeth, Baron Nicolas van den Branden, 259
de Seigneux, Comtesse Hydeline (author's grandmother, *see* Van de Velde), 26
de Zuylen de Nyvelt, Baroness Louise (author's great aunt), 26
Dillon, Gerald Dormer, 114, 115, 125
Dix, Francis and Eve, 221, 231
Douglas, Lord Alfred, 88
Douglas, Norman, 120
Downside (school), 35, 36, 49, 54, 56, 58, 59, 65-67, 73-75, 78, 81, 83-89, 103, 104, 106, 110, 111
Downside (monastery), 127-142, 144-151, 160, 161, 166, 167, 174-179, 181-183, 185, 186, 191-194, 197, 209, 216, 217, 219-222, 232, 233, 246, 254, 257-260
Driscoll, Mgr Michael, 259, 260, 263-267, 271
Dru, Alick, 75
Duchesne, Sacred Heart School, 252
Du Maurier, Gerald, 183
Dunstan, Father, O.F.M., 47, 49
Du Port, Antony, 81

Ellwood, coachman, 18, 19, 23, 25, 29, 72, 236, 237
Epstein, Jacob, 44
Eugenie, Empress, 235
Evans, Sir Horace, 239, 241, 242

Farm Street Church, 49, 236, 237
Farnborough Abbey, 147
Fitzgerald, Robert, 221
Foran, Father, 250
Ford, Miss, 67, 73
ffrench, Lord, 153
French, Lord, 153
Furrie, James, M.D., 251
Fyfe, David Maxwell- (now Lord Kilmuir), 114, 115

Gallagher, David, 259
Garvey family, 212, 247, 259, 265
Garvey, Hugh, 209-211, 216, 224, 260, 261, 271
Gautier, Marcel, 94, 95
Gerard family, 65
Gertrud, Reverend Mother, 263, 273, 274
Gill, Eric, 88, 89, 174, 196
Goosens, Emil, 104, 124
Gradwell, Leo, 115
Greenwich, Sacred Heart Convent, 215, 252
Groenthal, Dom Bruno, 156
Guadalupe, Our Lady of, Abbey, 276

Harding, Gilbert, 142, 143, 149
Harrison, Rex, 114
Harte, Bret, 235
Harvey, Father, 105
Hawtrey, Charles, 183
Headlam, Gerald, 208, 209
Hicks, Abbot Bruno, 161, 167
Hillier, Tristram, 75
Hinsley, Cardinal, 179
Hollis, Christopher, 182, 194
Huntsville, Utah, Cistercian monastery, 276

Jack, uncle, 71
Jackson, Mississippi, 251
Jacksonville, Illinois, 264-267, 271, 272
Jarrett, Father Bede, O.P., 86-90, 94, 104, 106, 108, 109, 113, 117, 130, 137, 138, 141-144, 148, 160, 161, 167, 203, 218, 244

INDEX

Jerome, Brother, 128

Kearon, Peter, 192
Kemmerer, Frannie, 252
Keogh, Dom Matthew, 128
Kitchener, Field Marshal Lord, 100
Knox, Mgr Ronald, 104, 143-145, 168-172, 179, 180, 182, 186, 194, 195, 203, 205, 210, 215, 216, 218, 219, 231, 234, 238-245, 259
Kynaston, Roger, 169, 170

Ladycross School, 167, 168, 173
Lancaster Gate, 4, 27, 29, 30, 33, 34, 38, 234, 235, 237
Lander, Mr and Mrs, 95, 97
Lane, Bernard, 75
Lauck, Father, 250, 261, 262
Lavanoux, Maurice, 259
Lavery, Dom Brendan, 190, 191
Lawrence, Colonel, 100, 182
Leonard family, 247, 263, 264, 272, 274, 275, 277
Lewis, Rosa, 124, 125
Leyne, Dom Christopher, 219, 220
Lindemann family, 37, 38, 41, 79, 98, 114
Lindemann, Helmuth, 37-40, 52, 53, 114
Lindemann, Hugo, 37, 114
Liverpool interlude, 111-117
Lourdes, 211, 277
Lovat, Lady, 241
Lunn, Sir Arnold, 194

McCann, Dom Justin, 180
MacDermot, chauffeur, 72, 80, 105
McGrath, Mrs, 25
MacGuire family, 230, 252
Macmillan, Harold and Lady Dorothy, 241, 242
McNerney, Frank and Martha, 238
Manhattanville College, 252, 267
Marcel, uncle, 14, 60, 62, 63, 120
Maria Laach Abbey, 151, 152, 155, 156
Marian, cousin, 61, 64
Maritain, Jacques, 212, 270
Marmion, Abbot, 118, 142
Marseilles, 20, 22, 95
Masterman, J. C. (later knighted), 240
Matthews, Timothy, 185-187
Maurice, uncle, 27, 63, 154, 155, 161, 236
Medievalists, the, 270
Merton, Father Thomas, 118, 119, 233, 252
Mestrovic, Ivan, 44, 78, 157, 174, 250, 261, 262
Michelangelo, 44
Mildred, cousin, 55, 65, 66, 70, 71
Milles, Carl, 174
Mooney, chauffeur, 105
Morey, Dom Adrian, 151, 152, 156
Mostyn, Father, 105
Mount Saviour Monastery, 251
Mundelein, Cardinal, 270
Murray, Dom Gregory, 209, 215
Murray, Mrs, 72, 73

Nelson, Edward, 110
Nelson Island, 37, 39
New Clairvaux (*see* Vina)
Newman, Cardinal, 118
Notre Dame, Indiana, 248-260, 270, 271

O'Clair, Dr Robert, 252
O'Gorman, Ned, 259
O'Higgins, Patrick, 186
O'Keefe, gardener, 63
Otmar, Dom, 155
Ottilienkolleg, 151, 225
Owen, Wilfrid, 88

Palette Club, 185
Paris, 5, 22, 24, 94
Parkminster, 148, 161, 163-166, 174, 186
Pascal, 175
Passmore, Dom Wilfrid, 198
Petre, Father, 166
Phillips, John, 198
Philosophy course, 141
Plutarch, 97
Pound, Ezra, 192, 267

Quinn family, 258
Quinn, Mary, 160

Racquets Club, 117
Ramleh, 8, 37
Ramsay, Dom Leander (later Abbot), 66, 86, 109, 110, 139, 144, 148, 244

René, uncle, 27
Retreats, 213-215
Reynolds family, 115-117
Reynolds, James, 75, 107, 111, 130, 149, 152
Richard, uncle, 27, 63, 64
Rita, aunt, 55, 65, 67, 69, 71, 76, 78, 80, 105, 147, 235
Riva Aguero, Marquis de la (author's great uncle), 26
Rocamadour, 211
Rochford family, 174, 247
Rodin, 44, 77
Rodney, 92, 93, 121, 122, 237
Romanes Lecture, 240, 241
Ronald, Tom, 114
Rospigliosi, Princess, 180, 196
Rutherford, Dom Anselm, 109, 117, 118

St André Abbey, 152, 153
St Bede Abbey, 213
St Bernard, 142, 211
St Mary's Hospital, Bristol, 188, 190, 191, 254, 255
St Mary's Hospital, London, 182, 183
St Walburga Convent, 229, 263-265, 268, 272, 274-276
Sandon Club, 117
Saslec, Major, 224
Sassoon, Siegfried, 88, 244, 259
Segrave-Daly, Reginald, 127, 128, 135
Shaw, Bernard, 183
Sheed, Frank, 219, 232-234, 270
Sheen, Bishop, 270
Silsileh, Fort, 14-16, 278
Stephanie, aunt, 154, 155
Stonor, Dom Julian, 268, 276
Suez crisis, 237
Sumner, Dom Oswald, 128

Talacre Abbey, 198-207, 276
Talbot, Father John, 108, 109, 117, 151, 162, 203, 216, 218
Tatton-Browne, Pamela, 51, 52
Taylor, Alma, 114
Teilhard de Chardin, Pere, S.J., 227, 228, 265
Temple Cloud, 157, 227
Theodore, Brother, 128
Theological studies, 141, 150
Thesiger, Ernest, 183
Thibaut, Dom Thomas, 153
Tomlinson, Mgr, 207
Tonitz, Josephine, 5, 11, 14, 15, 22, 42, 51, 56, 165
Trafford, Dom Sigebert (later Abbot), 75, 103, 176, 177, 203
Turnbull, Maurice, 75, 130, 135, 151, 184

van de Velde, Arthur, grandfather, 26, 27
van de Velde, Edward, great uncle, 26
van de Velde, Gabrielle, great aunt, 26
van de Velde, Hydeline, grandmother, 4, 25-27, 33, 46, 49, 235
van Zeller, Francis, father, 9, 12, 13, 16-19, 21-23, 30, 31, 36, 41, 44, 45, 48, 54-57, 63, 75, 77, 79, 85, 87, 98, 99, 100, 101, 137
van Zeller, Francis, grandfather, 6
van Zeller, Geoffrey, brother, xi, 5, 9, 15, 22, 24, 42, 43, 50, 51, 56, 76, 80, 84-86, 94, 96, 97, 102, 105, 107, 113, 136, 152, 191, 204, 205
van Zeller, Monique, mother, 11, 12, 14, 16-19, 21-24, 36, 41, 44, 50-56, 60, 76, 100-102, 145, 147, 148, 152, 187, 191, 204
van Zeller, Tommy, cousin, 16, 17, 55, 62
van Zeulen, Stephanie, aunt, 154
Vaughan family, 157
Venning, Hugh, pseudonym, 122
Vereker, Major, 157
Vina, California, Cistercian monastery, 238
Vladimir (Vlud), 192
von Doderer, Heimito, 1
von Halwyll, Hans, 26
von Knorring, John, 235

Water-Witch, 39, 50, 51
Watts, Nevile, 191
Watts, Peter, 45, 259
Waugh, Alec, 104
Waugh, Evelyn, 172, 194, 209, 210, 239, 241
Weld, Dom Hugh (Prior of Parkminster), 139, 161, 166
Wentworth, Lady, 187

Whitehaven, 159, 160, 227
William, cousin, 65, 80
Williams, Hugh, 113
Woodruff, Douglas, 231
Woodruff, the Hon. Mrs, 185
Worth (monastery), 167, 168
Worth (school), 172-175

Xenophon and his Baltic dream, 186

Yacht Club, 50, 51
Yolande, aunt, 3, 24, 27, 35, 60-62, 66, 77, 78, 84, 107, 113, 117, 125, 152, 160-162, 190, 204, 205, 235, 274

Zarima, Madame, 205, 251